Anonymous

Outlines of sermons to children

With numerous anecdotes

Anonymous

Outlines of sermons to children
With numerous anecdotes

ISBN/EAN: 9783337159962

Printed in Europe, USA, Canada, Australia, Japan

Cover: Foto ©Lupo / pixelio.de

More available books at **www.hansebooks.com**

The Clerical Library.

OUTLINES OF SERMONS TO CHILDREN,

WITH

NUMEROUS ANECDOTES.

New York:
A. C. ARMSTRONG & SON,
714 Broadway.
1886.

AUTHORS OF SERMONS.

Alexander Andrew.
William Arnot.
A. Bannatyne.
James Bolton.
Andrew A. Bonar, D.D.
Horatius Bonar, D.D.
Marcus D. Buell.
John Cairns, D.D.
Thomas Champness.
M. G. Dana.
J. Oswald Dykes, D.D.
John Edmond, D.D.
R. F. Fisher.
W. H. Gray, D.D.
T. P. Johnston.
J. Marshall Lang, D.D.
J. Ludlow, D.D.
Thomas Nicol, B.D.
W. R. Nicoll, M.A.
T. Teignmouth Shore.
E. Simon.
James Stalker, M.A.
J. Walker.
R. W. Weir, M.A.
James Wells, M.A.
George Wilson, M.A.
J. H. Wilson, D.D.
W. C. Wright.
J. B. Young.

I. God, the Creator. GEN. i. 31. "*And God saw every thing that He had made, and, behold, it was very good.*"

ONE of our pleasant duties is to lead children to see God in nature, to mix up loving thoughts of Him with all their enjoyments of it. It would be a wretched thing to live in a house which a kind father had built expressly for them, and furnished to their taste, and yet never think of him. And is it not worse to grow up, as so many do, in the midst of God's wonderful and beautiful works, utterly careless of the glorious Creator and gracious Giver of them? "The ox knoweth his owner, and the ass his master's crib:" but we eat and drink from God's hand daily, and are so engrossed with what the Hand contains, that we forget the Hand itself!

Now our text will help us to do better. It shows us "every thing," coming from God, fashioned by God, approved of God; God's eye is on it, His heart is in it, His arms are around it; "And God saw *every thing that He had made, and, behold, it was very good.*" This was how it appeared to Him as it lay fresh before Him six thousand years ago. He had just "finished" it; it was complete; and as He gazed upon it, as her mother does upon her newborn babe, it seemed, and it was, "very good." It could not be improved; it was perfect. How interesting it is thus to have God's own report upon it; to be assured that He was satisfied and delighted with it.

But now let us ask :—

Why it was "very good"?
What was "very good"?
How it was "very good"?
And then—Is it still "very good"?

I. *Why* was it "very good"?
Was it not because it was the offspring of *Infinite Wis-*
B

dom, *and Power, and Love?* These would be certain to produce what was "very good;" for Love would suggest it, Wisdom would contrive it, Power would do it. And there would be no flaw or failure; there could be none. Our rarest inventions, such as the watch or piano, fall short of God's commonest creatures, such as the fly or the robin redbreast; because we are finite—our wisdom, power, and love are limited.

Again: They were "very good," because they were *called and guided into existence by Jesus.* This is often plainly told us in the Gospels and Epistles. God commissioned His own, His only son, to do it. *He* was to have the honour of it, for God would put crowns upon His head from the beginning. Therefore, of course, God would rejoice in it, and consider it "very good." Even to earthly parents, what their children do is doubly sweet. Their rough sketches are more prized than artists' pictures, and their attempts at sculpture than Grecian statues.

Then, too, it was "very good," because there was *no evil* in it. There may have been unsightliness or ugliness, such as we have in toads and slugs; there may have been poison, such as we have in the berry of the laurel; there may have been ferocity, such as we have in the tiger or the eagle—we cannot prove that these are faults—but there was no sin. "Every thing" was innocent, untainted by Satan's touch, fit for God to move about amongst in His holiness.

And it was "very good," because it was *like God.* It was a reflection, however feeble, of His mind, as a book is of the person who writes it. When in the Great Exhibition there are spread before us the myriads of articles which human ingenuity and skill and industry have devised, could we not judge from them what the designer himself was? Will they not resemble him and "declare" him to be ingenious, and skilful, and industrious? We shall not have him visibly before us; and yet we shall get a glimpse of him from his contributions.

And so "everything that God made" is a manifestation of God Himself, and it must be "very good."

II. We ask, *what* was "very good"?

This we must answer in a shorter way. It was, "*every thing* which He had made." And if we say, What was that?

We have but to cause to pass before us the splendid panorama which Moses was inspired to describe for our learning. It opens with light dividing the day from the night, so that we might have a time for activity and a time for rest. Then follows the firmament, or heavenly dome, the space between filled with suitable air for us to breathe. Then there was a separation of the sea from the land; the sea for us to sail on, and bathe in, the land for us to tread and cultivate. And immediately the land was carpeted with soft grass, and stocked with shade and fruit trees and vegetables, and ornamented with ferns and flowers. Then the sun was ordered to shine warmly and nourishingly on it, and the moon and the stars to cheer its darkness. These were its fires and candles. Next we have feathered fowl to enliven it with their songs and variegated plumage, and fish to sport in its streams, and cattle to range its pastures, and wild beasts to inhabit its forests, and insects and reptiles to glitter as gems on it from pole to pole. Lastly, we have man himself, "in the image of God"—erect, shapely, comely, intelligent, speaking man—the king of this noble kingdom, to have dominion over it, and populate it, and replenish it, and subdue it, and use it!

This is an outline of what was "very good." You must resolve it into endless details and varieties for yourselves.

III. *How* are they "very good"?

In themselves. If the ocean or the sky, if a horse or a cow, had never been intended for us, still would they not have been "very good"—worthy of God's admiration.

"Very good" *in their purposes.* God meant them to be for our service. The vine to bear grapes for us, and the wheat, bread; the bee to provide us with honey, the sheep with wool, the cat to catch our mice, the dog to watch our property—how "very good" were these purposes?

And this being so, how very good they are *in their arrangements* for it. Suppose the camel had been as untractable as the zebra, could we ever have got it to bridge the sandy deserts for us? Or suppose the elephant had been as savage as the leopard, could we ever have got it to toil for us in India? But God arranged for it by implanting docility in its huge frame. Or suppose the hen had been as swift and shy as the swallow, could we ever have got her to drop her eggs and sit on them when we desired.

But God arranged for it, by implanting sociability within her.

Thus, however you turn it about, " every thing that God made was very good."

IV. And now we enquire, *Is every thing "very good" still?*

Here we are ourselves, "made" by God. Here, surrounding us, are ten thousand things which He pronounced "very good" ages since. Are they very good now? May not a thing be "very good," and yet have something very bad mingled with it? A bed of herbs is very good; but it may be choked with weeds. But, alas! if this is true of our fields and gardens, it is not true of us. There is nothing about us which is very good. Body, soul and spirit have been *spoilt* by the Fall, which brought the thorns and thistles into our fields and gardens. They have not been spoilt by it, though it troubles them; we have, for we were transgressors. When Adam and Eve ate of the forbidden fruit, we lost God's favour, and His frown is marked on us in our infirmities, corruption and decay. *We* are *not* "very good" now, but very bad, very weak, and prone to what is wrong, and ignorant of God.

But now observe that this will not be so always, for God is *fetching very "good things" out of this apparent frustration of His plan.* It is related that the best thing which ever happened to a tribe of Arabs was the sudden caving in of their common well, because they then resolved that they would cease to be dependent on such a frail resource, and each family should dig a well of their own. A farmer had his plot of Indian corn trampled on by a herd of bullocks. His neighbours pitied him sorely; but he ploughed it in and resowed it, and had a double crop from the rich manuring which the buried stalks supplied to the soil. So God will by-and-by reveal to the universe that what the serpent believed to be incurable damage to His "very good" things, was over-ruled by Him to be indeed "very good" for them.

And then remember that *He is restoring what is now very bad to be "very good."* Do you doubt this? It is going on hour by hour in those who have embraced the Saviour. In a horticultural, poultry, and agricultural show, you notice how everything is being wrought to a higher pitch of size and elegance. You are astonished as you compare the blossoms and flowers of your infancy with the blossoms there? "Can they be the descendants of these?" you say. But a grander movement than this is silently going on in some children. The Lord is *renewing* them into "His own image." They have washed their inward robes, and whitened them in the blood of the Lamb. They have received from Him a tender, penitent heart; and now they are increasing before Him, and under His nurture, in whatever is saintly and celestial. Already *that* in them is "very good;" and soon, when they quit this debased and diseased fleshly frame, they will be absolutely "very good." There will be no spot or wrinkle in them. And then at the resurrection it will be the same with that debased and diseased earthly frame itself; it will leave its mortality in the grave, and rise to God. Oh, how "very good!"

Is this your portion and prospect? If not, attend to it forthwith that it may be; for if it is not, you are "very bad" in God's sight, and you will be worse and worse, till you are ripe for a final outcasting from His blessed presence.

Do be persuaded; do turn to Jesus, and beseech Him to gather you into that happy fold which He will never forsake, till of the humblest lamb in it God Himself shall say, "It is *very good*."

J. B.

II. **Abraham's Trial.** GEN. xxii. 2. "*And He said, Take now thy son, thine only son Isaac, whom thou lovest, and get thee into the land of Moriah; and offer him there for a burnt offering upon one of the mountains which I will tell thee of.*"

WE will suppose that we are walking together on Mount Moriah; of course it is a walk in thought, like as it were in a dream. And, as we do in dreams we must mix things. Times, places, facts, fancies, must be mingled together; the teaching being, we trust, "truth as it is in Jesus." We will suppose that we are visiting Mount Moriah some time after the occurrences of which we are told in this chapter, and the heads of this sermon are certain things which we shall suppose to see in our walk up to the mountain's top.

I. There is a finger-post at the bottom of the hill, labelled with the name *Moriah*. Ah! then we are right. That is where we want to go.

But what can this name Moriah mean? Some learned people say one thing, some another; but you will not be far wrong if you say it means, the seeing of Jehovah; perhaps His seeing us, perhaps our seeing Him; or rather both in one. The Lord provides, foresees for us, and shows Himself so that we see Him. He provides by revealing Himself. There is another finger-post on the top of the hill. It covers the place Jehovah-Jireh—" the Lord will see." But Moriah is the same name turned round and made short. So the Lord, seeing and shining, showing the road by shining on it, is the beginning and the end of the path. Up the hill Moriah is up to the presence of God. It is the path of faith, "Offer on one of the mountains which I shall tell thee of," said God to Abraham; and He told him of it—showed it by showing Himself there. How He showed Himself we shall see. Meanwhile, let us go up this road of faith—it is rough and steep and hard. Ah! Abraham and Isaac found it so. All pilgrims find it so. But fear not; God sees and God shines. The walk of faith is with God and up to God.

Now we are at the top of the hill, we notice traces of burning.

II. There is a pile of ashes. Look down at this heap of ashes, and you may see written in it that "God did tempt Abraham," *i.e.* try him. You know that fire scorches, melts and tests things. The Bible therefore often compares trial to fire. It is a very touching figure. For, like fire, trial is keen and sharp; but it does not hurt or destroy everything that is worth keeping. It refines and purifies the silver by consuming the refuse. We read of many fire-trials in the Bible; some of them having literal fire connected with them. When Aaron saw his two sons burned up in their sin before the Lord, his heart was in a furnace of sore anguish. When Job heard tale after tale of dire loss, till at last he was told of the death of all his sons and daughters, it was like as if the lightnings which burned up his flocks had fallen on his own head to scathe him. Christ's cruel cross was a fire-trial such as never was passed through by any other. Nothing in Christ was condemned—for Satan had nothing in him. The last day will be a great fire-trial—burning up the earth and the works that are therein : and as Paul says in another sense, " The fire shall try every man's work of what sort it is."

The fire of hell is not said to be trial-fire. They burned refuse only in Tophet. The unquenchable fire is for chaff. Now let us consider Abraham's fire-trial. " Take now thy son." " Thy son." There is the first burning coal, for children are dear,—you would not vex your parents if you knew how dear they hold you. " Thine only son." There is another coal to the fire. One of two, or of many, had been hard ; but an only son!—that is hard indeed. Then, such a son—thy Isaac ; there is more fuel to the fire. Isaac is "laughter ;" and his very name brings back to mind how, after long, long waiting, father and mother rejoiced over their child. No wonder that it should be added " Whom thou lovest."

There is one faggot more: " Take thy son and offer him." To slay him ! Oh, what a flame burns there ! Yet there is something more—something that is like pouring oil in the furnace. This son was the child of promise. He was to be the father of a nation from which Christ was to spring. If he is killed, what becomes of the promise ?

Do you remember how Shadrach, Meshach and Abednego went through a fiery furnace and had not even the smell of fire on them after they came out of it ? So it was with Abraham. His faith kept him from being burned. He said to himself, "God will keep His word. If I must kill Isaac, God will bring him to life again." So, not to blind them, but in real hope, he said to the young men, " I and the lad will go yonder and worship, and come again unto you."

III. The sacrificial knife. There it lies among the ashes, with stains on it like blood-spots. There has been death here. Was Isaac, then, really slain ? No, but there was the offering of one in his stead. So we find an inscription on both sides of this knife. On the one side the word Surrender ; on the other, Substitution.

Surrender means giving up. Abraham gave up his son at God's word. It was not the first thing God had asked him to give up. He left his country and his kinsfolk at

God bidding. But God never asks us to give up anything except for something better than what we yield.

Surrender is a good motto for life. Give up—for the sake of others, for Christ's sake. You will be like your heavenly Father if you do.

"For God gave up His Son to die,
So gen'rous was His love.

He did not ask Abraham to do what He was unwilling to do Himself. His own, His only, His beloved Son, He gave for us.

The other inscription on the knife is Substitution. That is, one instead of another. The ram was offered instead of Isaac. It is hard to see the full meaning. The lesson that God taught Abraham was, Lord, Thy will! And what Moriah taught as a command, Calvary taught as an example. Look down through the years and see, on a little hill there are three crosses. One of them, the middle one, has One hanging on it who is the Lamb of God. That is the meaning of Jehovah-Jireh—"the Lord will provide." Abraham did not quite understand what he spoke, only he spoke in trust, and was sure to find the reality better than his hope, when he said "The Lord will provide a lamb for a burnt offering." He saw and understood afterwards, for Jesus says, "Your father Abraham greatly desired to see my day, and he has seen it and rejoiced."

J. E.

III. Isaac. Gen. xxii. 40. *"And Abraham stretched forth his hand, and took the knife to slay his son."*

This beautiful story wants looking into, if we would fully enjoy it and profit by it. It is like the brook in a meadow —pleasant to the eye; but the fish, and the water-cresses, and the polished pebbles in it, have to be searched for. It is not so much a mirror in which you have bright but shadowy reflections, as it is a microscope through which you see wonderful realities, which, but for it, must have remained hidden from us for ever.

Two persons are mixed up in it; a man and a lad, a father and a son. Now, if you were grown-up people, we should perhaps call your attention chiefly to the elder of the two—the man, the father; but as you are young yourselves, you will naturally be most interested in the lad, the son. Round him, therefore, let us gather; and God prepare us for the study!

We will consider him,—
I. As the beloved child.
II. As the pattern of obedience.
III. As the type of Jesus.

I. As the beloved child.

The Scriptures show us many such children. Joseph, the beloved of Jacob; Samuel, the beloved of Hannah; Solomon, the beloved of David. From the earliest ages God has provided that sweetest home and best school for childhood, the fond parental bosom. How dark and pitiable it would be without it! But nurtured in it the little one grows up in sunshine, to shine itself by-and-by.

Isaac was Abraham's only child by his wife Sarah, and that was a reason why he was beloved; but also, he was the child of his old age, given to him in his hundredth year, after he had been waiting for him, and hoping for him, and longing for him for half a century. "We dearly prize what cost us sighs," says the proverb.

Again, he was the child of promise—of *Divine* promise. In this sense, he was a special gift from God. God sent an angel from heaven to announce his birth, to assure his despairing mother that it should happen, though it would require a miracle.

Thus they had him in promise long before they had him in their arms. They saw him in the promise long before they kissed him in his cradle. He was beloved of them long before his infant face was there to claim it of them.

Directly he was in his swaddling clothes, they had a name ready for him. "We will call him Isaac," that is "laughter;" they were so glad, so happy. "God has made me laugh," his mother said.

How beloved he was of them as he grew up! This appears in the fact that he gave a "great feast" on his weaning day, and that they banished Ishmael from the house because he dared to mock and tease him. Not a hair of his head should be touched, not a tear should trickle down his cheeks, if they could help it. Then it appears afterwards in their care to obtain him a wife. How solemnly Eliezer the steward is summoned, instructed, and charged for that errand. It was as if they were a king and a queen setting about the marriage of the heir-apparent to a throne. I am sure if some of us had a quarter of the pains taken to find us Rebekahs, we should be too proud to speak to them when they alighted from their camels.

Thus, then, was Isaac beloved. This was his boyhood's privilege and joy. May it be yours abundantly; and may God enable you to value it, improve it, and be properly thankful for it! What a difference there is in bird's nests! How soft and warm are some—how hard and cheerless others! Should you not expect robins, and goldfinches, and nightingales, out of the wool, and moss, and feathers; and from the dry sticks, hawks, magpies, and jackdaws? And so it is.

II. As the pattern of obedience.

This was a further cause for his being so beloved, that he was such a dutiful child. He was himself lovely and lovable. You have to *try* to love those who are wayward —it goes against the grain to be kind to them; but those who are good lead you captive. You have to *tie* yourself to the former; the latter entwine round you. Positively it is quite difficult to smile (cheap as smiles are) on certain unfledged folk of my acquaintance, it seems so like smiling on toads or rattlesnakes. Isaac was none of these. I doubt not he was all that Abraham and Sarah could have wished him to be. What do we read to the contrary? What single instance have we of his troubling them? Rather, is not the narrative of his conduct here intended as a specimen of his conduct generally? And, now, observe it; it is unparalleled even in the Bible.

On a certain morning, Abraham abruptly informed him that he was to attend him on a journey, of the length and object of which he was perfectly ignorant. They started early and travelled far. That evening closed upon them, and the morrow evening as well, and still they went forward. Presently Abraham pointed out to him a distant range of mountains, those on which the city of Jerusalem now stands or which surround her as ramparts. Then Abraham commanded the escort to remain with the ass where they were, whilst he and Isaac should ascend the hill Moriah to worship God. But, ere they parted with them,

Abraham transferred the load of wood, which he had hewn in Beersheba, from the beast's back to Isaac's shoulders. Then, with a flaming torch in his grasp, and a steel blade in his girth, he and Isaac began the ascent. As they toiled up Isaac was struck with a sudden thought. Here is the fire, the wood, the knife, but where is the lamb for a burnt offering? How foolish of us—how useless to go on! the principal thing forgotten. So he opened his mind to Abraham—What are we about? What shall we do? Abraham had a knife in his girth, but I fancy that that question of his darling put a knife into his heart. I don't understand how he managed to answer him without choking or crying out to God! If he had flung himself on the ground in an agony and bloody sweat, and besought God to excuse him, this would not have surprised us. O Faith! what a triumph thou hadst here! Abraham calmly replied, "God will *provide* Himself a lamb for a burnt-offering." But did he say no more? I doubt it. I have a notion that then and there he described to Isaac the dreadful secret, and persuaded him to yield his free consent. He explained to him how God had selected *him* for the lamb—how there was no escape from it, but in resisting God—how God assuredly could and would raise him up from the dead if necessary! And Isaac, instead of being indignant or defiant, or breaking away and running, as we should have done, submitted without a murmur, and kept straight on for the fatal spot.

At any rate, when they were arrived there, he assisted Abraham in building the altar and spreading the faggots; and then, when Abraham advanced with the cord, he had no remonstrances, no further inquiries, no entreaties to be spared. He surrendered himself as quietly as a kid or a turtle-dove to be pinioned, to be lifted and laid on the altar; nay, when he watched the drawing of the dagger, when it was unsheathed and up it went to descend the next instant into his quivering flesh, even then there was not a word from him! He was content to die, and in that awful way, if Abraham required it of him. He might have appealed to him, reminded him of his faultless behaviour, begged him not to murder him, argued with him that it must be wrong He might have dared him to touch him, and walked off unscathed; but *obedience* forbade, and he preferred death to disobedience! What an example for us! what a practical illustration of that fifth law of the ten which is so apt to be forgotten in modern times, that we occasionally suppose the printers have accidentally dropped it from our Oxford and Cambridge editions; or is it that we are afflicted with short memories, as the pious labourer hinted to the farmer that *he* evidently had, when he was despatching him with a wagon to the hay-field on Sunday. "Short memory, sir," he said civilly, scratching his head; "Isn't it, *remember* the Sabbath day to keep it holy, sir?"

There is a nearly idiot girl in a village in America, who may be seen sitting by the hour by a well, to which her since buried mother directed her for drink, and into which she dropped the jug. She can't be persuaded that she did not grieve her; she can't forgive herself.

A band of schoolfellows were tempting a companion to steal his father's apples. "He won't be angry; he won't punish you if you are found out." "That," said he, "is just why I can't do it. He is so kind to me that I should be a brute to displease him."

Happy those who have right views of obedience both to God and man, who have resolved to abide by it at whatever sacrifice, who place it above their own whims and passions. It is a *strait* road, and it has thorns in it, but it is radiant with the light of God's countenance, and it ends in His blissful presence. To leap its hedges is to forsake our own mercies.

III. As the type of Jesus.

Isaac's obedience brought him this high honour of being the clearest type of Jesus that can be conceived. The animals which were actually slain in sacrifice were types of Him, but they failed in that they were merely animals. Noah and Job, and a list of men, were types of Him in His character; but they were not types of His atonement, and it was His atonement which was His glory—His crowning achievement! It was here that Isaac was so peculiarly distinguished. He prefigured that precious act, out of which has sprung such a harvest of blessings to our fallen race, such a harvest of praise to God, that it will occupy eternity to reap it.

What have we in possession or prospect which relieves

us of our load of guilt, which cheers us under bereavement, which robs the grave of its gloom for us, which will absolve us at the judgment seat? The sole solid foundation of that was exhibited as in a picture when Isaac, panting but passive, awaited the sharp stroke which should let out his soul.

As he had, so Jesus had, no will but His Father's: as he did, so Jesus walked, steadily though wearily, to His execution; as Isaac carried the wood, so Jesus carried His cross. But there we stop. Isaac was killed as far as his own and his father's determination were concerned, but Jesus was killed indeed. Isaac was not killed, because if he had been, he could not have expiated his or our transgressions, for he was himself a transgressor. But Jesus was killed because His sufferings were God's appointed and accepted atonement for the transgressions of the world. So, though Isaac was a lively type of Him, he was but a type. Jesus is our Isaac—the true " Laughter " of whosoever embraces Him and clings to Him for salvation.

The Lord Himself draw you to Him! Will you not visit Calvary at this season, and, in prayerful meditation, revive its memorable scenes? Be a witness of them, be a partaker in them, weep over them. Rest not until you can say at His pierced feet there, as you cannot say of Isaac—" He *loved* me and *gave Himself* for me!"

J. B.

IV. Joseph and his Brethren. Gen. xlv. 2. "*And he wept aloud; and the Egyptians and the house of Pharaoh heard.*"

THIS Scripture in the Old Testament reminds us of another in the New Testament, so like it and yet very different. " And at midnight Paul and Silas prayed, and sang praises unto God; and the prisoners heard them." Now we should have imagined that Joseph would have been the person to sing, Paul and Silas the persons to weep; for Joseph was surrounded with every happiness, whilst Paul and Silas were in a dungeon, in the dark, hungry and thirsty, their feet fast in the stocks, their backs torn and bleeding.

It is strange that though the two things—weeping and

singing—seem so opposite to each other, they are often hand in hand; tears never fall faster than when our hearts are bursting with joy.

It is an awful thing to hear a man weep aloud—generally he has good cause for it; well then, why did Joseph weep aloud? He has sent all his servants out of the room; he is alone with his brethren, and the first thing his servants hear is somebody weeping aloud! It is Joseph's voice. Not another sound but his convulsive sobs. Can you guess why he thus wept aloud! We shall give six reasons for it.

I. His pent up feelings.

When we give way to our feelings directly they affect us we can get through without much trouble; but when we hide and restrain them for a while, they become turbulent; just as a brook which has been dammed up with sticks and mud, will at last, with a rush and a roar, break the rampart and sweep all before it.

Now Joseph had been "refraining himself" for months and on several very trying occasions. Is it any wonder that when all this was at its height, it vented itself in these boisterous emotions?

II. There was the sight of Benjamin.

He was his own dear brother, "my mother's son," and for twenty years they had been cruelly separated. Would not the sight of Benjamin help to unnerve Joseph?

III. There were the thoughts of his father.

His brethren had been speaking much of Jacob—of the "old man," of his grey hairs, of how he pined for Joseph. This had stirred Joseph to the depths.

IV. There was his harsh treatment of his brethren.

This had been most difficult and yet most necessary. He had recognised them the instant they entered his presence, and as quickly he had determined to punish them for their own welfare. They had steeled themselves to his "anguish when he had besought them;" now he will steel himself to theirs, till they are humbled and contrite. He put them through a rigorous course of discipline. His lessons for them had cut them like knives. He had charged them with meaning treachery, theft, falsehood. They believed him to be a tyrant, and yet his heart yearned towards them.

V. There was Judah's earnest pleading.

Study that remonstrance for yourselves. There are not more melting words in the Bible. They would have softened a very stone, and Joseph, no marvel, wept aloud after that intercession.

VI. There was what he was about to disclose to them.

Startling news has a fashion of choking our utterance and paralyzing our tongues. Who has not wept aloud when he was about to relate what would be sure to produce weeping aloud? And here Joseph had it on his lips, "I am Joseph! I am he whom ye sold into Egypt! God hath made me lord and ruler throughout Egypt!" Is it surprising that with this disclosure on his lips, Joseph wept aloud ere he could stammer it forth?

But now arises the question, What do we weep aloud for? All of us have fountains of tears in us, and various things will set them overflowing. It was a custom with the ancients to have small bottles in which they caught their tears at their friends' sepulchres, and then these bottles were deposited in the urns which contained their ashes. David says, "Put Thou my tears into Thy bottle." What quantities of bottles some people could fill with tears. We will mention four things which we may properly weep aloud for, which we cannot bewail too much.

1. *Our sins.* They offend and dishonour God. They defile and wound and destroy our souls. They crucified Jesus. We are indignant with the Jews and Romans for piercing His precious flesh on Calvary; but our sins were what compelled Him to be so tortured, they were the nails which fastened Him there. Oh, weep over your sins, as Peter did over his denial of Jesus.

2. *Our unkindnesses.* We do not intend always to injure or distress; but we say what does it, or we do what does it, and then we treat it lightly, whilst the sensitive sufferer goes home refusing to be comforted. We wish children would learn and keep in mind these lines,

> " Evil is wrought from want of thought
> As well as from want of heart."

There is nothing which will so haunt us, when we are lying at the gates of death, as such unkindnesses. Then we shall bewail them; but it is better to do so now, when we can pick out the thorn both from our own consciences and the wronged one's side.

3. *Our ingratitudes.* Who has not these to mourn over? Ingratitude to God our Creator and Preserver; ingratitude to Jesus, who redeemed us by His own shame and agony; ingratitude to the Holy Spirit, who has sought our salvation when we have disregarded it; ingratitude to all those who are over us in the Lord. A young man whom he had rescued from drowning, was reproved by a Christian gentleman for Sabbath desecration; he actually swore at him, and bade him attend to his own business. But that base ingratitude rose up before him wherever he went. It wasted him; and when sick on his couch, he beckoned his sister to him, and said in broken accents, "I am sinking fast, I have never forgiven myself. If I could have met him, and acknowledged my wickedness it would have relieved me. Pray for me."

4. *Our wasted opportunities.* If a girl who had been strolling in the parks or meadows before breakfast, came in laden with bunches of primroses and violets, with cowslips for bracelets, with daisies for brooches, you would not reprove her, or consider that she had forfeited a splendid chance; but now if every pebble in her ramble had been a diamond or an amethyst, and yet she came in with nothing but these fading blossoms, would you not exclaim: "Silly girl! you have missed a fortune; you have despised treasures." And what shall we say of ourselves if we occupy ourselves in worldly vanities when God has strewn our path with what should enrich us for Heaven?

We might have gathered wisdom, which, "is above riches;" we might have gained God's favours; we might have adorned ourselves with virtues and graces; but we let the whole train glide by us, without seizing on a single gem! Weep for these lost opportunities. Pour your tears at Jesus' feet, and God will hear your tears and say, "I have blotted out as a cloud thy transgressions, for His sake who once wept aloud at Gethsemane for thee."

J. B.

V. Go Forward. EXOD. xiv. 15. *"And the Lord said unto Moses, Wherefore criest thou unto Me? Speak unto the children of Israel, that they go forward."*

"Go forward." This was the order which Moses was told by God to give to the children of Israel, and it was very needful that they should obey it. Pharaoh, king of Egypt, was pursuing and was not far behind them. They began to wish they had never left Egypt at all. But although they had lost confidence in God, Moses had not. He was sure that deliverance would come though he did not see how. He prayed to God, and the text gives God's answer.

But where could they go forward to? Before them, the mountains were high and threatening; and if they sought to climb them, they would become entangled, and separated from one another, and so become an easy prey for their pursuing foe. If they sought to go to the left hand, they must go into the Red Sea; for the ridge of mountains ran right into it, stretching into the water, and blocking up their path, so that they could not go along the shore. And if they went straight into the sea, it seemed as if they must be drowned. It stretched across for miles. Men could not wade in safety through it, much less could it be crossed by all these families of Israel. Humanly speaking, the way of the sea was the way of death. No doubt, there was an inviting valley on the landward side of that ridge of mountains; but that valley, though a pleasant and a tempting way, was a dangerous route for them to take. It would only lead them back, though by a winding way, to the land of bondage which they had left. It was in these circumstances that God told them to go forward, right into the bed of the Red Sea. They believed God, and they obeyed Him; and what was the result? A strong wind was sent to drive the waters back, and the people went through as if it had been dry land; but when the Egyptians, who were following them, were in the middle of the sea, the wind ceased, the waters flowed on as they had done before, and when the morning dawned, Moses and the children of Israel were standing safe upon the further shore, and "Pharaoh and his chariots and horsemen were overthrown and covered by the waters—

there remained not so much as one of them. Thus the Lord saved Israel that day, and Israel saw that great work, and the people believed the Lord and His servant Moses."

Good men in former times wrote all these things for our learning; and this is a kind of parable from which we are called to learn the truth we should believe concerning God, and the duty God requires of man. Those who live only according to their natural and corrupted feelings, without the grace of God, are more truly slaves than these poor Israelites were, for Satan is a harder taskmaster than Pharaoh. But a greater than Moses has come to deliver us from Satan's power; Jesus is our great King, guiding us from the enemy's country to the heavenly Canaan.

I. *We should believe in Christ, and also obey Him.*— These children of Israel believed in Moses, and they showed their faith by leaving their homes in Egypt, by going forth towards the wilderness, and by entering the channel of the Red Sea, though its waters seemed ready to devour them. Let us believe in Jesus Christ as the Son of God and the Saviour of sinners; and let us show our faith by our obedience to His heavenly will. Let us leave the land of sin, and follow Him through good and bad report.

But remember that God will neither have our obedience without faith, nor our faith without obedience. There are some who think they do not need to believe in Christ. They fancy they can themselves do all that is required; but, indeed, they cannot. They are every day sinning against God; and if they have no Saviour to believe in, how are they to find mercy to pardon them for the past, and grace to help them for the future? Without believing in Christ, we have no true love to God in our hearts; and without love, we cannot give Him the obedience of children; and it is this obedience of the heart which our Father wishes, not the outward obedience only of works—it is the obedience of children, and not of slaves.

There is a sense in which even good works will not please our Father. It is when they have not right motives, and when we have not first given Him our hearts. Then our best works are but whited sepulchres, which inwardly are full of rottenness and dead men's bones. Therefore it is that, when the sinner asks, "What must I do to be saved?" the answer of God is not, "Do good works," or even, "Do your duty;" it is, "Believe in the Lord Jesus Christ,"—believe so as to love, and then from this fountain of love, let the pure stream of obedience flow forth. But though we must first believe, we must go on to obey. It would not have done for the Israelites to say, "We believe in God and in Moses, and we do not need to go forward, we only need to stand still and see the salvation of the Lord." We are not meant to stand still, merely saying, "we believe," until we die. "Faith without works is dead." We have spiritual diseases, even the youngest of us. It is not enough for us to say we believe in Jesus Christ, as the Physician who can heal us; we need to prove our faith by going to Him, telling Him how we feel, hearing what He orders, and doing what He prescribes—otherwise our faith will not save us from death. This is what you must do, if you believe in Christ, and hearken to His teaching. Each of you has a garden to keep. You must not let it be overrun with weeds and thorns and thistles. You must take the good seeds which God provides for you, and sow them in it. There are good plants that you can care for, and good trees that you can prune and watch, that they may bring forth good fruit. Your heart is like a castle, and you can take care to whom you open the door. Keep it shut against the enemies of God, and of Christ, and of your own souls. Open it to Christ, and to all His servants and friends. And as you have power, so far, over your thoughts, so have you power over the language of your lips, and over the actions of your life. You must not think this is trying to save yourselves. It is because you believe in Christ and love Him that you know what to do, and wish to do what pleases Him. You listen to His voice, and you are *able* as well as wishful, in believing in Him, to do what is good; for, in His name, you pray to God for help to keep your garden and your castle as you should, and you get that help in answer to your prayers. At the same time, you daily feel that you cannot keep them rightly, and believing in Christ, you pray for the pardon of all your sins, and hope to be saved from deserved punishment and wrath, through Him.

II. We are taught here also that we *should both worship*

God and work for Him. Moses cried unto the Lord, and it was good for him to pray, but God told him that there was duty as well as devotion to be attended to. He had to stretch his rod over the Red Sea, and to lead the Israelites across. He had work to do as well as worship to engage in, and it must be so with us.

I have heard of a heathen king who was wounded in battle, and who, in his dying hours, sending for his trusted servant, said to him, "Go, tell the dead I come." That soldier-servant, without hesitating for a moment, drew his sword and stabbed himself to the heart, that he might go to the dead before his master, and prepare them for his coming. Oh, that we had this spirit of service and of sacrifice for the King of kings! In His dying hour, He also said to us, "Go, tell the dead I come." He asks us to go to a world dead in trespasses and sins, to tell them of His coming, and to preach to them glad tidings of great joy. Alas! how many of us are content to worship Him, and say, "O King, rule for ever!" without spending and being spent, that His kingdom may come, that His will may be done on earth, as it is done in heaven. Remember this, then: As we must not only believe in Christ, but also obey Him; so must we work for God, as well as worship Him in spirit and in truth.

III. This passage further teaches us, that *while we enjoy religious privileges, we should seek to make yearly and daily progress by means of them.*

Like the children of Israel, we have knowledge, and benefits, and hopes, which heathens, who are still in Egyptian darkness, do not possess. To whom much is given, of them the more will be required. Having these privileges, therefore, we should make corresponding progress. Knowing the way, and the truth, and the life, we should go forward, year by year, and day by day. Our hearts should become purer in its thoughts and desires. Our language should become more truthful and loving, our life humbler and holier, our work more directed for God's glory and man's good. We should become liker to Christ, and seek to learn more perfectly the language of heaven. In one sense, the work of our salvation is already perfect. Christ's work *for us* is complete. In another, it is far from being perfected as yet. Christ's work *in us* is only begun,

—if it is, indeed, begun at all,—and God loves to see His believing children growing in likeness to that Elder Brother who is the very image of Himself.

If you ask me why you should thus go on towards perfection, I answer, in the *first* place—*It is the will of God.* We are to be perfect as our Father who is in heaven is perfect; and we see, from all that goes on around us and within us, that this perfection is not to be reached by a single effort, or in a single day. The flowers do not get all their beauty at once. Fruit trees show their blossoms first, and then produce their fruits, which ripen slowly day by day. It is good to see the blossoms and promises of youth. It is better to see the fruits of faith. Let piety, and love, and patience, and gentleness, and humility, and truth, and all the graces of the Spirit, grow and ripen day by day. Ministers, and teachers, and parents have been sowing the good seed in your hearts, "that ye may be born again, not of corruptible seed, but of incorruptible, by the Word of God, which liveth and abideth for ever." We expect to see the results of our sowing.

But not only should we go forward in obedience to God's will! We should also feel that it is needful for our own sakes to obey our heavenly Father.

For first, if we refuse to go forward it is ruin to our highest interests. If the Israelites had stood still, would they have been safe? Pharaoh would have soon come up to them, and made them his captives. We may lay a flower on the stream, and leave it there untouched. But it does not remain where it was; it is floated away. We may leave a dead body undisturbed, but it becomes more corrupted day by day, It does not remain as it was; it becomes loathsome and foul. So we are sailing down the stream of life, though we think we are not moving at all; and our souls are becoming more corrupted year by year, if we allow them to remain just as they are, without spiritual life, and dead in trespasses and sin. We cannot, therefore, stand still. If we do not go forward, we must be going backward. Even if we could always remain where we are, sin prevents us from being safe. The fire is raging, and is coming nearer and nearer, till it shall destroy us. We are lying on the railway track, and the engine of death is coming nearer every hour. We have to go on to

Canaan, to be like Christ, and to learn the language of heaven. We have to be God's servants, and every day to do our Master's work and will. It is not enough, therefore, to say that, though we are not learning the heavenly language now, we remember what little of it we have learned; that, though we are not serving our master now, we are doing nothing against him; that, though we are not going forward to Canaan now, we are not going backward to Egypt. Not to go forward is to disobey God, and the wages of our sin is death.

But, as it is death to disobey; so, second, *It is life to go forward.* The Israelites went forward through the Red Sea at God's command, and it was well with them. On the morrow, "they sounded the loud timbrel o'er Egypt's dark sea," proclaiming "Jehovah has triumphed, his people are free;" and though, in their wilderness-wandering, they had not the fleshpots of Egypt, they had special blessings from the God of Israel. They had manna from heaven to eat, and water from the rock to drink. They had the consciousness of God's presence, the knowledge of His gracious character and of His holy law, the protection of His mighty arm, and the enjoyment, at last, of His heavenly Canaan. And so, it is our life to go forward in the way of believing obedience and persistent service. The pleasures of sin, indeed, we cannot have. The lusts of the flesh, the lust of the eyes, and the pride of life, we dare not indulge. But the Christian's is, after all, the better part. "Godliness is profitable unto all things, having promise of the life that now is, and of that which is to come." We have the light of Christian knowledge, the blessings of religious faith, the hope of a happy immortality, and the blessedness of holy love. Amid all the inconveniences of our homeward journey, we can look up to our Father, and go forward leaning on our Elder Brother's arm. Not only can we endure, without harm, the trials of life; we can feel, in our happy experience, that, because we love God, through faith in Christ, all things work together for our good. We are perfected by suffering; and the storms which threaten to make shipwreck of our faith, only drive us nearer to the haven of eternal rest, where we shall be safe in the arms of Jesus, and perfect as our Father in heaven is perfect.

Before I conclude, let me give you this one counsel : Do not, as pilgrims of immortality, think lightly of *little steps*. These Israelites had to go all their long journey to Canaan one step at a time, and so it is with you. And, alas! you may go a far way from the path of duty, and the path of safety, though you only take one step at a time. We see a lovely flower, and it seems but a little step away from the pathway, and we go to pluck it, and other flowers tempt us, and we go away, step by step, after them also, into the fields of sin ; but the end of these things is death. How often do we read of youths, inclined to goodness, who thus take one step in evil after another, until they become monsters of iniquity. I have read of the wicked and cruel Emperor Nero, that in his youth he burst into tears when asked to sign the order for a criminal to die. Yet it was he who, going step by step into and through the fields of sin, and vice, and crime, laughed like a fiend to see the burning of the city, to which, it was said, he himself set fire. He murdered, without feeling any stingings of conscience, his nearest relatives ; he wrapped Christians round with sheets of canvas steeped in oil and covered with pitch, and then lighted them as torches for his garden-grounds and palace-halls. And, as bad persons become wicked step by step, so it needs many little steps to go forward to the love and likeness of Christ. Even Paul had to forget the things behind, and press on to the things before. The youngest of us may make some progress in the Divine life, and the oldest and the best of us have great progress still to make.

It was told of a painter, that he had "no day without its line." Every day he added some touches to his picture. So let it be with ours. Thus we shall make it liker and liker to Christ, the perfect Image of the invisible God.

W. H. G.

VI. **What is it to be to me?** JOSH. iii. 4. "*Ye have not passed this way heretofore.*"

LIFT up your eyes to the heavens, and look at the fair stars that are shining there. Can you count them ? No. But God has counted them, and given all of them names of his own, far better than ours. How great must that God be who counts the stars, and gives them all their names. They are very beautiful, especially in the winter nights; and tell us what a great, wise, good, and holy God it was who made them. "The heavens declare the glory of God." These stars toil not, and spin not; yet "Solomon in all his glory was not arrayed like one of these."

A learned man, who thought himself very wise, once wished to puzzle a poor man whom he met going to church.

"Where are you going?" he said.

"To church," said the poor man.

"What are you going to do there?"

"To worship God."

"Is your God a great God, or a little God?"

"He is both."

"How can that be?"

"He is so great as to fill the heavens, and yet so little that He can dwell in my heart."

These heavens above us are not dumb. These stars of God have a voice that never ceases to speak to us; and often when I have looked up to them at the close of one year or the beginning of another, they have seemed to "utter speech" more loudly, and to sound through the silent heavens of midnight the name of the great God who made them, and kept them shining so brightly above this little Earth of ours. Every ray that comes from them says, not merely "God is great," but "God is love;" for He who created them was none other than the Son of God, as it is written, "All things were made by Him, and without Him was not any thing made that was made" (John i. 3); and it was He who gave His life for us.

As Earth is only as a grain of sand in the midst of these innumerable stars, so is that little bit of time that we call life, in the midst of the awful Eternity which surrounds us. What is an atom of dust in comparison of the great mountains? and what is a year of our life here in comparison with the ages that are to roll on for ever?

Yet that little life of ours—even the life of the poorest and the youngest—is precious beyond all precious things, and important beyond all the important things of the greatest cities or kingdoms here; and that which makes it so precious and so important is this, that it must either be full of joy, or full of sorrow, for ever and for ever.

Another bit of this *little* but *great* life of our closes on the thirty-first of December; and another bit of it opens on the first of January. On that closing and that opening scene, these clear stars are looking down; nay more, on that closing and opening scene angels, brighter than these stars, are looking down, though we see them not. For "he gives His angels charge concerning us," and they never forget their charge. They are watching this closing year, to see what it has done for us; and they are earnestly looking into the coming year to see what it is to bring forth. They do not weep; but if they could, oh, how they would weep over the wasted days of the year that has passed away! Yet, though they do not weep, they can rejoice; and, oh, how they would rejoice even over one life made happy, one soul saved!

The gate of the new year has now opened upon us, and we must all go in, whether we will or not. But the question is, What is that going in to be to us? with whom are we to go in? and who is to walk with us through its months and days?

The new year will do nothing for us unless we enter on it in the company of the Son of God. Without this, there can be no "*happy* new year." At the very entrance of it, Jesus meets us in His love, and, taking hold of our hand, says to each of us, "Wilt thou go with me?" His company would make life happy; his love would sweeten every change, and brighten every hour.

H. B.

VII. Gideon. JUDGES vii. 5-7. "*So he brought down the people unto the water: and the Lord said unto Gideon, Every one that lappeth of the water with his tongue, as a dog lappeth, him shalt thou set by himself; likewise every one that boweth down upon his knees to drink. And the number of them that lapped, putting their hand to their mouth, were three hundred men: but all the rest of the people bowed down upon their knees to drink water. And the Lord said unto Gideon, By the three hundred men that lapped will I save you, and deliver the*

Midianites into thine hand: and let all the other people go every man unto his place."

THAT is a strange story. Gideon was a great leader of the army of Israel; and the enemies of Israel had gathered together so that when Gideon and his army were on the mountain tops the hosts of the enemy, we are told, were like grasshoppers. Israel had to fight against this great army, and she gathered together about thirty-two thousand men for the purpose. Now I shall explain first, how Gideon was chosen to be a general over this army, and how this army of thirty-two thousand men was gradually reduced to three hundred, and how these three hundred went and fought and defeated the enemy.

First, the Israelites, who had been worshippers of the one true God, as often happens, when they became happy and prosperous, fell into evil ways, forsook God, and worshipped idols. Now Gideon was living in the house of his parents, and they worshipped idols, and Gideon and all his people were brought up to worship false gods. We read that Gideon built an altar to the Lord, and when he rose up early in the morning the altar of Baal was cast down, because he feared God; and he also feared his father's house, and he did it by night and not by day. Gideon, you see, was afraid to do it in the day—he was not a very brave man—still he was a true man. And thus God gave him a very glorious part to play. He was given a curious proof to show he was chosen to lead the army of Israel. There was a fleece of wool put one night in the open, and lo! in the morning this was covered with dew, although all around was dry; and the next night it was the opposite; the fleece was dry though all around was wet. That tells us why God chose Gideon. He was unlike the rest. Gideon was wet with the dew of God's blessing when all around was dry. He was the exceptional man.

I have found this in the home. One boy or one girl living a better life, striving quite timidly or frightened, like Gideon, to live an unselfish, holy life, the dew of God's blessing resting upon them. So Gideon, because he would serve the true God, and was unlike the rest, was chosen.

How were these three hundred men chosen? First, twenty-two thousand fell off because they were not brave enough to go to the battle. All who fight must be determined to fight till the last. The three hundred were chosen in the way I have read. The army came to a stream of water. "Here," said God, "I will try who are the true men. A great many were weary and hot, and they lay down. There was the water running down, so cool and refreshing after the weary march. There were three hundred men who did not lie down, but said, "We will have no rest until we defeat the enemy." And so they lapped the water like a dog. They did not lie down; they simply caught a handful of water and went on to the battle. Now you see why God chose these men; they had something to do in God's name and they would do that thing before anything else. They were men of one great object for the sake of God. You know, boys and girls, when you see people get on in the world you often say, "I should like to be successful like that one." You do not see all the toil and devotion which they have had to do. You see, afterwards people envied these three hundred men. But Gideon took them with him to the battle because they were men of a single eye, and that eye was fixed upon duty.

What is the lesson of all this for us? It is, if we do not do well, if we do not seek to do God's will in, the small things of life, God will not give us the opportunity to do them in the great things. In your home, you say, "When I am grown up and married, and at the head of the house, then I will try to set a good example." You will do very much when you are grown up what you do now. The little boy or girl who is selfish and makes the home unhappy will do the same when they are grown up. The selfishness will not leave you, believe me, when you become a man or woman. You think childhood is a gay and happy time. It is, and God desires and loves you to be happy. How many things indeed He has given you so that you may be happy. But oh, God gives you childhood to prepare you for manhood and womanhood, and if it is thrown away and wasted you will never recover it. There is no limit to God's mercy, but you can never make up for a wasted, selfish, and sinful childhood.

Remember, that as the men were chosen for the battle, so the leader was chosen himself, because he was a man of some courage in his own home. Home, I may tell you, is the very hardest place in which to show ourselves true and faithful servants of Jesus Christ. Pray God to give you the courage to be true to Him, and then you will be like Gideon, brave in the battle afterwards. Try and live like these three hundred men. There will be all kinds of streams of pleasure to lead you astray; but remember your purpose in life is to serve God for the sake of Jesus Christ, to fight all the enemies of the soul, and to permit none of these things to lead you away from God. Touch them lightly as these men took the water in their hands. Enjoy them as God has given them. Oh, never lie down by any stream of human pleasure as if it were your resting place.

Try to begin early to live as soldiers of the cross, try to learn early to be brave as He who died on the cross for you, try and learn in early life those lessons of obedience, self-sacrifice, and love, which will make you good servants and soldiers of Jesus Christ in the great battle of life hereafter.

Perhaps, God may not give you anything great in this life; but you do not know what God has for you hereafter. Do not think when you pass away from this life that you pass quite away from activity. God has work enough for his saints to do. Oh, early childhood! I beseech you, cherish it as the time during which God is fitting you by all the experiences of life for the more solemn duties which He will give you soon, and for the more glorious duties of the life which is to come.

T. T. S.

VIII. A Ministering Child.

1 SAM. ii. 18. *"Samuel ministered before the Lord, being a child, girded with a linen ephod."*

HERE you see the child Samuel busy in his early years with that which was to be work of his life. The scene to which you are taken is a place called Shiloh, situated among the hills of Ephraim, not far from the spot where Jacob, when flying from his father's house, dreamed of the ladder whose top reached to heaven, on which the angels of God ascended and descended, and above which stood the Lord God of Abraham and Isaac. There was the tent which served as the house of God. There lived the old priest Eli, whose two sons, by their bad conduct, made men abhor the offering of the Lord. There, too, was the Samuel of whom it is said that "he ministered before the Lord, being a child, girded with a linen ephod."

In this verse, there is the picture of a life surrendered.

In this verse, there is a service which is the sign of a life surrendered.

In this verse, there is a separation which is the sign of this service.

I. There is first the picture of a life surrendered.

It was surrendered to God by a pious mother, given by her as a life for a life. She had asked a life from God; when the child was born, she called him "the asked one," Samuel. And because the Lord had given her her petition, she lent or returned him to the Lord. In the hour of her gladness, when the sweet cares of motherhood were opening upon her, she solemnly dedicated her firstborn to the Father of fathers. And so the child grew up, knowing that the fixed point of his existence was that, whether he lived or whether he died, he was the Lord's. I hope that your parents, my dear young friends, have done as Hannah did; that from the earliest moment of your history, they gave you, in willing consent, in earnest prayer, in true act of devotion, to God your Father, Saviour, and Sanctifier. We, who are Christian fathers and mothers, should settle it in our hearts that our children are to grow up in the knowledge that they are not their own, but God's.

Happy, happy they whose first years have been infolded in parental piety, who begin their course in this world with a religious atmosphere about them, taught, as the beginning of all instruction and all discipline, that they are partakers with those whose name they bear, of the one blessed nurture, the nurture of the Lord, heirs with them of the one blessed grace, the grace of the eternal life. Thank God if you are the children of many prayers. "Who cares for mother?" said a boy one day to his sister, who told him that mother wished him to leave his play on the sand and come home. "My boy," said a gentleman who overheard the remark, "don't speak thus. I despised my mother, and took my own way, and broke her heart. But, after her death, oh, what would I have done to be able to call her back! I was miserable until I remembered how she taught me to pray; and I cast myself on her God, and He has heard me. Oh, how much I owe to my mother and her prayers!" The boy's eye kindled, and his voice trembled, as he said, "I will never speak lightly of my mother again."

It is a very touching picture this picture of Samuel and his mother. Do you not think that she would have liked her darling child beside her? that she must have shed some hot tears when she left the little fellow behind her at Shiloh, and went back to the distant home, and saw the little cot he was never more to sleep in? But she will not recall her gift. She lent him to the Lord. That life at Shiloh is his, not hers. Ah! when fathers and mothers grudge their children for some work of God, refuse to part with them that they may go forth and be Christ's ministers, let them reflect on Hannah and Elkanah, without a murmur, nay, with holy joy, yielding up their dearest to the ministry of God. Some of you may have read the life of good Bishop Patteson. Do you remember how beautifully the old judge, Patteson's father, folded his son in his arms, kissed him, and bade him go and preach Christ's gospel to the heathen, although he felt sure that he would never see him again?

Well, the life surrendered by the mother is, by his own free will, surrendered by the son also. There is no gap, it would seem, between the parents and the self-dedication. Sometimes, alas! there is. Sometimes mother's and father's eyes are sealed in death before the one whom they gave really gives himself to God. The child Samuel was always holy to the Lord. No break in his history. The Divine life filled him, and set its seal on him from early youth.

And yet there was an awakening hour—an hour in which he understood, as he had never done before, who was dealing with him, and what his life-work was to be; an hour in which there came a new earnestness into his character, a new sense of his calling as the servant and prophet of God. That hour is beautifully set before you in the third chapter. It was the Lord's call to Samuel, the revelation to him of the Word, which he had not yet known. What I feel is this: a child, in early childhood receives of the life that is around, the life of the home, or the influences immediately surrounding; and when that life or these influences are good, inspired by the Holy Spirit of God, there is often, although not always, a gradual unfolding of the beauties of holiness. But there is needed a moment in which the soul hears God calling to itself, and in which His Word—the Word which it may have been taught—is revealed, is lighted up with meaning, comes home with force; and the soul sees what before it heard and partly felt, and consciously answers God's call. That is the great moment in the history.

Then the picture of our verse is truly fulfilled,—the life is surrendered in sweet trust and willing obedience to the Lord.

II. But now observe the sign *of this surrendered life*—Service. "Samuel ministered before the Lord, being a child." He waited on the old priest, ready to go on his errands and attend to him in any way he wished. Perhaps he had some care of the lamps in the temple.

"Being a child." Sometimes God lays a heavy charge on even children; "being a child" is *not* something which stands in the way of service. You must not say, "Oh, I am only a child; I have nothing to do for God." There is the ministry of children as well as of grown-up people. In God's temple there is room for the young no less than for the old. Both the little Samuel and the old priest Eli are there.

The great word for all service is, "Before the Lord." When we live our life every day before the Lord, we are always ministering to him. The most ordinary thing done in his sight is a sacred thing. If you have the feeling of God in your heart, and the fear of God before your eyes, you are ministering when you are at school repeating your lessons, when you are at home learning them, when you are in the house and by the way. That which consecrates all is the direction of the mind. Look up; look to Jesus; carry the thought of Him with you wherever you go; ask His blessing on whatever you do; go only where and do only what you can feel sure He is pleased with and will bless, and you are dwelling in God's temple as truly as Samuel was, and ministering as truly as he did. Here is a grand text,—"I will walk before the Lord in the land of the living."

The secret of ministry is being ready, asking constantly "What wilt Thou have me to do." Samuel was taught the servant's answer, " Speak, Lord, Thy servant heareth." That is the way for us, to wait and be willing to be anything to do anything that God commands us.

III. The dress he wears is a sign of his consecration.

Now the ephod has disappeared, belonging as it did to the old priesthood of Israel, but the truth signified by it will never disappear—that God's servants must come out and be separate from the world.

J. M. L.

IX. Samuel. 1 Sam. iii. 7. *" Now Samuel did not yet know the Lord."*

WHEN you see a very old man, with white hair and wrinkled face and tottering steps, it is difficult to conceive that he was ever a child. And when you hear an old man of God pray—perhaps it may be your grandfather in your home, or the minister in the pulpit, or some one at the prayer-meeting—it is difficult to think that there was ever a time when he was not a true believer. I have no doubt the children of Ramah, where Samuel used to live, felt the same difficulty. When they saw the grand old man, who had been the judge and the king-maker, moving about the streets, they looked after him with awe ; how could they think he had ever been a boy like themselves? When they heard him at a sacrifice praying in his solemn tones, or in a meeting of the people, addressing them as a prophet in the very words of God, how could they think of a time when he did not know the Lord?

Yet there was such a time. He was a child once just like you, and he did not know the Lord. But one night God came and revealed Himself to him ; and from that time forth Samuel did know the Lord.

Three things are noticeable about Samuel at the time when he did not yet know the Lord :—

I. *Though he did not know the Lord, he knew about Him.*

He could not help learning a great deal about God, for he had a good father ; and his mother was one of the best women that have ever lived. She prayed a great deal for him ; and when he was born, she composed a beautiful hymn of thanks to God. They both wished their boy to grow up and be a godly man; they prized that far above wealth or station. They wished him to be a priest, and so they brought him to old Eli, and left him with him. He lived in the very house of God, and was a child-priest, in his little white linen ephod lighting and trimming the sacred lamps, and opening the doors of the tabernacle at daybreak. When his mother came year by year to see him, bringing his little coat, she must have spoken about God to him. And old Eli, who loved him as if he had been his own child, and made him his companion, must often have spoken to him on the same subject. He breathed an atmosphere full of religion; he saw the sacrifices offered and the incense rising every day; and the friends about him were all talking to him of God. If there was one child in all the country who knew far more about God than all the rest, it must have been he. Still, "he did not yet know the Lord."

Now, your lot may be very like his. Your father and mother are godly persons. You know they pray earnestly for you every day. They wish above everything else that you should turn out to be a genuine Christian.

Yet, for all that, perhaps you are like Samuel—you do not yet know the Lord.

It is one thing to know about a person, and another to know him. Some of you are learning languages, and may be aware that in most languages these two kinds of knowledge are distinguished by two different words,—in Latin, by *cognoscere* and *novisse;* in German, by *wissen* and *kennen;* in French, by *savoir* and *connaître*. The one of these words is used for knowing about a person or a thing, the other for knowing a person.

But you are all aware of this difference. You know, for instance, about the Queen. Perhaps you could tell her age, and when she came to the throne, what have been the chief events of her reign, and what are the names of her children. You have heard that she is good and noble; and you may admire and love her. But you only know about her. Your knowledge of her is not in the least like your knowledge of your own mother. It is a cold and distant kind of knowledge compared with this. You do not only know about your mother; you know her; you

D

are acquainted with her. It is because you live in the same house with her; because she speaks to you every day; you speak to her and confide in her; she belongs to you and you belong to her. It is a close and warm knowledge. It sets your heart on fire. She clasps you close, and says, This is my child. You clasp her close, and say, This is my mother.

Now, that is just the difference between knowing about God and knowing Him. Merely to know about Him is a cold and far-off thing. You may know about Him, and yet never think of Him except when you are being spoken to about Him, and you may not love Him in the least. But to know Him is to be acquainted with Him. It is to realize Him with you always,—in the daylight and in the dark; when you are working and playing, and lying awake. It is to speak to Him every day, and confide to Him all your secrets, as you do to your mother. It is to love Him, and to be able to say, He is my God—not only, He is God; but, He is *my* God.

Now, my children, do you know the Lord, or do you only know about Him? When Christ's name is mentioned, does it fall unheeded on your ears, or does it make you thrill with joy and love? When you think of Him, is it as one who lived long ago in Palestine, and is now far away up in heaven; or is it as one you spoke to this morning, and will speak to again to-night, and who is near you every hour? Is He your companion and your friend?

II. *As long as he did not know the Lord he was exposed to great dangers.*

Although he did not know the Lord, Samuel must have been in every way a child to love. We naturally think of him as a beautiful and noble-looking boy. Dressed in his pure white ephod, and the coat adorned by the loving fingers of his mother, he was fit to move about among the sacred objects of the tabernacle. His heart was still tender, and his mind unspotted by the world; he was sheltered in the holy place from temptation, and had not seen the vile deeds or heard the vile words of bad men. Still, any one, however good and sheltered from temptation, who does not know the Lord, is in danger. There is no safety for us till Christ has become our Friend and Saviour.

There was one danger close at hand. Eli's sons were very wicked and tempted those unto sin who came to worship. What if Hophni and Phinehas had cast their eyes on Samuel, and being angry to see his soul so white, had laid their black polluted hands on it and made it like their own? Sinners always wish to make others like themselves, and it is a delight to them to corrupt young souls.

Samuel was exposed to another danger. His heart would soon have grown hard. It was soft when God came to him; and that was why, as soon as Eli informed him who was calling, he answered God so heartily.

If you do not know God, you must be becoming a greater sinner every year. That hardens the heart against God. It will make you afraid of coming near Him.

There was another danger for Samuel as long as he did not know God. God intended him to become a very great man and do a great work in the world. He had gifted him with talents for this, but Samuel's life would have been lost if he had not learned to know the Lord.

Perhaps God intends some of you children to be great. It may be; but this is certain, that God intends you all to become true and noble men and women, to do good in your day in whatever sphere you may be placed.

Now you cannot do so unless you know God. When winter walks forth over the earth his breath brings death everywhere and his icy hand is laid with a deadly chill on the face of the old man in his bed and the baby in its cradle. But when summer goes forth over the world, joy and life spring all around her; where her footsteps fall the flowers spring up, her fingers touch the trees and they smile with blossom and verdure; all the birds on the boughs sing their finest songs to welcome her, and the rivers dance in the bright sunlight with gladness. Will your march through life be like winter's, chilling and killing; or like summer's, blessing all about you and gladdening their hearts? It depends on whether you know the Lord or not. All the good Samuel did in the world dated from the night when he learned to know Him.

III. *Because he did not know the Lord, he did not recognise God calling him.*

The boy-priest used to lie in the tabernacle all night. He slept alone. Many a one would have been afraid to sleep in that awful place, but Samuel slept soundly and had no fear.

But one night, when the darkness lay upon all the earth outside, when everything in the tabernacle was as still as death, and Samuel lay in the deep sleep of boyhood, a strange loud voice broke the silence in the chamber, and he started up with his own name ringing in his ears—Samuel, Samuel. It was God's voice; but he did not recognise it, because he did not yet know the Lord.

My children, you will never hear a voice like that from heaven breaking the silence of the night in your bedroom. But God calls to you just as really as he did to Samuel, though, like him, you may not have recognised the voice.

He calls to children in many ways. You notice sometimes the anxiety of your parents or your teachers about your soul. They speak to you; you know they pray for you; you have been surprised at the strange, yearning look of love in your mother's eyes sometimes, or the pain shooting over her face when you committed a sin. Who do you think put that love and anxiety there for you? It was God. He put it there because He loves you far more than either father or mother. It is Christ who pleads with you through human lips. But perhaps you never recognised that; you thought it was only man's call.

Perhaps death has entered the families of some of you, removing those you loved. That was God calling; but perhaps you did not recognise Him.

God is calling you. Will you not do as Samuel did? He went back alone to his room. With what awe he must have entered it! How different it was from what it had ever been before! It was full of God. Often he had prayed there before, but God had been far away. Now He was beside him. Will you do that in your bedroom to-night? You have prayed there often before, but God was far away. But when it is dark, will you try to realize that Christ is just beside you? Will you speak to Him soft and low, telling Him you wish Him to be your Saviour, to be your friend and companion for life; that you wish Him to take your sins away, and to keep your soul safe till it is in heaven with Himself? Samuel's true life began that night; perhaps yours will begin to-night.

J. S.

X. The Ark of God. 1 Sam. iv. 10, 11.

"*And the Philistines fought, and Israel was smitten, and they fled every man into his tent; and there was a very great slaughter; for there fell of Israel thirty thousand footmen. And the ark of God was taken.*"

THIS, you see, is an account of a battle which took place many many years ago between the armies of Israel and the forces of the Philistines. And the Israelites were beaten, and the ark of God was taken. This last fact is mentioned as the most terrible thing that could have occurred. You know that if the French or German or English soldiers were beaten they would tell you with shame that so many standards were taken. The ark was to the Israelites what the cross of our Redeemer is to us. It was a representation to them of their country and of their religion; and so when the account is written here of how the armies of the Israelites were beaten, it is all summed up in these words—" The ark of God was taken."

I want first of all to speak to you about the ark itself. You must not confuse it with the ark which Noah built; the ark here referred to was quite another thing. First, let me tell you what it looked like. It was a box or chest made of acacia wood—a wood we read of in the Bible—it was the wood of the acacia tree. The box was some six feet long and three feet wide. This ark or chest, for the word in the Hebrew means chest, was covered with inlaid gold, and on either end of it were the cherubim. These were two figures, one at each end, each figure being called a cherub. Cherubim, I may explain, is the plural of cherub. These cherubim were also made of gold. There were four rings, one at each corner of this chest or ark, and through these were poles, and the men whose duty it was to carry the ark carried it through these poles resting upon their shoulders. These were the Levites, who were especially privileged in this respect.

This ark was placed within the Tabernacle. This simply meant a tent. In those days, when people were moving about like the Arabs, they did not live in houses but in tents. Just as you see in the English army rows of tents and a big tent in the centre with the colours of the army standing in the corner; so with the ark of God.

This ark was covered with a curtain. So sacred was the ark that though they took it out of the tent to carry before them, it was covered with richly embroidered cloth so that no one could see it. The ark was for the Israelites a type and an emblem of God. We know that God is with us, but we cannot see Him, and so the ark was to them a type of God's presence. In the ark were three things; first, the tables on which Moses wrote the law of God, to remind the people always that they were to keep God's laws; secondly, a little pot of manna with which they were fed in the wilderness; thirdly, there was in it Aaron's rod which budded. You remember that when the people rebelled against Aaron, his rod blossomed forth. This was to remind the people that they were to obey God.

So you see that the ark was a sacred thing to the people of Israel. When they came to the River of Jordan, and they distrusted God, the ark went before them and the waters were divided and they passed safely over, and when they came to a fortified city the ark was carried around that city, and after a while the walls of the city fell. It was the ark that reminded them of God's tenderness to men, and so it was a terrible thing to them when it was captured by the Philistines.

What was the object of the Philistines? They thought, if we can get this ark we shall get the victory over our enemies, as by its aid the Israelites have won their battles.

The lesson I wish to set before you is, that though a thing may be very good for some it may be very bad for others. This ark helped the Israelites and preserved them; but when the Philistines got it into their possession it was no good to them, and in the end it got to be such a curse to the Philistines that they very soon got rid of it. This was because God had not given it to them, for they had stolen it from the Israelites. It all turns on that. Are you born rich, of high station, with many friends; or are you born poor, of low estate, and almost as it were alone in the world? It is good whether you are rich or poor, because God has so ordered it. Remember, the ark became a great curse to those who had no right to it. Where God has placed you, whether rich or poor, you are not to be discontented with it. I hear some say: "If I was like so and so I could be of such use!" My little friend, if you do not use the place and opportunity that God has given you, and do not use the blessing which God has bestowed upon you, depend upon it, it does not matter in what rank of life you are, or how rich you are, you are not acting right. God gives wealth and rank, which is much, and He gives poverty. That and nothing else is good for you—what God has given you.

A great and distinguished man gave a little girl a plant which he had brought from a northern climate, and she was told by this man—he was a great traveller—to put this plant into a particular part of the garden, where the cold wind beat upon it. And the little girl looked upon this plant day after day, and it seemed to her that it was withering up. She went into the conservatory in the heat and there she saw the grand plants blossoming even in the midst of the heat. She hesitated a moment, then went and dug up her little plant and placed it in a pot in the conservatory, and thought that in that warm place her plant would become as glorious as any in that conservatory. The next morning she went to look at it and it was dead. The heat had killed it. What made the others blossom, according to God's law of nature, had killed the plant which only blossomed in the cold.

And so it is, boys and girls, in your life. If God has put you in a place, preserved by those who love you from all cold blasts, be satisfied; but if He ever places you in His mercy and love where the storm of trial and temptation will beat upon you, it is only there you will blossom. The ark which blest the Israelites to whom God had given it, cursed the Philistines who stole it.

T. T. S.

XI. "Send and fetch him." 1 SAM. xvi. 11. "*And Samuel said unto Jesse, Send and fetch him.*"

MANY years ago, there was a farmhouse in the quiet village of Bethlehem, in which lived a man called Jesse. He had a large family, and some of his sons were very fine-looking men indeed. One day the quiet of the place was disturbed by the report that the prophet Samuel had come.

The people did not know what to make of his visit; but though he did not tell them his errand, he managed to make them feel easy. Very soon there was some stir in the old farmhouse. "I want to see your sons." "Very well," said Jesse; for fathers like to show their children, and especially when they are as handsome as many of his sons were. No one of them knew that Samuel was looking for the future king; but when the tall and manly figure of Eliab came, the prophet thought, "This must be the man. He is fit to be a successor to Saul." But God said, "No." The fact is, God does not go by outward appearance. He looks lower down. There are some of you very fine-looking fellows; but, "*Handsome is that handsome does.*" You may be big and strong, and only use your strength to bully other boys smaller than yourself. You may be a very pretty girl, and yet your beauty may only be a mask, and your real nature be ugliness itself. Remember, "*The Lord looketh on the heart.*" What does he see in your heart? Does He see a great tall body, hiding a little cowardly heart? Does He see, behind a lovely face, a vain and deceitful heart? If so, you will not do. You are not yet fit to be one of God's kings or queens. But you may have the heart changed. You may have a beautiful mind given to you, and then it will not matter so much whether you are good-looking or not.

When the old farmer had sent in his sons one after another, and God had refused them all, Samuel asked, "Are here all thy children?" He was told that he had seen them all except the youngest, and that he was in the fields taking care of the sheep. "Ah well," said he, "let me look at him. '*Send and fetch him.*'" Send for whom?

I. *A boy neglected.* It is plain to be seen that David's brothers, if not his father, did not care for him as much as he deserved. Perhaps, like another younger brother, he had dreams of a bright future. A lad with such mettle in him as David had, must have felt at times that he would like to be a soldier, or in some place with more life and stir than Bethlehem. But his brothers seem to have sneered at him; and when Jesse sent for his sons, instead of Eliab saying to one of the servants, "Here, take care of these sheep till David comes back," he left the boy in the field, just as he did afterwards when he went to war. Though his big body had a heart too small to go and fight the giant, he could sneer at David when he felt that *he* should like to have a try at ridding his country of such a plague.

Well, and supposing there is some little fellow who is quite overshadowed by his big brothers, or some little girl who is quite forgotten when her elder sisters are playing on the piano before the visitors, don't let it spoil you, and make you sulky. David did not grow peevish because no one noticed him. He looked cheerful when he came before Samuel. So *you* must remember that neglect will not make you any worse, for sooner or later your turn will come. When a collection is made in a church, supposing a gentleman should put half a sovereign in the box, and then threepenny pieces, and sixpences, and pennies are put on the top of it, and hide it, so that no one can see it; by-and-by the box will be taken into the vestry, and overturned upon the table; and some one is sure to see it and say, "Here's a bit of gold," and he will put it by itself. And if *you* are *gold*, it does not matter how the big penny pieces try to hide you; sooner or later you will be seen, and made a great deal of.

"Send and fetch him." Whom?

II. *A boy minding his work.* Yes, he was a picture of Jesus, the Good Shepherd. He stuck to his work, and it was from his lowly duty he was sent for to be anointed King of Israel. It was dangerous work. The other day I saw a beautiful picture of the shepherd lad standing on a dead lion. There was the king of beasts dead on the plain, and a pool of blood under him; and the brave lad was standing on him, as he afterwards stood on Goliath. And all round him the sheep and goats were bleating, and saying in their language, "Oh what a brave shepherd we have!" If David had run away from either the lion or the bear, and left the sheep to be killed by the wild beasts, God would not have chosen him to be a king. Boys! stick to your work! Never mind how difficult it is. Conquering here, you shall fit yourself for other duties. Be brave, and never flinch from your tasks.

It was, when not dangerous, very tedious work. For a lad so active as David was, the work would be very dull; but it was his duty, so he kept at it. He made the time pass quickly by improving himself in the knowledge of music, and became a very skilful player on the harp. Some of you would have gone to sleep; but David wanted to make a man of himself, and so kept practising on the harp, until it was difficult to say whether he was a better shepherd or musician. After a while, King Saul became very unhappy and low-spirited, and some of his friends advised him to have some one who could cheer him by music; and then David was called for. One of the king's nobles said, "I have seen a son of Jesse the Bethlehemite, that is cunning in playing." So one day the old farmer found some men who had come with a message from the palace: "The king said, '*Send me David thy son, which is with the sheep.*'" You see they did not think David not fit to come to the palace because he had been taking care of the sheep. It was well known how he had spent his time. He who can kill lions or bears when they come, and fill up his time playing on a harp in the style David did, need not fear that he will suffer in the estimation of the great because he has to mind sheep; for it is true now, as it was in the time of David's wise son, King Solomon— "Seest thou a man diligent in his business? He shall stand before kings; he shall not stand before mean men."

"Send and fetch him." Whom?

III. *A boy who feared God.* It is very plain to be seen that David was a good lad. It is most likely that while he was keeping sheep he made some of the beautiful psalms, such as the eighth and nineteenth. It will be worth your while to go through the psalms and pick out those you think likely to have been made while he was a shepherd lad.

Perhaps some lad here is saying, "Ah! I am sorry that I am not brave. I am sure that I should have run away from the lion, and let him eat the kid, and its mother as well." You don't know that. If you had been called to it, maybe you would have had courage to fight as David did. In rambling about the world as I have done, by sea and land, I have found that some of the timid and nervous people have, in danger, done better than some of the loud blustering ones.

Is there some one who would like to have the chance to do something brave? Well, I want you to turn back a lion! "What's that?" you say; "turn back a lion!" Yes. The next time you are tempted to sin—to tell a lie, or to disobey your mother—you may turn back a lion, for that is what Satan is like—"*As a roaring lion, walketh about, seeking whom he may devour.*" "*Resist the devil, and he will flee.*"

Oh! my young friends, be good. Love that Saviour who died in your place. Do as God tells you to do; and then, though you may have to live in Bethlehem all your life, and never be known outside of your own quiet street, yet God will know all about you, and the day of your coronation will come. Then shall the King greatly desire you, and shall say to his angels,—

"*Send and fetch him.*"

Let us then do our duty, and thus prepare for future honours.

T. C.

XII. Parting Alike. 1 Sam. xxx. 24. "*As his part is that goeth down to battle, so shall his part be that tarrieth by the stuff: they shall part alike.*"

THIS is a law that was made by David, and was kept till the time this book was written, and it was ordained that the one that went to the battle and the one who tarried by the stuff were to part alike. What does "part alike" mean? It means there was to be a division of what was captured in war, parted alike—divided equally. Now the way it came about was this; David was going down to a battle, and he took 600 men with him, and 200 were left behind. They occupied themselves in guarding the stuff, that is the household things that were left behind. It would be hard if those who went forward and defeated the enemy and took an immense deal of spoil had come back, and those who had been left behind to guard the camp—though equally ready to go forward—had no share in the spoil; indeed on one occasion, when no one had been left behind to guard the camp, the enemy had come in and captured the camp, so that the men who were actually victors in one part of the battle had lost their stuff or household things; and so it was found necessary for some to guard the camp while the others went into battle. It was therefore laid down by David that the share was to be equal between all the men. That is, if a man was doing his duty by guarding the camp, he was to share in the spoils the same as the man who had done *his* duty by going into action.

That is what David, a man after God's own heart, settled, and that is what God settles for us now.

All who do their duty will have an equal reward from the Captain of our Salvation. Now, boys and girls, that is a lesson to you all. The hundreds of you who come here to listen to me cannot all become famous in this world; but do not imagine that they only who become famous will share the spoil. The share will be equal to all if you do your duty to God and to man. Though the leader in the great battle gets the glory and honour, he could not win the engagement without the help of all those who take part in the engagement. A great poet—Tennyson—tells of the captain of a ship who had been very cruel to his men, a very unusual thing for the captain of an English ship to be. And the men dare not rise against him in mutiny. They simply waited their time. These men resolved when the day of danger came that they would do nothing for the captain. So one day, when the ships of the enemy came into sight, the men went to their guns but they resolved not to fight. The captain called to the men, but they were silent. The captain was a brave man, but what could he do? Shot after shot of the enemey poured in, and the ship went down. The men sold their captain into shame. They had forgotten the great lesson which we all have to learn.

The question is not "What have I to do?" but "How am I doing it?" It will be nothing but shame if you are not doing your duty well. You may be in the humblest condition of life, but if you do your duty well it will be noble in the sight of God. There was living a short time back, near Charing Cross, a harness-maker. He was in a very humble position in life. He had three sons—one son became a Lord Chief Baron, a second became a Field Marshal in the army, and the third became the Lord Chief Justice of England. One of them died only the other day. When a man—not unkindly so—reminded the Field Marshal that his father had been a saddle-maker near Charing Cross, the old soldier replied: "I know he did his work well; I should be ashamed if any one said he did his work badly." Noble words! It is not what you do, if it be only to tarry by the stuff; if you do your duty you will all share alike in God's sight.

I have a word to say to you particularly, little girls. Your true position in life is to tarry by the stuff, to keep to the home. You have a noble duty to do there. The father or mother goes out into the battle of life and becomes a great soldier or preacher of the gospel. You have your own duty to do—to make home the best place where your brothers or, in time, your husbands can be; and your portion in the great share of the spoil of the world will be share and share alike. To you, girls, who tarry by the home, comes an equal share. Some of the greatest in heaven are those women who ministered to the Son of man.

The best place to learn this is in the life of Jesus Christ. Three and a half years of toil and shame, and then the Cross; but, oh, after that the glory of the Eternal Son of God. Remember His life, His death; think ever of His cross and passion, of His eternal glory; and pray and strive night after night, day after day, when you rise in the morning and when you lie down at rest, pray that you may do nobly the duty God has given to you to do. Do it in humble trust, not in your own strength, but in the strength of Jesus Christ, who loved you and gave Himself for you.

T. T. S.

XIII. Solomon's Prayer. 1 KINGS iii. 7. "*I am but a little child.*"

WHO is the little child that says this? It is curious, but it was not a little child at all. Trace the words up, and you find that they came forth from the lips of a full-grown man. He spoke them in a dream by night. Follow him next morning, and you will see that he is a king. He wears a crown. Yet here he says "I am but a little child." What made him say it then? He had ascended the throne of his father David, who had trained him in the nurture and admonition of the Lord. So he was humble, and thoughtful, and distrustful of himself. "I am but a little child." But his people—Judah and Israel—were many. "They cannot be numbered," he says; and they are God's chosen people, and a great people. They required therefore a monarch who should be worthy of such a people. God knew this too, and He intended to furnish Solomon with those very things.

But He will try him first, and before giving them, will have him ask for them. Accordingly in a vision, as Solomon slept, God said to him, "Ask what I shall give thee." Now the uppermost thing in the new king's mind was a desire for wisdom. So after a short and beautiful preface about his beloved father and God's faithfulness both to him and himself, he lets the secret of his soul spread its wings and fly heavenward in the cry "I am but a little child: I know not how to go out or come in. Give therefore Thy servant an understanding heart, that I may discern between good and bad."

That cry went up (far above the soaring, singing lark) to the ear of God. The answer descended, silently as the rain on a blossom, straight as the dove on Jesus, abundantly as the dew on Gideon's fleece. Solomon from that hour was the wisest man there ever was, or will be. "Neither after thee shall any arise like unto thee."

You would be delighted to have such a vision as that, and to have it prove true. But is it not so that God bids us all ask what He shall give to us? "Ask and it shall be given you." Does He not say to us, "If any lack wisdom let him ask of God, and it shall be given him."

I. Remember though you are "but a little child," God notices you.

If He notices those who feel themselves to be but little children, He surely notices those who are little children. We see this notice of them very frequently in the Bible, such as Moses, Samuel, the captive Hebrew maid, the mere babes blessed by Jesus. God notices you. He marks all your ways and doings, at home, in the street, at school. The bedridden lad in the garret who said to the city missionary, " I'm left alone from breakfast to supper, but mother locks Jesus in with me when she takes the key, and I have such sweet times in talking to Him and repeating my hymns and texts to Him," that little lad realized that God noticed him.

II. We are taught that though you are "but a little child," He would have you pray. He said to Solomon, "Ask what I shall give thee," that is, pray to Me. "They that seek Me early shall find Me." A little child once wrote a letter to Jesus, directed it to Him and dropped it into the post-office. He had seen his father writing letters to his friends and getting replies from them in the same way, so he determined to use the same plan in addressing Jesus. That was very simple faith in Christ's willingness to be addressed by a little child, and doubtless it was lovely in His sight. But prayer is the right and certain plan of addressing Him. You may be as confident that He is listening, as if you were kneeling at His feet, or exchanging telegraphic messages with Him.

III. We are taught that you should ask God for wisdom. You may think that it is too glorious a thing to expect. God offers it freely to you little children. This is Solomon's testimony about it, " Her ways are ways of pleasantness, and all her paths are peace." Whatever you want, wisdom will supply it; it will help you to fight against temptation, to subdue a naughty temper, to bear a reproach, to be cheerful under trouble. In short, when God gives an "understanding heart" He gives a new heart. When He gives us wisdom, He gives us His Holy Spirit, and that is better than the fairest face, the costliest dress, the most splendid fortune.

IV. We are taught here that if you ask for wisdom, God will give it you, and other things too. God does give wisdom to little children who ask for it, and He has given all little children the capacity for it; and He now wants to put the pearl into the casket, when they shall open it to Him and ask Him to put it in. Then He will be able to add other things to it without doing you harm. Where the "understanding heart" is viewed and treated as the first thing, He can give besides wealth, or friends, or pleasures, or beauty, or all of them together. At any rate that is the gate out of which they issue as blessings, and if we enter at it, we may look for them, or else settle it with ourselves that God withholds them because they would not be blessings to us.

Will you let Solomon's prayer for an "understanding heart" be yours? Will you let it be your prayer all through, till your rosy cheeks are exchanged for grey hairs, nay, till the last milestone is passed and the next is your own tombstone.

If so, we can promise you a childhood of joy, a youth of success, a manhood of influence, an old age of tranquillity.

"Get wisdom," and you have got all this, and eternal "riches and honours" besides.

J. B.

XIV. The Little Maid. 2 Kings v. 1–27.

IN former days, when one king ruled in Scotland and another in England, the people near the borders very often fought against each other, even when the two countries were at peace. At one time the English would cross the borders and carry away from Scotland all they could get, and at another time the Scotch would march into England and burn English castles, and drive off English cattle, and bring back English prisoners.

Something of the same kind went on between the Israelites and the Syrians, about 2,700 years ago. Once when the Syrians marched into the kingdom of Israel, they carried off among their captives a young girl. The Syrian general saw her, and was so much pleased with her appearance, that he took her home to be a little servant to his wife. Naaman was the name of this general. The Hebrew slave girl soon noticed that there was something wrong with her master. He was captain of the host, a great man with the king, and held in honour by all the people as a mighty man of valour; *but he was a leper.* Everybody young and old has some *but*. We would be happy, *but* for this. We have some things, *but* we have not that. Naaman's *but* was a very serious one. His seems to have been a case of white leprosy. Little white spots appeared on the face and then covered the whole body, till the leper became as white as snow. These spots grew to the size of a pea or a bean. The nails of the hand and feet became scaly. The teeth began to drop out, and the fingers and toes to drop off. The whole body became a mass of disease, and the poor victim was often thankful when death came to end his misery. The general was not very bad yet. But if he had been in Israel, even as he was, he would not have been allowed to command the army. He would have had to live by himself. Even in Syria he knew he would soon have to retire into private life. The little maid saw and heard something of all this. She knew enough to make her very sorry for her master. So one day she said to her mistress, " I wish very much the general could go to the Hebrew prophet in Samaria, for I am sure *he* could cure him of his leprosy." She was *a very good girl*, and she *did a great deal of good*.

See what a very good girl she was. Hers was a very hard case. The soldiers had carried her away captive, and Naaman was their general. Many a one in her place would have said, " I hate these Syrian soldiers and everybody connected with them. My master is their captain, and has been the means of killing and making slaves of many of my people. I am very glad to see him suffering so much, and to see his wife so sorry. I have my revenge." Even without going so far, she might have fretted and brooded over the past, and taken no interest in her master or mistress. But she did not cry and sulk. She was like a little flower plucked from a far-off garden, and taken away to be all alone in a strange place. But, like that flower, she carried a sweet fragrance along with her, and filled her new home with a delightful odour. She was not revengeful, but forgiving ; she was not selfish, but thoughtful of others, and thankful for their kindness. She felt for others, and tried to make them happy and to do them good.

But besides this, the little maiden showed she had not forgotten the religious lessons of her childhood. She had no mother now to tell her about the God of Israel. The people she lived among were worshippers of idols.

E

But she remembered what her mother had told her of the True God and of the great works He enabled His servants to do. She had heard of the prophet of the Lord, Elisha, who lived in Samaria, and she believed that he could heal the sick and do great wonders by the power of God. And so she said to her mistress, "I wish my master were with the prophet that is in Samaria, for he could recover him of his leprosy." Some of you remember about the great woman of Shunem. She made ready a little room for Elisha, and called it "The prophet's chamber," so that whenever he passed that way he came and dwelt in it. She was married and, like everybody else, she had a *but*. She had no family. Afterwards, however, she had a child, and he became a fine boy. One morning he was on the harvest-field with his father looking at the reapers who were busy cutting down the grain. All at once he cried, "My head, my head." His father told one of the lads to carry him to his mother, and he sat on his mother's knees till noon, and died. Elisha raised this little boy to life again, and said to his mother, "Take up thy son," which she did very gladly and thankfully, you may be sure. Now the little maid remembered this, and she believed that the man who could do that, could cure her master's leprosy.

She told her mistress about Elisha, and soon the king of Syria heard what she had said. And the king of Syria sent a letter to the king of Israel. And Elisha heard of it, and said, "Let Naaman come to me, and he shall know that there is a prophet in Israel." Then Naaman went to Samaria, with a grand chariot and fine horses, and a number of servants. I cannot tell you all that happened, but Naaman was cured by going, as the little maid desired. The result was that the God of Israel was made known to the heathen as the Great God to whom all should look for help. Naaman himself said, "Now I know that there is no God in all the earth but in Israel."

Now is this not a good example for boys and girls, and for men and women too? We should all be forgiving and thoughtful of others. We should try to make one another good and happy, and not bad and miserable. And whatever you young people forget when you go from home, you should remember what your fathers and mothers, and ministers and Sabbath-school teachers have told you about your heavenly Father and Jesus Christ His Son, and the Holy Spirit, and the Bible, and the way of salvation from sin and misery. You see, too, how much one person can do. This little maid sent a great man to God's servant, and his leprosy departed. And boys and girls still can be the means of sending persons— who may be very clever and rich and great, but who have a sad spiritual leprosy—to the Son of God, who is a Great Physician, able to save to the uttermost all that come to Him. And remember a boy or girl may do a great deal of *evil* as well as a great deal of *good*. Let all of my young friends be like the little maid and try to do good, and every little will help to make the world good and happy.

> " Little drops of water, little grains of sand,
> Make the mighty ocean, and the solid land ;
> Little deeds of kindness, little words of love,
> Make our earth an Eden, like the heaven above."

W. H. G.

XV. Where to Carry our Sins. Ps. xxxii. 7.
" Thou art my hiding-place."

YOU often see your minister look very severe when he speaks about sin. Your Sunday-school teacher tells you about fighting a giant, though it turns out that she means no real giant, but some habit of wrong-doing. And David, in his thirty-second Psalm, calls what kind of a man very happy or blessed? The rich man? The educated man? The famous man? No; neither of these; but the man who has somehow got rid of his sins.

Now, you may not know it, but you are all on the side of preacher, teacher, and Psalmist. Your fist was doubled up last week as decidedly as if you really had a giant on hand to fight, and your face was as earnest as David's must have been when he began this song of his. A boy in school had told a falsehood about you. Tell me, what did your clenched hand and your scowl mean? They meant that just then you keenly felt hatred for one sort of sin. We always despise sin in others when that sin makes us suffer or lose anything. But very often we see that we ourselves have done before now the very things we loathe so in others. Our eyes seek the ground when we straightway remember some falsehood of our own, some bad thought we once harboured ourselves. We become very wretched indeed. Paul tells us, in Romans, that we feel then as if our souls lived inside a dead body, and that we could cry out: "Oh! wretched man that I am!"

I. The remembrance of our sins is grievous to us. They are like a corpse in our charge: where shall we bury it from sight? Poor David shows us in this Psalm that he imagined he could bury them in his own bosom. "I kept silence," he says. So you have more than once made up your mind, "I'll say nothing to anybody about my sins, and I'll stop thinking about them myself." But, with Israel's king, you have found that silence is not peace. "My bones," he writes, "waxed old," or, literally, rotted. The body of death is not yet buried. His friends may think well enough of him, but God reads his heart with an eye as piercing as the Palestine sun, which, you know, seeks every blade of grass and withers it. "Day and night Thy hand was heavy upon me: my moisture is turned into the drought of summer." It is certain, you see, that we cannot bury our sins where they will cease to trouble us.

II. The covering of sin. Was not the covering of his sins the very thing that David was rejoicing about as he began his Psalm with "Blessed is he whose sin is covered"? Yes; but the next verse tells us who it is that covers sin: "Blessed is he to whom the *Lord* imputeth not iniquity." It is very joyful news to us that the Lord who buried Moses's dead body where no one could find it, has undertaken to bury the body of our sins. When the sun comes out after a gloomy rain, on some of these May afternoons, remember that He said: "I have blotted out, as a thick cloud, thy transgressions."

III. How the Lord hides sin. David makes haste to tell us how the Lord hides our sins: "I said, I will confess my transgressions unto the Lord." That means that we may make our Heavenly Father our Confidant, and with sorrow tell Him the very worst secrets of our hearts. No mother was ever so gentle and gracious with us as He is. We have no sooner cried in bitterness of soul, "God be merciful to me a sinner," than He bids us "Go in peace." This is just what the beloved disciple teaches us. "If we say that we have no sin we deceive ourselves, and the truth is not in us ; if we confess our sins, He is faithful and just to forgive us our sins and to cleanse us from all unrighteousness."

A year ago a friend of mine was trying to cross the Simplon Pass into Switzerland. While he was in one of the tunnels near the summit an awful avalanche of snow thundered down the mountain side. It did not harm him, though, because he was hid away inside the rocky tunnel. There are worse things than avalanches hanging above the path each of you must travel before you die : grief, pain, temptation. Where will you hide in the day of trouble ? The ostrich, when chased, buries its eyes in the sand, and thinks itself safe from the hunter because it no longer sees him. Foolish bird ! But too many a boy and girl tries to forget sin by turning the mind away from it. Why not learn a lesson from your baby brother ? When he hears a strange knock at the door he runs and buries his face in the skirts of his mother, and is safe. Why not, when you feel troubled about your sin, go away to Jesus, with the words of David here : " Thou art my hiding-place ? "

M. D. B.

XVI. The fear of the Lord. Ps. xxxiv. 11. *"Come, ye children, hearken unto me: I will teach you the fear of the Lord."*

I WANT to talk to you for a few minutes about why the Bible was written.

Some of you when going to school in these days carry a parcel or a bag of books, and if I met you on the way and said to you : "What's this book for ?" I suppose you would be able to answer, "Oh! that is a geography." "And what is this book written for ?" "That is a grammar." "And what is the use of that one ?" "Well, that is an arithmetic." And so I could go on, through all your bag of books, and you would be able to tell me generally why the books were written. One was written to teach arithmetic, another history, and so on.

Now, I wonder if I asked you for what purpose the Bible was written, what sort of answer I should get. I will tell you what David thought about it. There is a beautiful verse in one of his Psalms which I think specially belongs to children, and it says something about the purpose for which the Bible was written.

"Come, ye children, hearken unto me: I will teach you"—who can finish the verse? "The fear of the Lord."

I think, then, that the Bible was written in order to teach us that. David wanted children to listen to him, and there is a great deal in this Old Testament that we have from David, and it seems to me that when he was writing for other people it was to teach them that beautiful fear of the Lord. Now, if you will "hearken unto me" I will try to teach you what this fear is. We must first of all try to find out what it is not. There are some kinds of fear which are not quite like the fear that David talks about. My home was in a very lonely country part, and the nights were very dark, and there are woods not very far away, and I did not like being sent out into the dark. Well, just imagine a boy coming home one night full of fear and trembling, yet not knowing what he was afraid of. The moon was not shining, so he could not be afraid of his own shadow. And coming on along the quiet road he hears a noise with every step he makes, a sound of a horse's feet or of the sheep rapidly running away as they hear his lonely step. And the fancy keeps returning that he hears an unusual noise, and at length he hears that there really is something coming nearer.

What shall he do? His courage nearly all deserts him; he does not exactly know what to do Perhaps it would hardly be safe to whistle, nor yet to turn out of the road. So he comes on with fear and trembling until he sees it is some person, very tall and strange-looking, and as he comes nearer he stops, and the man says—what? "Is that you, my boy?" "Ah! yes, father!" What a wonderful relief it was. And that little boy was very full of fear, and was specially afraid of that dark object as it came nearer and nearer.

But was that the sort of fear, was that the fear of the Lord that David wanted to teach the people? No! we learn that sort of fear soon enough—directly we have done wrong—and we learn it without any teaching. Can you tell me of anybody who was afraid of the Lord much in the way I have described? In the Book of Genesis, the very beginning of the book, some one was afraid. "Adam and Eve"—some one says—were afraid. Yes! when they heard the voice of God, when He was walking in the garden in the middle of the day, they went and hid themselves; but depend upon it that was not the sort of fear that David wanted the children to learn. "The fear of the Lord" was not to be afraid of Him, was it? And now let us try to find out what it was, for it is much more important to know what it is than what it is not; perhaps it is more difficult to find out what it is. When I find a thing difficult I generally like to illustrate it by a story. Now, I know a true story that has something to do with "the fear of the Lord."

A little friend of mine, a charming little girl, is the subject of my story. Some of our best stories, I suppose, are not true, but truth is stranger than fiction. This true story is of this little girl. She went to stay with her auntie out in the country, and there were a great number of damson trees in her auntie's garden, full of their purple fruit. Mary was fond of any ripe fruit; she liked to go and pick the fruit off the ground, to shake the lower branches and pick up the fallen apples or damsons. And one day damson pudding came on the table, and little Mary enjoyed it very much until her aunt looked across the table and said, "Mary dear! what are you doing with the stones?" "Why! swallowing them auntie." "Oh! but you must not swallow them." Well, Mary was a curious little girl, so she said, "Why may not I swallow them?" Now her uncle was a funny fellow, and he said, "I will tell you Mary! if you swallow the stones they will grow, and if one grows out of the top of your head it will spoil your best bonnet." But Mary said, quickly enough, "Oh! then I can easily shake the tree and down will come the damsons."

But her aunt said, "Mary! you are too young yet to know why it is wrong for you to swallow the stones, but you are old enough to know that it is wrong to do what aunt tells you not to do; and if you do, it will make God sorry." Then said the little girl, "I will never do it again if it makes God sorry." Next day there was some sort of damson again, and Mary was very proud of her new virtue, and so she placed the stones in a nice row round her plate. But very soon auntie was called away from the table, and when she came back all the stones were gone.

"Where are they?" "I have swallowed them, auntie," said the little girl, sobbing. "Well, never mind, darling, I will forgive you." "But" came again through her sobs, "God is sorry." Then her aunt saw that it was not enough to comfort her, and so she took her away out of that room into another. And they both knelt down and prayed to God a prayer something like this: "Dear Jesus! please to forgive Mary for doing what her aunt told her not to do, and for making you sorry. Amen." And then she came out, feeling quite sure that though God had been sorry for her disobedience, He had freely forgiven her.

And now, ever since I heard that quite true story, I have felt that I knew what the fear of the Lord was, and that it was the fear of making God sorry. It is to be afraid of anything that would grieve Jesus; and I say the Bible is written to teach us that very thing, how not to grieve God and not to make Him sorry. I am afraid this purpose is often forgotten, and here I must speak to the elder ones. It is frequently forgotten when we attend our Bible classes from week to week. It is right for us to want to know the facts of the Bible, but are we not often apt to forget this ultimate purpose for which the Bible was written? I think some persons reverence the Bible as a man does a telescope who does not use it. There it is! a beautiful thing, to be kept nicely polished, placed like a handsome book on a nice little table. I say nothing against having a nicely bound volume; I am not sure that I am not pleased when I see it. But let it be for use as well as for ornament. If a man has a telescope, a valuable one, the proper thing is for him to use it in reading the heavens and bring them nearer.

And so it is with the Bible. It is a telescope by means

of which we can get to know these things. I say sometimes, too, that it is intended to be used like a time-table, to tell about the starting of trains and the journey. Fancy a man studying Bradshaw's guide, and going on to the Continent without it; he may easily miss finding some high mountain or finding time to ascend it because he goes without his guide. The Bible is intended to be of spiritual help to us, to assist us to scan the heavens and to help us to learn the fear of the Lord.

Now, there are reasons given in this thirty-fourth Psalm where David wants the children to learn the fear of the Lord. One is this: "The angel of the Lord encampeth round about them that fear Him, and delivereth them." To have the fear of the Lord is to have angel guardianship.

I need only just remind you of that scene in the Old Testament, where one of the prophets sees his servant greatly alarmed because the Assyrian armies were round the city. But the prophet prayed that God would open the eyes of the young man that he might see the mountain afar off covered with chariots and horsemen. "Far more are they that are with us than they that are against us." To have that fear of the Lord is to put ourselves under Divine guardianship. "Fear the Lord! Oh ye His saints, for there is no want to them that fear Him." That is the thing we are to have if we like. We ask for foolish things sometimes; but if we learn to fear the Lord, we shall be anxious to please Him. He will take care that what we really want shall be given to us.

Then there is another fine saying; "The fear of the Lord is the beginning of wisdom." Depend upon it, we are quite foolish if we have not learned the fear of the Lord, for it is the very alphabet of wisdom.

I trust the young men will not get the absurd notion that in order to seem manly and wise they must throw off their beloved Sunday school, their attendance there, their reading of the Bible; and yet they must do all this if they would seem wise in the eyes of those whom they would please.

But, depend upon it, the profoundest wisdom is here, and he only gets enlightened by it who begins with the fear of the Lord, the fear of making God sorry; and I am sure this fear will grow in us. If we are only studying Christ we shall get to understand Him better, and what He has done for us. Our hearts will be drawn out towards Him, and we shall very naturally fear to grieve Him; not because of the consequences, but because we never like to grieve those we love; and if we learn to love God and Christ, then we shall soon learn to know what the fear of the Lord is about which I am speaking, and which the Bible was written for the purpose of teaching us.

May every one of you learn to use this Book wisely, and you will soon learn the sweetness, the happiness of this fear.

E. S.

XVII. Summer and its Lessons. Ps. xxiv. 18.
" Thou hast made summer."

SUMMER! Is there not a wonderful charm in the word! During the bleak days of winter or spring how often we send our thoughts a little way forward and say to ourselves, It will be summer soon. So through many a long hour the poor sufferer has been cheered, almost fed, by the hope of the warm sunshine and the blue sky of summer.

I. What does the summer say concerning Him who made us. The power to discover the beautiful and appreciate it is a great gift of God. All do not possess it in equal measure; but most of us have it to some extent, and we should cultivate the capacity far more than we do. Is not summer a time for so doing?

What do we discern of God, who is the Everlastingly and Infinitely Beautiful, in all the works and glories of the summer?

One thing we observe: *how much is done, and yet how simply all is done.* There is a marvellous force and variety of life, so that you never see two things "twins at all points." How many purposes are served by the same objects! The grass, whose soft green refreshes the eye of man, sustains the life of numberless creatures. The hills both secure the rainfall and protect from the sweep of winds. What ministries are fulfilled by the river and the wood! All are so ordered, so adapted, as to serve and assist in the working out of some benevolent aim. And how simple are all the laws and ways by which the great world is made the workman of God! You think of the sunshine which is the blessing of summer. How is the earth gladdened by the sun? The old pagans used to think that the sun swam around the sea during night, that he might be in his proper place in the morning. We know that the earth is made to turn once a day before the sun, now one part and now another thus receiving of his light and warmth. And so with regard to rain: the sun is made to draw water up from the sea and the land, and the vapour makes the cloud, and the cloud makes the rain. And, in this way, all who are wise and observant may learn every hour that the most wonderful thing about the mind of God is the manifoldness, and yet the simplicity, of His wisdom.

Another thing which strikes us is: *how constantly, through all God's works, we can read the blessed name—Saviour.* Some of you, perhaps, are not too young to have felt that there is a peculiar, I might say, an unspeakable emotion excited by the loveliness of a lovely summer day. It is a luxury merely to exist. Nay, that is not all. When you get away from noise and stir,—away beneath the mountain-shadow, or at the river-side, or in some sweet chapel of the great universe-temple, away where the mountain and the hill seem to break forth into singing, and all the trees of the field to clap their hands—there are feelings and thoughts awakened which you cannot express. It is the feeling of love, and that is the healing power of summer. We want to get away from town and breathe the fresh air, and live in the health and sweetness of nature. It is the touch of God the Saviour that is felt by the weary, worn-out man.

Yes; the summer preaches Christ. It preaches Christ both by what it has and by what it has not. It has not the way of happiness. You can be in the midst of all the beauty, and yet be miserable. The sun and the moon cannot tell you whether God will forgive; they cannot give a peace that will keep your heart and mind; they cannot make you holy; they cannot lead you to glory. The Milky Way is not the way to Heaven. No; you need another Book along with the Book of Nature. When the one is in your heart, oh, how glorious in its teaching is the other!

Thus it is that all the loveliness spread around us seems to say, "Come, ye children, hearken unto me: I will teach you the fear of the Lord."

II. What does the summer say concerning us for whom it was made! We notice first how silent and how gradual the progress of life is. Is not this suggestive of what is true concerning us all? We move from one stage to another, and we scarcely notice it. As the days pass we are leaving ever so many things behind; there are unconscious influences which are making ever so many things new.

Why the growth, the ripening, which in summer we see? First, it is because seed was sown at an earlier time. Was it bad seed? You can tell that by the result. Was it good? You can tell that too. Further, even during spr ng you know that in regard to some things a certain protection was necessary. The geraniums, the asters, and so forth, were kept from the cold; they could not be bedded out until the soil was ready, and the agencies which develop life were more powerful. Nay, further still, you can tell me that in the bright summer-time it is quite needful to be ever and again weeding and hoeing and caring for the plants and the grain. Now, do you understand that what we have thus traced is a parable of you and me? This is your morning, and parent and teacher and minister are sowing the seeds of knowledge and goodness, hoping and praying that God may give the increase. And because you are not yet able to do for yourselves, you are held in the wholesome discipline of home and the gentle restraints of school. The hour is coming when you will be planted out. Oh, how anxiously do those who are interested in you think of that hour!

Summer, with all its loveliness, seems to say, "*The time is short; watch, and pray, and work.*" Already we have passed the longest day. A few weeks and the foliage will begin to shrivel, the glory to depart from the earth. Yes, the time is very short. Cannot some of you feel this, who cast your eye back twelve months, and remember that then there were hands which touched yours that have vanished, and voices which spoke to you that are still?

Very short! But we must not cry over water that has been spilt. Gather up your hours, redeeming the time. We can all glorify God; for we can all, in His strength, be dutiful and make others happy.

J. M. L.

XVIII. "The Joyful Sound." Ps. lxxxix. 15. *Blessed is the people that know the joyful sound.*"

THERE are two things in this text to be noticed. There is something joyful—the joyful sound; that is the thing spoken about. Then there is the other thing—the people that know it. That is quite a different thing. There may be a joyful sound and I may not hear it. I may have no ears to hear it, or I may shut my ears.

I. What is this joyful sound? There are many joyful sounds in the world. Music is a very joyful sound, and you are often trying to produce that joyful sound. But there is something sweeter than music—a sound which reaches to the inward ear, to the soul. The sweetest of all sounds to the soul is the love of God in Jesus Christ. Was that known when this eighty-ninth Psalm was written, hundreds of years before Christ came? Yes; because Christ was always going to come, and there were people who knew about it—prophets who taught about it, and priests who offered up sacrifices pointing forward to the Lamb of God that taketh away the sin of the world.

They did not know so much about it as we may do, but they knew enough to make them happy, and to save them, and take them to heaven. And the children knew too, for parents were told to tell their children.

Now what are some of the things that make this sound joyful? It is joyful because it tells us how we are to get our sins forgiven—all sinners, old and young. It is only in one way that our sins can be forgiven—through the blood of Jesus; and if we come to that fountain filled with blood all our sins will be washed away. Will you not know this joyful sound, and take it into your hearts, and receive Jesus?

This is a joyful sound because when we receive it we get our hearts made new and clean. What a beautiful thing it would be if our hearts were made clean and white as Adam's was when he was in his innocence; and how much better still if they were made pure, like the heart of the Lord Jesus. That is what Christ does for us—for old and young. Our hearts are far from being so pure and holy and loving as they should be, while we are here; but they are beginning to be so, and they will be so fully in heaven. Take this joyful sound as yours and then your hearts will become pure.

II. The people that know of this.

There may be a great deal of happiness we do not enjoy because we do not know about it. If any one left you a sum of money in a will, that would be a joyful sound; but if you did not know about it you would lose the blessing. There is in the Gospel something like this; it is called a Testament. Christ left us this Testament to enjoy, after He died. We publish this to the heathen that they may enter into possession of this treasure. If a treasure is left us, we must go and claim it; we must know of it; we must believe and take it. Receive this precious legacy of eternal life. "Peace I leave with you, my peace I give unto you; that is, to all of you that will take it. God offers pardon and peace to all the world, to whosoever will take it. Come to Jesus now, and then you will know the blessedness of feeling your sins forgiven; you will anticipate your heaven below, and at last you will have perfect blessedness.

J. C.

XIX. The Spread Net. Prov. i. 17. "*Surely in vain the net is spread in the sight of any bird.*"

THERE are two opinions as to what this means. Some say that no bird is so foolish as to go into a net which he sees you spread for him. He has a little head and little brain, but not so little wit as to do that. Others think that Solomon means to say that, even if a bird sees you spread the net, he has not wit enough to know what it means, and will hop into it.

But though we are uncertain what Solomon thought the birds would do, there is no doubt at all as to the lesson he would teach us. He is talking to young people, and means to say that some of them are silly enough to go into the net of sin in order to get a few crumbs of pleasure, even though they ought to see that the devil was spreading it for their destruction. He is saying how easily "gulled" young people are by temptation. You know we get that word "gull" from the birds which come down from the Arctic regions, and fish in flocks in our harbours and along our coasts, and who, some people think, are easily caught. But that is a mistake; for those who have tried it say that it is rather an insult to the gulls to think that they are so easily gulled as some men fancy they are.

We sometimes think Satan is so very shrewd that he can deceive any human being. But God does not allow him to deceive those who keep their eyes and ears open. The deceit is in ourselves; for the Bible says, "The heart is deceitful above all things." The Bible also says, "The devil goes about as a roaring lion, seeking whom he may devour;" but God makes him roar first, so that everybody can get out of his way. If any of us die through sin, God will write this epitaph for us, "Thou hast destroyed thyself" (Hosea xiii. 9). He compels Satan to spread his net in our sight.

We can see him spread it with the eye of *Conscience.* The smallest children as well as the lowest savages have a conscience which tells them right from wrong. When Stanley, the great traveller, started through Africa, he knew that he would find wild tribes who could not understand his language, but he knew that they understood the language of conscience—the same in him and in them. So he ordered his men never to steal from a savage, never to break a promise, however insignificant it was, and never to harm a human being. One day he met the fiercest of the tribes. Expecting that they would attack him as the other tribes had done, he was surprised at their kindness. When he learned to understand a little of their language, he asked why this was. They said, "Because we sent a canoe up the river, with a woman and a boy, and plenty of provisions. If you had been bad people, you would have taken that canoe. Then you would have had to fight us; but, see, we have left our spears on one of the islands." Stanley was right in supposing that the language of conscience was universal, and had not been confounded as our tongues were at Babel. So there is not a boy or girl who does not know what is right and what is wrong. All sin is as clearly seen as if you could watch the devil's fingers setting the net.

Then the *Bible* tells you what is right and what is wrong. As if a good man who loved the birds should shout and drive them away when they hopped too near the net, the Bible calls out (Prov. iii. 15), " Avoid it, pass not by it, turn from it, pass away." God shouts over the net, " The soul that sinneth, it shall die." Solomon represents Sin as sitting down by the door of a house, and saying, " Whoso is simple, let him turn in hither. Stolen waters are sweet." But as policemen stand by the doors of some of the gambling dens in our city to warn the thoughtless not to enter, God's prophet stands by Sin's door, and says, " The dead are there. Her guests are in the depths of hell." It is as if the floor were one great trapdoor, which tilted the silly victim down to perdition.

Then *other people's experience* of the consequences of sin shows us that it is the devil's net. If you knew how many are suffering from their evil habits, you would turn from yours as you would from a rattlesnake's den. They say you cannot catch the birds if you leave the dead bodies of those already caught around the cage. But Satan's net is surrounded with the piles of his victims. I was once asked to bury a man whose name those who asked me would not tell. He died in a hovel, with such pain of body, such horror of mind! He had held the highest offices in the land ; but sin had so ignominiously slain him that no one wished the world to know it.

And perhaps some have found out that sin is Satan's net by *their own* sad experience. Your bad habit makes you feel so condemned, so mean, so weak, that you have said to yourself, the end of this is destruction. A bird whose leg has been broken in getting out of the net has been known to fly straight into another ; and some young people do the same thing. In hunting deer at night we creep up to them and suddenly flash the light of a dark lantern into their eyes, and, while they stand a moment wondering at its meaning, the fatal bullet pierces the deer's heart. I have tried to shoot a deer who sprang into the thicket at the first gleam of light. It had no fascination for him, because he had seen it before and been wounded by the bullet. But I have known young men who would stand and be shot again and again by temptation, though it seemed as if Satan had opened the door of hell and flashed its firelight into their very faces.

Are you the victim of any sinful habit? I doubt if you can deliver yourself. You may be like the fluttering bird who entangles himself the more in the meshes. But Christ came to "proclaim deliverance to the captives, and to set at liberty them that are bruised." By the power of His cross He destroys the meshes of guilt, and by His Holy Spirit He heals and strengthens the moral purpose which has been weakened by the habit of sin. But if, my young friend, you have not yet entered the net, give Him your faith, and He will answer the prayer which he has taught you: "Lead us not into temptation, but deliver us from evil."

J. L.

XX. The Treasure Trove. Prov. ii. 1-15.

My son if thou wilt receive my words, and hide my commandments with thee; so that thou incline thine ear unto wisdom, and apply thine heart to understanding; yea, if thou criest after knowledge, and liftest up thy voice for understanding; if thou seekest her as silver, and searchest for her as for hid treasures; then shalt thou understand the fear of the Lord, and find the knowledge of God."

You will first of all take notice how in this passage God speaks to you as to children. It is God that speaks, though Solomon writes the words: and He says, "My son." Here, then, is the word of a Father addressed to you in love; of a Father, moreover, who never makes mistakes, who knows what you really need, whose care of you is constant and tender, and whose light to guide you is of the highest kind. Hearken, therefore, to what God your Father says.

Remark this also, that your Father speaks to you one by one. As if each of you were His only child, He says,

"My son." Suffer His word to come close to you; hear it as if you were in your closet, and a gentle voice you knew to come from glory were speaking to you.

In truth, the voice is gentle, for wisdom is no other than the Lord Jesus Christ.

Notice four things here brought before us.

I. There is a precious treasure.

You can tell what it is. It gets three several names in the text, but they all mean the same thing,—wisdom, knowledge, understanding. You know that wisdom is the opposite of folly. Folly chooses show, wisdom takes substance. Folly is all for the present, wisdom takes into view the future. If you took folly into a room where there were glittering gauds of no value lying beside unpolished jewels, it would covet the trifles that shone, and despise the worth that was dull.

Nearly fifty years ago, there was a long, severe frost in London, and the river Thames was frozen over for weeks. So the people built streets of shops over the icy surface, and there was driving and buying, and all kinds of pleasuring upon the river. But one night, suddenly the thaw set in, and the solid ice heaved and cracked and broke away into pieces, and booths and merchandise were hurled down the flood. Suppose some man had said, it would be far nicer to live in the beautiful ice street, than in the narrow lane where I now stay, and had moved all his furniture and all his family into a new dwelling on the river, what would have become of him and his that night? This supposition goes to show how folly takes up with the present merely. Heavenly wisdom, taught of God, says of sinful pleasures, they are not what they seem to be; they are fine coloured fruit, but hollow and corrupt within, and they do not last. Wisdom does not lay up treasure on earth, but in heaven; for it says, I must soon be done with earth, and heaven abides.

II. The field where the treasure lies.

The field is the Bible. It was while walking and digging in this field that young Timothy found it. From a child he had known the Holy Scriptures, which were able to make him wise unto salvation. Sinners need wisdom for salvation; they need to be taught how to be reconciled and restored to God; and that sort of wisdom is to be found nowhere else. If we should go down to the sea-shore and say, Oh, great salt ocean, canst thou wash my soul clean from the stain of sin? the ocean would reply, no, not with all my waves. But go to the Bible, and you will get knowledge how to get quit of sin, both in the guilt and the power of it. Salvation is revealed in the Bible. Whoever recalls and remembers the words of the Bible, has the treasure in his very heart and mind.

III. The search after the treasure.

To find the treasure lying in the Bible you must read it with a purpose, wishing to find wisdom. Gold must be searched for with care, even where its glittering grains mix with the river's sands; they must be diligently sought out. So any reader who would find wisdom unto salvation in the Bible must be in earnest about it, and think, and search, and compare, and pray. Persevere; seek till you find. The gold digger does not soon get weary; many a disappointment love of riches overcomes. Do not say it is hard work to search. For besides that the reward is great, the very search is sweet. A literary man of name is reported to have said, that if God should give him his choice of two things, truth, and the search after truth, he would rather take the last. The quest, with all its toil, is good for us. It is training, it is health.

IV. The discovery of the treasure.

The glad thing to know is, that it is sure to be found by searching. It is not every digger that finds store of gold. But seekers after wisdom are sure to find. Then, when it is found, it is a very precious treasure; "Then thou shalt understand the fear of the Lord, and find the knowledge of God." We shall find Wisdom, the Lord Jesus. To find Him is joy and peace.

If we find wisdom we shall understand the fear of the Lord. It is easy, without search, to know the dread of God. But fear that adores, stands in awe yet rejoices, can only be taught by Jesus. He shows us how God forgives and brings our hearts back to Him in childlike trust.

Have you found this treasure? If so, ye are rich indeed. See that ye hold fast the treasure ye have gotten.

Have you not yet found this treasure? Oh, ye are poor and wretched. Away to the field and dig. Read, think, pray. Hear what Jesus says, " Whoso findeth Me findeth life, and shall obtain favour of the Lord. But he that sinneth against Me wrongeth his own soul: all they that hate Me love death."

J. E.

XXI. Knowledge and Wisdom. Prov. x. 14.
"*Wise men lay up knowledge.*"

THE Bible has a good deal to say about wisdom and about wise people. It is hard to tell exactly what this word "wisdom" means. Great men have often tried to define it, but sometimes their descriptions of it are harder to understand than the word itself. Sometimes it is supposed that folks who know a great deal are always wise; but that is certainly a mistake. A man may have a good deal of knowledge in his head, and yet have but very little wisdom.

Wisdom tells us what to do with things—how to use them.

When people get to be wise, then, they learn how to use things properly. Here in the text we are told what wise men do with knowledge. They do not neglect it, or pass it by as of no account, or forget it; but they lay it up. They store it away as a man does his gold in the safe or bank, as a farmer does his hay in the mow and his grain in the bin, ready for use when it is wanted.

How are we to lay up knowledge and thereby gain wisdom?

I. The first rule we must follow is this: *Apply the mind to it.* Some of you have found out already that this is hard work. The mind does not usually want to be applied to study. It is like a wild, skittish colt. Did you ever see one running loose in the pasture? It does not know anything about pulling a load or carrying a saddle, or being led by a halter or driven with reins. It has to be taught gently and by degrees; maybe it will have to be whipped a little; it must be encouraged, and broken in, and then, by and by, it will apply itself to its work; it will pull at the heavy load until it starts the wagon; it will mind the word of the driver, and go, or back, or stop, just as he wishes.

Now, the mind is like that wild colt, and needs to be

broken in, too. Our minds will never mind unless we make them mind.

Now, there are many people who grow up with minds which have never been trained. They cannot think easily, or remember well, or study at all. They are not fond of reading, and do not love books. When they were young they did not apply themselves, and now that they are grown up they are too old to learn very much. They miss a vast deal of pleasure, and are not worth nearly so much to themselves or to others as they would be if they had studied hard in childhood and youth.

You have often seen soldiers marching on parade. They step all together as if they were one man. At the command, their arms are brought all at once down at their sides or placed up on the shoulder. It all looks very nice and easy; but if you would ask them how it was done, you would find that they had to be drilled and disciplined a long time in the armoury and in camp before they learned how to go through with what they call the manual of arms. They had to apply themselves in order to lay up their knowledge of military matters.

By following this same rule a child can grow up to be master of his mind just as the soldiers and sailors learn to use with ease and skill their hands and arms and limbs. He will learn how to think and reason; how to get at the truth and find out things; how to use his eyes and ears and voice; how to observe what is going on in the world about him; how to treasure it all up; and how to enjoy for ever the true, the beautiful, and the good.

II. The second rule that must be followed in order to lay up knowledge is this: *Remember.*

The Wise Man in the Bible—you know who this is, do you?—says, "Get wisdom;" and then he adds to this the counsel, "Hold fast instruction." It is not enough to get knowledge, but we must keep it. We do this by a wonderful power which the mind has, called the memory.

Did you ever try to carry water in a sieve, or colander, or in a straw hat? If you have tried such a foolish undertaking you have failed. You found that all the water quickly ran out. Now some people have memories that are like a sieve. Nearly everything put into them runs out again.

Yet, hard work as it is, if you keep adding a little every day to your store, you will by and by have saved up abundance of knowledge and wisdom.

III. The last rule to be heeded in laying up knowledge is : *Seek the right kind of knowledge.*

There are many sorts of knowledge. Much of it is worth a good deal. The branches that you study at your school will be of service to you for years to come. When you go to college, if you wisely use your time and opportunities, you will get knowledge there, and something better than knowledge—command of your mind, control over yourself—which will be a blessing to you throughout life. But, after all, there is a higher knowledge than any you can get in schools. There is a wisdom which you can learn only from God's Book. St. Paul knew much about everything that men thought good and great in his day. But he says : " I count all things but loss for the excellency of the knowledge of Christ." The Saviour calls this precious knowledge of Himself and of the way of life " the pearl of great price." This knowledge will teach you how to control your bad temper, how to fight bad thoughts, how to be useful to others around you, how to do work which you ought to do in life, how to grow up to be strong, good, true, courageous men and women. Whatever other knowledge you lay up, dear children, be sure that you lay up this best of all sorts of knowledge—the knowledge of the Saviour and of eternal life.

J. B. Y.

XXII. The House of Wisdom. Prov. ix. 1-5.
" *Wisdom hath builded her house, etc.*"

I. THE HOUSE.—The house is the house of wisdom. In this house is the fear of the Lord, and in every part of it is written, Holiness to the Lord. It is a very strong house ; it rests upon seven pillars. Nobody can pull it down. Satan has been trying for six thousand years, but he has not pulled it down yet. And wicked men have been trying to pull it down, but they cannot do it. It won't come down ; let them try to pull it down—they will not be able. The foundations are sure, very sure and very deep.

It is a large house. It can accommodate millions. It is a well-built house, like the well-built city in the Book of the Revelation—the New Jerusalem.

It is this large, strong, beautiful house of wisdom that we ask you to enter. We ask you to enter, for God is here, Christ is here, the Holy Spirit is here; wisdom is here, and life and peace and joy. It is a house full of song and of gladness,—a house in which God delights to dwell.

II. THE OPEN DOOR.—It would be of no use to speak to you about the house, though it was large and beautiful and strong, if there was no door, or if the door was not open. It is always open; it is never shut, day nor night.

Do you remember any one that spoke of Himself as the door? Christ. What did He say? "I am the door." Christ was the house and also the door of the house,—that is the wonderful thing; just as He is the Shepherd, the fold, and the door of the fold.

It is an open door; any one can go in at any time. Men shut the doors of their houses and shops at night, but the door of this house is always open, day and night, summer and winter; you can always get in at this open door.

May any one get in? Yes. In some exhibitions I have seen written up, "Children under twelve not admitted." Is that written up over this door? No. May a child of twelve years old get in—of ten, of five years? Yes. May a little babe get in? Yes; for Jesus has said, "Of such is the kingdom of heaven." It is an open door; you don't require to open it; you can just walk in. It is free to the young and to the old, to the rich and to the poor. The door has been standing open very long—ever since Adam fell, six thousand years ago.

And it is large enough to admit all. Suppose there was a great crowd wanting to get in, could they all get in at once? Oh yes. Suppose all Great Britain,—Scotland, England, and Ireland,—suppose all Europe, all the earth,—America, Asia, Africa,—were wanting to get in, they could all get in, for it is a wide door in one sense, though narrow in another, and it is always open.

Do you need to wait to get in? No. If I wanted to get into one of the Queen's palaces I should have to go for an order. But you don't need to go for an order, for a line or certificate, to get into the house of wisdom. You have got an order already.

If you were invited to visit the Queen, you would have to put on particular clothes; you would not be admitted without. What kind of clothes are you to put on before you go into this house of wisdom? You are to go just as you are.

Is there anybody standing at the door to hinder you going in? Is there an angel standing there to hinder you? Or ministers? No; they stand there to help you in. Christian, in the Pilgrim's Progress, saw a man trying to get in at the gate of a palace, and he had to fight his way in, because Satan would have hindered him. But a sweet voice was heard from the top of the palace, saying,

> " Come in, come in,
> Eternal glory thou shalt win."

This is what I would sing, and what angels sing from the heavenly towers—

> " Come in, come in,
> Eternal glory thou shalt win."

It is an open gate, for the young and for the old, for the rich and for the poor, for the foolish as well as for the wise; and no man was ever kept out because the door was not open. Thousands have been kept out because they would not come in, but no man was ever kept out because he could not get in. I was once kept out of Jerusalem. The sun had set and the gate was shut. I knocked, but could not get in. I did not like to have to wander round the walls all night; robbers might be there, and jackals, and dogs. I took out a piece of silver, and the man inside saw it, and ran and got the key. I should not have got in if I had not paid that piece of silver. Is that the way with this door of the New Jerusalem? No; the angel that keeps the door does not say, You will not get in unless you pay me a sum of money. He say, " Glad to see you; come in, come in!"

III. THE FEAST.—There are a great many feasts

spoken of in the Bible, both in the Old Testament and in the New. Lot made a feast, Abraham made a feast, and Isaac and Jacob. Feasts were joyful things in those times, and people gathered round the table to be happy together, —not in sin, not to get drunk, but to be happy together. There are one or two special feasts mentioned in the Bible. Our Lord speaks of a marriage feast, and the invitation went out, Come, for all things are ready! And we have the Lord's Supper. There is still another supper that has not yet come,—the Marriage Supper of the Lamb. In this house of wisdom there is a feast, a wonderful feast, something for us to feed upon, something that will satisfy our hunger and quench our thirst—something of which if a man eat he shall never hunger, and of which if a man drink he shall never thirst.

What is the first mention of food in the Bible? "Of every tree of the garden thou mayest freely eat." After that, you find in the Bible a great many things concerning food. Israel ate manna in the desert; there was the shewbread in the tabernacle; and there is what is called the hidden manna. Jesus says, "I am the bread of God which came down from heaven; My flesh is bread indeed, and My blood is drink indeed." I put all these together, and say, Here is God's feast for the foolish, for the hungry and thirsty. It is a Divine feast. Should not you like to sit down at this heavenly table? This feast is free, free!

IV. THE COMPANY.—It is a curious company that are gathered in this house of wisdom. It is the lame and the halt, and the maimed, and the blind, and the leper. All are sick, foolish, sinful; but then they are all changed. Once they step across the door of this house of wisdom, everything becomes new; for "if any man be in Christ Jesus, he is a new creature." He gets a new heart as soon as he comes in,—new clothes, white raiment; new eyes to see, new ears to hear, new hands to work, new feet to run; all things are made new.

The company you find here is a wonderful company. It is a company of sinners, and yet it is a company of saints. If you want to know their character before they come in, you have just to look about you in this wicked world. And then read in the seventh chapter of the Book of Revelation,—"I beheld, and lo, a great multitude, which no man could number, of all nations and kindreds and people and tongues, who have washed their robes and made them white in the blood of the Lamb." They were foolish before; they are wise now. They were wicked before; they are holy now. They did not love God before; they love Him now. They loved sin before; they hate sin now. They did not care for Jesus before; they care for Him now. They find round about them men like themselves, a strange company of the redeemed, from Abel down to the present day. What a blessed thing to be in the midst of such company as this,—Abel, Enoch, Noah, Abraham, Isaac, Jacob, Moses, David, Solomon, and Paul and John and Peter. That is our company, and will be our company for ever and for ever. What a blessed thing to be in such a house and in such company through all eternity!—the company of God, of Christ, of angels, of saints! And how awful to be shut out from such company!

V. THE WELCOME.—Is everybody welcome? Yes. Do you remember when the prodigal son came back to his father's house, what the father did? "When he was yet a great way off, his father saw him, and had compassion, and ran, and fell on his neck, and kissed him." That is the sinner's welcome from God. God wants you to come back, every boy and every girl. But does He know your name? Yes. And if you go to His house, what will you say to Him? The prodigal tells us what to say. "Father, I have sinned." That is the way to go back. When will you go back? If you go will the angels say, It is too soon; you must come back to-morrow? No; they will say,

"Come in, come in;
Eternal glory thou shalt win."

But if you go just as you are, will they say, You cannot be admitted with such a dress? No. Did the father say that to the prodigal son? No. What did he say? "Bring forth the best robe and put it on him, and put a ring on his hand and shoes on his feet." The prodigal did not need to make the robe, nor to buy it, nor to buy the ring and the shoes, nor the fatted calf. The father provided all these, and gave a father's welcome to his boy. He was glad to get him back again, and He wants you back. He does not want you to wait till to-morrow. He says to young and old, Come back, with all your sins, and come to-night where all good things are, and you will get of My abundance, drink of My wine, and be refreshed with the pure water of the river of life, and feed on that tree of life which is in the midst of the paradise of God. Welcome, welcome! is what God says to you ; and if Satan says you are not welcome, tell him he is a liar, for God says you are welcome.

Enter this house, to find the joy, the life, the love you cannot find anywhere else, and that God is so willing to give you, to make you happy for ever. Come unto Me, all ye that labour and are heavy laden, and I will give you rest! Come unto Me, all ye that hunger and thirst, and I will give you meat and drink! Ho, every one that thirsteth, come to the waters! Behold, now is the accepted time ; behold, now is the day of salvation !

H. B.

XXIII. Bad Company. Prov. xiii. 20. "*He that walketh with wise men shall be wise; but a companion of fools shall be destroyed.*"

It is as if the text said : "Don't, on any account, make companions of the foolish." If the *wise* are such *as fear God*, the *foolish* must be such as *don't fear God*—such as have no fear of God before their eyes,—the ungodly. Look at some of the *marks* of these : *flattery, dishonesty, idleness, evil-speaking, Sabbath-breaking.*

I. Beware of FLATTERING friends. I shall try to explain. A companion wishes you to do what is wrong. He knows you would refuse if he were directly to propose it. So he makes great professions of friendship : he is more anxious to be friends with you than with anybody, you are such a fine fellow. Having thus paved the way, he makes his proposal : "Come, join us in this. If it had been a bad thing, you are the last I would have thought of coming to. It will do you no harm." That is one of the "crooked ways"—the serpent-like ways, in which some succeed in tempting to sin by *flattery*—praising you, and pretending to be your friend. Many fall in this way who else would stand firm. There are flatterers among children as well as among men. A companion of such shall be destroyed.

II. Beware of DISHONEST friends. I mean both plain, downright stealing, and something else. I know some are thieves whom people would little suspect. I warn you of them. Our prisons have had more than one young thief from schools and churches like those which you attend. Solomon says regarding such : " My son, if sinners entice thee, *consent thou not!*" Refuse,—say *No*. But I don't merely refer to the stealing of money, or fruit, or such things. There is a scholar copying from the slate or book of another, or gaining a place in his class by unfairness. That is *stealing*—that is *dishonesty*, whatever may be thought of it. Say, "It is wrong ;" say, "God sees!" A companion of such shall be destroyed.

III. Beware of IDLE friends. Indolence and idleness are little thought of, yet are they very sinful and very hurtful. Some one has said that the devil tempts the busy, but the idle tempt the devil. And—

"Satan finds some mischief still,
For idle hands to do."

Now you must have noticed that idlers try to keep other people from working. You see it in our streets,—you see it at school. No good ever comes of an idle scholar ; and he is a dangerous person to have to do with.

IV. Beware of EVIL-SPEAKING friends. I refer to tale-bearing, which is ever a mean, low, vile thing; but I also refer to all kinds of improper language—low, trifling, wicked words. Like bad books, such words pollute the minds of those who hear them, and leave marks which perhaps will never be wiped out. Those who use low, bad language must have a bad heart ; and it is sure, sooner or later, to end in a bad life. Don't laugh at such, don't go in their way ; put your finger in your ears, and run out of sight. And what shall I say of *swearing*, which also is too common, even among the young ? Flee from the presence of a swearer, be he young or old. It is not manly—it is not gentlemanly ; it is base—devilish—it is the language of hell. A swearing companion *must* be bad ; a companion of such shall be destroyed.

V. Beware of SABBATH-BREAKING companions. This is a very common but very grievous sin. I have seen the effects of it but too often and too sadly. It leads to many other sins, and often comes to a sad end. He who would tempt you to break the Sabbath is one of your worst enemies. Tell him that God is wiser and more your friend than he, and that God says, "Remember the sabbath day, to keep it holy." How many mournful cases show that the companion of Sabbath-breakers shall be destroyed!

Such are some of the bad companions against whom we are warned. *Why* are we to beware of them? Because, as in the other case, we are in danger of growing like them. As in the case of some terrible, infectious diseases, if you go near, it will be a wonder if you do not catch the infection.

Beloved young people! don't be laughed into what is evil; don't be threatened into what is wrong. Make a companion of your *Bible:* you will find it both safe and profitable. Still more, make a companion of Him of whom it tells—*Jesus.* Whatever other friends you have, make sure of the friendship of Jesus. Take no friends as yours but those who will be friends to Him. And in order to have Christ as your *Friend,* you must have Him as your *Saviour. That* is the *only way.* He is willing to be the Friend of the youngest, of the poorest, of the most wicked. He says to-day, " Come." He says, " I will in no wise cast out."
J. H. W.

XXIV. Left to Himself. PROV. xxix. 15. "*A child left to himself bringeth his mother to shame.*"

A CHILD left to himself! I daresay, my little friends, you have often pitied a child left to himself. When you have been going through some poor street you have perhaps seen a poor child ragged and forlorn, and cold and hungry. The whole look of the child seems, " I am left to myself." The cold wind pours through his ragged clothes—a child left to himself. I have seen a very sad sight sometimes; a little child of eight, nine, or ten years old, who has committed some crime, and has been brought before the judge. Such a child, knowing neither how to read or write, has been found to have been left to itself.

I want to tell you of a sadder thing still. It is a very sad sight to see a child so uneducated and left to itself as to suffer in its body. But in that sense none of you are likely to be left to yourselves. You are well cared for, you have warm clothes, and kind friends whom God has given the means to care for you. But there is a sadder thing than all that I have just spoken of—it is a child's soul left to itself—a child who has not heard about Jesus Christ. This is why I speak to you at these services. These services are for you, boys and girls, that you should not be left to yourselves. I want to say a few simple words about coming to church in the afternoon.

Always be here in good time. You know very well that if any of you got a message from the Queen you would not be late in attending. You would be in a state of anxiety all the morning in order to make sure that you would be in time. Here is the King of kings waiting for you to learn the lesson which His Holy Spirit teaches. Be in time.

When you come in, pray to God. Do not look around to see any of your friends, but pray to God.

And then remember, in the next place, that you do not come to hear the sermon only. You come here, of course, to listen to what I have to teach you—so far as God gives me the power to do so—but first of all to tell God all you need, all about your sins, and to ask God for His dear Son's sake, Jesus Christ, to save you. Remember the prayers, remember the hymns, these are parts of the service you come here for as well as the words which God speaks to you through His servants.

Listen to the sermon as a lesson from God to you. When God makes me speak to you of some fault do not say, "That is for my little friend, or brother or sister." Ask in your own heart, Am I not the one? And then I tell you of Christ's great love, of how He died for you when there was not a being in God's world that cared for you. Put your whole trust in Him, cast yourself upon Him as a drowning man upon a plank. He is your Saviour. All you have to do is to put out your hand and say, "God be merciful to me a sinner."

And then one more word about coming here. Come here expecting that God will give you some good. I do not think you will get much unless you expect it. Come here and say, "I am determined something or other shall be made mine." If you were starving, and saw a table laden with meat and fruits, you could not be satisfied with simply looking at it. It will not do to look around on others getting God's blessing; all that is no good except you take it for yourself. Say, all the blessings here are for me; all Christ's love is for me. It must be all taken for yourself to be any good. God never leaves any man, woman, or child to himself. God sends to some danger, and to others blessings and joy; but it is all for the best. The most awful thing written of any man is written in the Bible. A man had turned to idols, and God said: "Let him alone." The most awful thing that can happen to you is not pain or sorrow, but the one awful thing is, "Let that one alone." You may thank God even for the pain, even for the trouble or whatever it may be that oppresses you; it shows that God is not leaving you alone, but is determined to have you Himself, through Jesus Christ. As long as you can feel a single sentiment in your heart of pain when you hear of evil, or of joy when you hear of the glad things of Jesus Christ, you may be certain that God is not leaving you alone. In moments of lying awake at night, in times of sorrow, in times of danger, in all these ways God is coming to you, determined not to let you alone. In the cold, it is only when he falls asleep that a man is in danger.

A strong man coming home at night one cold day after his work, laid down in a lime kiln for warmth, and fell asleep. Next morning his comrades found not the man, but merely the cinder of what had been the man. The man had never felt the fire; if he had felt it he would have been saved. So long as you feel, there is hope; the only danger is when you become dead to God's voice. Then we must leave you in God's hands. Try to make these services a blessing to *yourselves*. Then is the message for you. God says, "Give me thine heart." Remember who asks for it—Jesus Christ, who came from heaven to earth, and went through the agony and shame and death—He who had no sin Himself, but bore all that to save you, and who rejoices againand again over every one who cometh to Him, for none shall be cast out. "Give me your heart," said God. Can you refuse when you think who asks you? It is Jesus Christ.

T. T. S.

XXV. The Good Example of Four Wise Creatures. Prov. xxx. 24. "*There be four things which are little upon the earth, but they are exceeding wise.*"

A MAN called Agur once said, "There be four things which are little upon the earth, but they are exceeding wise: the ants are a people not strong, yet they prepare their meat in summer; the conies are but a feeble folk, yet make they their houses in the rocks; the locusts have no king, yet go they forth all of them by bands; the spider taketh hold with her hands, and is in king's palaces." The wisdom of those creatures is worth thinking about, and worth imitating. We will take them one by one.

I. "*The ants* are a people not strong, yet they prepare their meat in summer." As instinct makes certain insects prepare for winter, when they will be certain to suffer if they have no store of food, so experience teaches thinking creatures that they ought also to prepare for the future. Many, unfortunately, are not so wise as these insects, and waste money and time to such an extent that when sick, or without work, or in old age, they have to seek that help from others, which, had they been more thrifty, they never would have required.

There are other ways also in which a like want of wisdom may be shown. For example, the entrance to most professions is now obtained only after passing strict examinations, and failure in these is a certain thing to those who will not carefully prepare beforehand. In the same way, all life is just a series of trials of the results of previous preparations. Men and women are useful only when they have such qualities as honesty, truthfulness, energy, courage, kindliness, good temper, prudence, and some learning. These good things are thoroughly obtained only after long efforts, and they who do not begin early and persevere diligently in seeking them can never be as useful as they might have been. Then when we recall how our good qualities are put to the test here, we cannot but remember that hereafter all shall be judged "every man according to their works," when the results of our lives here will have a tremendous influence on a great future elsewhere—a day when the books will be opened.

We may thus all desire that which may make us care for our future, as much as instinct makes some insects care for their future.

Seeing thus how much depends on a preparation for the future, we ought to seek strength to become "diligent in business, fervent in spirit, serving the Lord." That strength is given to those who acknowledge and serve Jesus Christ.

II. "*The conies* are but a feeble folk, yet make they their houses in the rocks." There are no conies in our country. The creatures in this country that they most resemble in their habits are our wild rabbits, who, like them, are but a feeble folk, and yet often make their homes among rocks, or in stony places. A feeble creature can make itself strong by thus going where its enemies cannot reach it. Foxes, hares, and rabbits, when driven from a low-lying country, take refuge in the hills and among the rocks. Men hunted by enemies have often had to do the same. Sir William Wallace, King Robert Bruce, the Covenanters, Prince Charles Edward, and many others that you read about in Scottish history and elsewhere, had to do this. As instinct and experience thus prompt all creatures to seek safety in strong places, so all wisdom tells us that we ought to seek safety from troubles and temptations and the fear of God's anger. As children go to their parents in distress, so we ought all to go to our Father in Heaven, who is said to be "our refuge and strength." Thinking of this, we may remember what our Lord said about the house built on the rock and the house built on the sand; and we may remember also how many who have been in trouble about us have been able to say:—

> "Rock of ages, cleft for me,
> Let me hide myself in Thee."

III. "*The locusts* have no king yet go they forth all of them by bands." Locusts are large insects that travel together in great companies, and eat up everything in the fields, so that, where they go, no food is left for cattle or for sheep, and great distress is caused to all the people who live there. They are to be dreaded, because they go in such numbers. If they were few in number, or if they were scattered over the country—a few here and a few there—they would have little power. To be wise, then, as the locusts, we must learn to work together. What a number of people scattered about, and working without direction, cannot do, the same number working together, under orders, can easily do. It is the long pull, the strong pull, and above all, the pull altogether, that does the work. We must all try, then, not to quarrel with one another; but to be helpful to one another, to obey orders, and to do our duty well. The one careless, bad-tempered boy or girl in the family, or school, or workshop, is not much; but his or her badly done work hurts the work and the tempers of others; and the strength of the whole " band " is lessened. We, as Christians, are the subjects of the kingdom of heaven, and we ought, therefore, to be as a "band," not spreading desolation, but peace and happiness. Each one can do a little to help this great good.

IV. "*The spider* taketh hold with her hands, and is in kings' palaces." Every boy or girl has heard about Robert Bruce lying down and thinking that he was quite beaten, and then taking such encouragement from the sight of a spider trying again and again to make a web, that he roused himself to new exertions that ended in great success. The spider gives a wonderful example of perseverance, as all the girls who have to clean rooms know only too well. Sweep as you like, the cobwebs will appear, and that even in "kings' palaces." To be wise as the spider we must try, and try, and try again. There are lessons to learn, bad habits to be overcome, bad tempers to be mastered. When you find that these are difficult, think of the spider, and be wise as the spider.

God has thus given us a good example in these four creatures, and as we ought to know much more than ants, conies, locusts, and spiders, we show ourselves to be both wicked and stupid if we do not learn, like them, to provide for the future, to seek true safety, to work well together, and always to persevere.

R. W. W.

XXVI. The Words of King Lemuel.—Prov. xxxi. 1.

"*The words of king Lemuel, the prophecy that his mother taught him.*"

THAT is the beginning of the chapter, and the chapter is full of lessons of wisdom. What I want to speak to you about to-day is, that here is a chapter in the Bible, and the writer commences by saying that King Lemuel learned these words from his mother. What honour is here put upon his mother and upon her teaching! If you ask me who King Lemuel was, I know nothing but his name. If you ask me about the one who taught him these words, I do not know her name, but that she was his mother.

And so what I want you to learn from it to-day, my young friends, is the immense importance of what you learn while you are young. Here are the words of a mother, taught to her child. A mother is the dearest thing we have. Do you ever think, boys and girls, how a mother looking at the little one coming into the world, wonders what manner of child it will be? A good child is a great blessing and a bad child is an awful thing. And so this mother thought when she looked at her little one, "What manner of child shall this be?" and she resolved so far as in her power he should grow up brave and strong and good. It is a little matter whether we become great in the world, but oh, it does matter everything whether we are good. A good mother! You know David was king of Israel. God had shown him great kindness, but he committed the most terrible sins. He became a murderer among other things, and yet though he had committed an abominable murder, he came back in tears and penitence to God, and he pleaded with God. He prayed God to turn to him again and save him. And what do you think he called himself? "The son of Thy *handmaid*." He pleaded the memory of his mother in prayer to God. And so Lemuel—whoever he was—was well looked to by his mother as to his character.

There are two things I want you to remember. They are not simple, these two words—character and reputation. "I would like to be a person of good reputation," a boy will say. Now, what is the difference between character and reputation? Your reputation is what other people think of you. Well, if they think according to what is true, it is of importance for you to have a good reputation. But character means what God sees you to be. That is far more important. Character is what you are really; reputation is what people think about you. And so when we find the mother of Lemuel looking after his character and life, his reputation can take care of itself. Let us be pure, true, faithful, holy in the sight of God, and then we shall be able to say with one of the noblest men who ever lived, St. Paul, "With me it is a small matter with any man's judgment. He that judgeth me is the Lord." He did not care about reputation. The mother of Lemuel said to him, " My son be true, be pure, be loving, be faithful to God; and then let the world say what they like about you."

Boys and girls, we shall never know till the great day, when all things are made known, what a blessing a mother's words have been—what an influence the things we have learned when we have been young have had upon us. The things we learn when we are young are infinitely more important than when we are old. " Train up a child in the way he should go, and when he is old he will not depart from it." Augustine was a heathen and a man of great intellect and great power to do good or evil. His mother prayed him to be a Christian, and he struggled against sin; and when he was really won to Christ, the mother of Augustine said, " I have nothing more now to do on earth. Why should I remain here? I only wished to linger here to see you a Christian. Now God has given me this, I want no more." Three days afterwards she died. And though perhaps our mothers are not the saints and heroines the mother of Augustine was, still, if we treasure up the words of kindness our mothers give us, they will be of use in the days to come. I want you to know, my young friends, the tremendous importance of the things you learn while you are young; and oh, when you come to be old you will find the things we meet now—the friendships, the love, the lessons, the joys and fears—linger on with a strange power ever after.

I have been told the story of a pit far away in the coal country. When the miners had penetrated to a certain place they came to what was once an old mine, but owing to an explosion forty years before, it had been given up. And there they found the body of a young man. He was quite fresh, with no signs of decay, because when the explosion had taken place, and he had been working there, the explosion had so driven the earth that he was covered in in the cold mine; and his body had been preserved there by the strange action of the gas. The body was brought up to the surface, and there stood a wondering crowd of men and women, and this body, forty years buried there, had still the freshness and form of youth. And in the crowd there was one old woman of sixty, who was known to spend her life in doing good, and was called "Mother" by every one. She rushed forward with a wild shriek and flung herself on the body, and kissed what had been a corpse for forty years.

She had grown old; he had remained young though dead. That was the lover of her early days. They were to be married the day after the explosion which had killed many, him among others, and left his body in the mine.

It seems to me, some old forgotten love of early life, some memories of a loved home, some words of a favourite hymn, some words of a loved text, some words of a loved father, some words of a loved mother—these lie buried for years and years; but they come back some day with all the freshness and all the beauty of their early utterances. Treasure them, boys and girls, and lay them up, so that in the days to come the words of your mother may be your help and strength.

T. T. S.

XXVII. White Garments. Eccles. ix. 8. "*Let thy garments be always white.*"

WHITE is a favourite colour with all of us. There is something heavenly about it; and so the Bible describes the redeemed as wearing "white robes," and the throne of judgment as being a "great white throne."

There is nothing prettier for children to wear than white. So we robe our babies in it for their baptism, our brides for their marriage, our May queens for their court on the lawn.

But there is a certain responsibility about these "white

garments." They are easily soiled, and what is more offensive than soiled white!

Now Solomon took his figure from this universal love of white garments, and yet the quickness with which they get defiled. A Christian's conscience and character are his white garments. The conscience is the inner, hidden garment. The character is the outer, visible garment. Sin is what defiles them both. Disobedience, temper, envy, vanity, falsehood, selfishness—these are some of the common spots which appear on them, and it is to put us on our guard against these that our text whispers in our ears, " Let thy garments be always white."

Now none of our garments are white by nature. We are born with sinful hearts. None but the Holy Spirit can make them white, or keep them white afterwards. He makes them white by convincing us of sin, bringing us to Jesus for forgiveness, and implanting a hatred of sin in us.

The Holy Spirit advises us how to keep our garments white, and promises the grace for it. We have to use both the advice and the grace to keep our garments white. There must be a constant attention to five things.

I. The Bible.

The Bible teaches us what is sinful, where it lurks, how to avoid it, and what God thinks of it, how it grieves Him and dishonours them.

" Wherewithal shall a young man cleanse his way? By taking heed thereto according to Thy Word."

Half the stains on some Christians' garments can be traced to neglect of the study of the Scriptures.

II. The Cross—the blood of Jesus.

Doing our best, sins of infirmity will break out. What are we to do? Look to Jesus. To that fountain opened for sin and uncleanness we must repair daily and hourly. Do not be afraid of His rejecting you because you are children.

III. Prayer.

By this you will ask and receive grace from Him to resist evil. If you trust to your own power, Satan will be too strong for you. In the battle you will rely on your own armour, and he will treat you as Goliath of Gath fancied he could treat David. What is your shield that it should parry his stroke, or your hand that it should fence with his!

But if, by humble prayer, you draw down on yourself the might of the Mightier than he, then you will be a match for him, and he will flee before you.

IV. Watchfulness.

We must keep on the alert always if we desire white garments. No sleeping, no throwing the reins to the horse, no yielding our boat to the tide.

V. Self-denial.

This is a hard part of our task, but if we are resolved to gratify self, it will lead us into hundreds of defiling things. "I cannot do this, I ought not, I will not," are difficult expressions to utter, but they are the secret of garments "always white."

"That "always" is emphatic, it points to ceaseless anxiety and effort.

Never till death translates us beyond temptation can we consider that our warfare in this matter is accomplished.

There are four reasons why we should cultivate holiness.

1. Because it insures peace. 2. Because it insures your being useful. 3. Because it insures your nearness to God. 4. Because we shall then be prepared for death.

J. B.

XXVIII. "Rock of Ages." ISA. xxvi. 4. "*Trust ye in the Lord for ever: for in Jehovah is the Rock of Ages.*"

MANY young people who know and sing the hymn,—

"Rock of Ages, cleft for me,"

would perhaps be at a loss to find out, in the Bible, the place where that name of our God and Saviour occurs. We are familiar with the words, but are they in the Scriptures?

Do you find that name of God anywhere in *the Bible?* It describes Him, truly and gloriously, as unchangeable and sure, and at the same time as a refuge and shelter to which we may run and be safe. It speaks of security for us in Him who, like a great rock, is the same yesterday, to-day, and for ever. But is it a *Bible name* for God, our Saviour?

"Yes," says one of our readers, who in reading the word turns his eye at times to *the margin* as well as the text, "I have found it! It is in Isaiah xxvi. 4: '*Trust ye in the Lord for ever: for in Jah Jehovah is the Rock of Ages.*'" In God Himself, says the prophet, in God, who alone has the name "Jah" and "Jehovah," you find an immovable, unchangeable, safe, secure refuge and shelter and home.

Toplady, the author of the hymn, was an eminent and devoted minister of Christ, who died about a hundred years ago. On his deathbed he had days of sunshine from the presence of the Lord. He fed upon the Word, and sometimes broke out into utterances of adoration and joy, as if already in the third heaven. This hymn, so well known among us, "Rock of Ages," was a favourite one with himself. In publishing it, he described it as "A living and dying prayer for the holiest believer in the world."

A beautiful incident in connection with it occurred a year ago. One of the "Jubilee Singers," a black student of Fisk University, in America, was on board a steamer that took fire. He had presence of mind to fix life-preservers on himself and his wife; but in the agony of despair, when all on board were trying to save themselves, some one dragged off from his wife the life-preserver, so that she found herself helpless amid the waters. But she clung to her husband, placing her hands firmly on his shoulders as he swam on. After a little, her strength was exhausted. "I can hold on no longer," was her cry. "Try a little longer," was her husband's agonized entreaty; and then he added, "Let us sing 'Rock of Ages.'" Immediately they both began faintly to sing, and their strains fell upon the ears of many around them, while they were thus seeking to comfort each other. One after another of the feeble and nearly exhausted swimmers was noticed raising his head above the waves and joining in the prayer,—

"Rock of Ages, cleft for me,
Let me hide myself in Thee," etc.

Strength seemed to come with the song; and they were able to hold out a little longer, still faintly singing. A boat, a life-boat, was seen approaching, and they did get strength to keep themselves afloat till the crew lifted them on board. And thus Toplady's hymn helped to save more than one or two from death by sea, as it has often helped to save souls ready to perish.

But what does that line mean that speaks of the Rock as "cleft," comparing it to Christ's "riven" or "pierced side"? It refers—1. To the smiting of the rock at Rephidim (Ex. xvii. 6), when waters flowed forth like a river for the thirsty people. 2. To Moses being placed by God in a cleft of the rock (Exod. xxxiii. 21, 22), perhaps just above where the waters gushed forth when the rock was "smitten." It was there, standing in that cleft, that Moses saw as much of glory as he could bear, and heard God Himself proclaim His glorious perfections. Put these two together—the rock cleft that the water might flow forth, and Moses standing in the cleft—and you have a type or picture of a sinner hid in Christ, who was smitten for us, and from whom flow all the streams of blessing to our souls.

Tell all men of this Jesus, "the Rock of Ages, cleft for us;" tell sinners young and old, at home and abroad; tell the Jew and the Gentile. But all the time see that your own heart is full of what you tell to others. Indeed, if you yourself are finding a heaven in "the Rock of Ages, cleft for you," your joy will affect others who see it; just as the singing of that hymn, to cheer their own souls, drew the attention of so many others ready to sink and perish.

A. A. B.

XXIX. The Secret of true Strength. Isa. xxx. 7.
" Your strength is to sit still."

WHICH of us does not wish to be strong? Strength is such a fine thing. It brings us fame, it makes us independent, it is a well-spring of joy in us. We cannot help admiring it in others, we cannot help coveting it for ourselves.

I. *There are many different kinds of strength.*

There is the strength of the crane, which can lift a couple of tons as easily as we could a couple of ounces. There is the strength of the engine, which can drag a train fifty times as long and as heavy as itself. There is the strength of gunpowder, which can tear a solid rock to pieces, or throw an immense cannon ball a mile and a half. There is the strength of the elephant, which has to be measured by dozens of horses. There is the strength of giant men, whose fist falls with the weight of a sledge hammer.

Then there is the strength of countries, such as our own: their power to defend themselves and conquer their enemies. There is the strength to bear up under trouble, to resist temptation, to overcome evil, to do what is good. And lastly, there is the strength which comes of the feeling that we are *safe*, because we are doing what is right and have God on our side.

This is the strength spoken of in our text. The Jews wanted to have a sense of security in the midst of foes. They sought to get it by forming an alliance with their ancient masters and oppressors, on the banks of the Nile. God was angry at this, and tells them that the strength of Pharaoh shall be their shame, and their trust in the shadow of Egypt their confusion. They may try, but they cannot profit them. "Therefore," says the prophet, "have I cried to them, that their strength is to *sit still*." This leads us to our second point.

II. *The secret of true strength.*

The key to the armoury or arsenal is a little thing; but it lets you in to the stores with which you could equip an army or a fleet.

Now a lion's strength lies in his shoulders; a giraffe's in his legs; an eagle's in his wings. Samson's was found to be in his curly locks. A fortress's is in its walls; a ship's in its keel; a nation's in its wealth, and the number and bravery of her sons. Strength to endure affliction is in a courageous heart; and strength to triumph in the arts and sciences is in a gifted mind. But the strength which we are talking of is where we should never have expected it to be—in *sitting still*. Is not that curious? You would have thought that it was just the opposite, and that to have it you must be busy and bustling, and running hither and thither, as the ants do to collect their winter stores. You say, suppose the ants should sit still, what would happen to them? or suppose the squirrels should sit still when the nuts and acorns are dropping from the trees ; or suppose the bees should sit still when the dandelions and violets are scenting the hedgerows ; or suppose the birds should sit still when the nest-building month has begun,—would *they* find that it was "their strength" to sit still?

But do not let us forget, that, as Solomon says, there is a time for everything. There is a time for activity and a time for sitting still. I shall answer your questions by similar questions. Suppose that the ants ventured to run about when there was an ant-eater ready to lick them up with his tongue. Suppose that the squirrels ventured down on to the ground when the boys were pelting them with stones. Suppose that the bees ventured to fly abroad when the thermometer was below zero. Suppose that the birds ventured to leave their eggs to be hatched by the sun.

So, you observe, that there is a season when the "strength," even of ants, and squirrels, and bees, and birds, is to sit still. If they refuse to sit still they expose themselves, and will perish. And are there not those of our own race whose strength is nearly always to sit still—infants, invalids, prisoners, and the poor slaves! What will they gain by restlessness, resistance, and determination to follow their own inclinations? Would you not "cry to them concerning this, Your strength is to sit still?" You, baby, will only hurt yourself scrambling about. You, invalid, will only hinder your recovery by exertion. You, prisoner, will only lengthen your punishment by endeavouring to escape. You, poor slave, will only tighten your chains by striking before deliverance is at hand.

And now let us transfer this idea to ourselves. May it not often be our strength to sit still? There is weakness in much of our fancied strength. We are as foolish as the ostrich, which thrusts her head into a bush, and then believes that she is safe from her hunters.

So we fret and wear ourselves out about things which really do not "profit" us, and which, in the hour of trial, would be a "shame" and a "confusion" to us. What a deal of looking to creatures there is—bruised reeds at best. What a deal of unnecessary work, and reading, and fidgetting, and worrying, and chattering there is. Is it not quite the fashion of the day to live publicly instead of in retirement; noisily instead of peacefully; as turbid cataracts instead of gentle flowing rivulets? My experience of most modern children is, that they are either overdriving themselves, or being overdriven on hard and dusty racecourses, when, as colts, they should be feeding and training out of sight in green pastures. I pity them. I remember a childhood of "quietness and confidence," which has ever since been my strength, and sigh when I notice how the sheltered fold is kicked at, and the youthful graces are sacrificed for an early show and admiration.

Now will you listen to advice which is not mine, but your Creator's, Preserver's, Saviour's? Will you ponder this heavenly counsel? "Your strength is to sit still."

III. I will mention four ways of sitting still and gathering strength.

(1) In shunning the glare and excitement of the fashionable world. How this dissipates, exhausts, and enfeebles! It drains you as you drain an orange, till nothing remains but the empty skin. Cultivate modesty, simple tastes, self-discipline, the habit of reflection. Do not be "careful and cumbered" as Martha was; but listen, and learn, and love, as Mary did. Sit still in the study—in the sweet fields, where nature opens her book to you—in the closet where God draws near to you.

There is no mistaking those who sit still in these respects, and how they gain strength in so doing.

(2) Sit still at the feet of your ministers and teachers. Don't imagine that you are wiser than they, and can be your own pilot. You have scarcely touched the ocean's brink, whilst they have traversed it in frequent voyages, and seen its rocks and shoals, its tides and storms. They can direct you to lamps by which you can walk in the darkness, and to planks on which you can cross precipices, and woe to those who will not be guided to them. Submit yourselves to them in the fear of God. Do not be ridiculed into self-conceit and presumption. The wild asses in our schools and congregations who snuff at the bridles and traces generally end in being strangled by the lasso. Ah! how they mourn at the last, and say, How have I hated instruction and despised reproof.

(3) *Sit still at the cross of Jesus.* This is the sitting still

which obtains us salvation. The ceasing from striving to restore ourselves to God's favour by our own deeds, by repentances, mortifications, amendments, charities ; and the embracing of Christ as our perfect obedience, atonement, advocate, Friend. It is the *beholding* the Lamb of God, and not the earning God's mercy ; it is the yielding ourselves to Him and His righteousness, and not the struggling to establish a righteousness of our own.

How blessed a privilege, to fetch our load of sin, our wounds and fetters, our obstinate will, and our depraved affections, and cast them there before a bleeding Redeemer, and then sit still under His championship for evermore!

(4) Sit still under God's providence. Do you not grow calm in danger when your father plants himself between you and it; when he says to you, " My darling, it shall not harm you." With your father with you, you will dare the midnight gloom, the churchyard ghosts, the sea's crested waves, the herd of cattle—you sit still, as it were, under his protection.

Now God's providence is a thousand-fold what the tenderest father's protection is. For God is omnipotent, and He is aware of whatever there is in the future ; and He is infinitely compassionate ; and He has said that not a sparrow dies but He permits it. He clothes the lilies, and feeds the ravens, and counts our hairs. He has sketched out our path from the cradle to the grave, and what He has ordered He can control. He will be our shield in battle, our watcher in sickness. He will be our pillar of cloud and of fire in the wilderness. Cannot we sit still then under this providence, and silence our murmurings and doubts ; and when Satan says to us, Flee or be overwhelmed, reply, I am sitting still under the banner of Jehovah, and you cannot overwhelm me.

In conclusion : those who do this will nourish and cherish their strength as the flowers do theirs by underground roots and imperceptible dews. Resolve to be docile, attentive, humble, prayerful. Be fond of shining rather as the glow-worm in the lanes, than as a sheet of tin or a bit of broken mirror in the street.

Collect strength now to use it by-and-by. The Lord Himself was an example in this, when He went down from the Temple to Nazareth, and was subject to His parents for twenty years. Could He "sit still" to mature His "strength" for twenty years—He who was God manifest in the flesh—and will you be impatient of sitting still, when your strength is but as a blade of grass compared with His? May He who was your example in this, as in everything, aid your doing what is so difficult for you to do, and you will prove the truth of the old proverb, illustrated by the fable of the hare and the tortoise—*hasten slowly.*

J. B.

XXX. The Lamb Slain. Isa. liii. 7. "*He was brought as a lamb to the slaughter.*"

MOST of us have never seen lambs "brought to the slaughter." We have only seen them on their way to it, with the butchers shouting and the dogs barking. Then the pretty creatures rushed in at the fatal door; and when we saw them again they were hanging dead in the shop window! meanwhile, in that dreadful house they had been tied with cords, the cruel knife had drawn their blood, and they had given up their lives to be food for us. That seems hard, very hard; but it is going on every hour. Hundreds of thousands of lambs are thus "brought to the slaughter" year by year in England. Now mark what is said in this short text, of the death of the Lord Jesus Christ—"He was brought as a lamb to the slaughter." It would be solemn if He had died peacefully, as our beloved parents do; but He died violently by the hands of wicked men. We have to think of Him being "crucified and slain,"—"brought as a lamb to the slaughter." Oh, have you no tears for this scene? And do not say, "but it happened more than eighteen hundred years ago; I could not help it, and He does not care about it now." Do you not know that *your* sins brought Him to the slaughter; that He was "bearing your stripes" there; that it is as fresh in His recollection as if it was but yesterday; and that if you are ever to be forgiven, and to get to heaven, it will be by simple faith in what He then and there suffered *in your stead?*

This is salvation!—Looking up at the Son of God nailed on the cross, bleeding, fainting, thirsting, crying, breathing out His soul in that sigh, "It is finished," and saying

"He was brought to that slaughter" for me; "He loved me, and gave Himself for me."

But now let us ask and answer some questions.

I. Who was the "Lamb?" The Lord Jesus Christ.

What the prophet says before and after about Him leaves us in no doubt about this. Read it for yourselves, and say if it is not the Gospel of St. Matthew or St. Luke in a parable.

But what a Lamb was this! the Lamb of *God* surely,— God Himself manifest in the flesh. Study His miracles, His teaching, His character, His work, until the apostles and martyrs, until kings, and until the angels themselves appear utterly unworthy to loose His shoe's latchet. There never was such a wonderful, beautiful, glorious being on earth. The marvel is that all creation did not crowd down here to behold Him, and worship Him, and shout His praise! And yet *He* here was brought "as a lamb to the slaughter."

II. What was the slaughter?

Sad as this is, we must not hide it from our eyes. The Bible is full of the minutest details about it; the mock trial, the scourging, the crown of thorns, the spitting and blasphemy; then the weary walk to Calvary; then the executioners driving in the spikes; then the scoffing, the languishing, the few brief utterances, so expressive of intense pain; then the darkness; then the last loud wail; then the sudden silence.

It was a slaughter so brutal that we would not inflict it on a savage; so shameful, that it was reserved for Roman slaves; so public, that the sun itself interfered to veil Him from those rude gazers; so agonizing, that the soldiers themselves wanted to stupefy Him with myrrh and vinegar.

And not a friend but John and His mother to stand by Him! the rest were actually rejoicing in His torments, and taunting Him as if He had been a dog.

The slaughter of the lamb is purest mercy in comparrison! What mortal terrors would scourge us if it was allotted to us.

III. What "brought" Him here to this slaughter?

You say the malice of the Jews and the order of Pontius Pilate. These, indeed, were the immediate instruments of it,—these were His betrayers and murderers, and nothing can lighten their crime. But still He need not have been delivered up to them. He could have escaped from them as easily as an eagle from a flock of sparrows. Did He not say this as they bound Him in the Garden of Gethsemane? But if He had so escaped, how could He have wrought out our redemption? Therefore we must remember that He was bound for this sacrifice by a threefold cord,—

The will of the Father.
His own consent.
Our guilt.

The will of His Father, who laid this commandment upon Him,—" Go, obey and atone for them ; drink up the cup of My wrath for them ; bear their chastisement."

His own consent.—" Lo, I come to do Thy will, I *delight* to do it. Thy law is *within My heart.*"

Our guilt.—He was wounded *for our transgressions ;* He was bruised *for our iniquities.*

Had He broken away from this threefold cord, as He might if He had chosen, He could not have ransomed us from hell. But He was quiet under it as a lamb,—submissive as Isaac to Abraham.

So it was this that "brought" Him to the slaughter. It was the fulfilment of His covenant with God, for nothing could turn Him from that. When He was perfectly free and at liberty, and no one dreamt of His arrest and slaughter, He said " I have a baptism to be baptised with, and how am I straitened till it is accomplished!" We do not, then, excuse the Jews and Pontius Pilate ; but we will not forget the determinate counsel and foreknowledge of God. The Jews and Pontius Pilate could not have brought Him to it without Divine permission.

IV. *Why* was He brought to the "slaughter?"

Ah! why? God had no pleasure in it. He did not deserve it. It was not an accident. It was not for His own advantage. Then why did He, the infinitely Holy, yield Himself to it? There is but a single reason : it was for His people. They were doomed ; He would endure their doom. They were accursed ; He would expiate their curse. They were shut out of God's favour : He would reconcile them to God by surrendering Himself to God's indignation. Therefore it is said, " He (Jehovah) hath put Him to grief. He hath carried our sorrows. He was smitten of God and afflicted."

That was *our* punishment; but He said, "Inflict it on Me, and then pardon them for My sake."

It was pity for us, it was the resolve to open the door to the many mansions to us, that "brought" Him to the slaughter.

That accounts for it,—it was paying there the price for His Church; and the price was sweat and pangs and crimson drops that stained the grass of Golgotha.

In conclusion. How real a thing is Adam's fall!

It brought Immanuel to the slaughter. How fearful, hateful, must those offences of ours be which rendered His slaughter necessary! They are as bad as the Jews and Pontius Pilate.

How easily God can receive us back to His bosom now! The spotless Lamb has been treated as if He was the "blackest of the black" for us!

How fervently we should thank Him, and how closely cling to Him! Who has done us a kindness? are we not grateful to him or her? But who was brought as a lamb to the *slaughter* for us?

How we should try to imitate Him. "As a lamb"—so meekly, patiently, gently! so should we conduct ourselves in trouble, whether it be from God or our fellow-creatures.

Has this precious Lamb won our affections yet? Have we felt His grace, confessed His right to us, and thrown ourselves at His feet! If not, let us lose no time. He is waiting to embrace us. Conceive what it would be to have wilfully neglected Him "who was led as a lamb to the slaughter" for us. He says to us, "Is that *nothing* to you, all ye that pass by?" And what will we reply to Him?

J. B.

XXXI. Gates. Isa. lxii. 10. "*Go through, go through the gates.*"

In riding across the country, especially in the neighbourhood of noblemen's estates, there are so many gates to go through, that you carry a whip which is made on purpose to open them; or, if driving, the people in the carriage take it by turns to jump out and open them, unless little rosy-cheeked boys and girls are at hand to save you the trouble for a halfpenny. In some parts of America the gates or "bars" are so numerous, that to go through on horseback is about as severe a penance as the Pope can order you, yet it is the only road to the doctor's or the mill. Have you ever noticed the double and treble sets of gates to a prison? You would despair of getting through them without the warder's key, or a miracle such as we twice read of in the Book of Acts. God sent His angel to unlock them, and at his presence or touch they yielded, and the Apostles went through.

I remember when a child, a certain day when Queen Adelaide was to come in a chariot and four from Oxford to Windsor. As the scarlet liveries were seen approaching, the turnpikes flew wide—who would have dared stop that company for toll, or anything else? Was it not the royal command, "Go through, go through the gates?"

Now so in our text; it was a royal command. It was God's voice to the Jews. For their transgressions they were exiles in Babylon. For forty years their captivity had lasted; but there was to be an end of it. They were to return to their own beloved land. King Cyrus would issue the decree (Ezra i. 1–3). The brazen gates of the heathen city, so long closed against them, should let them pass out, and they should depart for Zion with song, and everlasting joy upon their heads. This was God's promise to them. It was about to be fulfilled, and already the prophet cries aloud to them, "Go through, go through the gates!"

Gates are useful things. They keep out stray animals which might otherwise wander into our fields and gardens, and ravage them as the hippopotami do the rice plantations on the banks of the Upper Nile. They are also useful in keeping in our flocks and herds, so that we can leave them at night without tethering them, as the Indians and Arabs are obliged to do theirs. They are useful, too, as landmarks—they answer the purpose of mile-stones and signposts, in reminding us where we are, and how our journey is progressing. Without these breaks in it, we might forget how far and how fast we are travelling. And then they are still further useful as drawing forth our activity; if we are lazy or timid, they will check us.

In the Bible we have a variety of gates spoken of. There **was** the gate of Paradise, out of which Adam and Eve actually had to be driven—through which they were hurried, weeping and woful; and then it was guarded by the flaming sword of the cherubim.

There was the gate of Sodom, out of which Lot and his wife and daughters were urged by their heavenly visitors. Had they not gone through it, they would have been burnt alive; for hardly were they escaped, when the storm of fire and brimstone burst over that guilty race.

There were the gates through which God led the Israelites from out of the bondage of Pharaoh into the possession of the land flowing with milk and honey. He said to them, " Go through, go through the gates!" when the gates were the dry bottom of the Red Sea, with the waters piled on the right and the left; and when they were the dry bottom of the river Jordan, with the waters cut off and "piled in a heap" a league above.

There were the gates of Jerusalem, through which David fled before his wicked son Absalom; through which Stephen was dragged to martyrdom by the mob; through which our Lord walked, bound and surrounded by soldiers, who had just arrested Him in Gethsemane, and through which, a few hours later, he issued bearing His cross towards Calvary, and followed by the lamenting women. And there were the beautiful Temple gates, through which the worshippers went in to the altar, the table of shewbread, the golden candlestick, and the veil which hid the sacred ark. You will think of more, it may be; but now I want to talk about the gates which we ourselves have to go through:—

There are gates which we cannot help going through.
There are gates through which we should escape.
There are gates which we should strive to enter.
There are gates which shut us in for eternity.

First, there are two gates which we *cannot help going through*. I mean we have no choice about it—we have to go through them whether we will or not. We are not asked· if we will, or would rather not; we go through them as a chrysalis is changed into a butterfly, and as a caterpillar is changed into a chrysalis. What gates are these? The gate of life and the gate of death. God arranges our going through these gates for us—the how, the when, the where; and who would not leave it to Him? who would have to fix it for themselves? No; we cheerfully and thankfully confide it to infinite wisdom and kindness: they have tenderly brought us through the one; they will as tenderly bring us through the other.

Secondly, there are three gates through which we should *escape*, as Lot and his wife and daughters did through the gate of Sodom.

The gate of Sodom through which it was possible to escape, was apparently the sole good thing about it. Now, as we are "by nature children of wrath," we are born into the kingdom of sin and Satan and the world, a kingdom in rebellion against God, a kingdom which hates His holy laws and fights against Him, and would, if it could, be independent of Him. To remain in this kingdom is to remain in corruption and bondage, under God's frown, under condemnation!

We must "go through, go through its gates," as for our lives; through the gate which is opened to us out of *sin*, so that we shall not continue in the enjoyment, excuse, and indulgence of it; through the gate which is opened to us out of the power of *Satan*, so that we shall not for the future be his slaves, compelled to do what he bids us, and yet hating ourselves for doing it; through the gate which is to open to us out of the allurements of the *world*, so that it shall not bewilder and drug us with its sweets, as the poisonous flower does the flies which settle on it.

Oh, we must "go through, go through these gates," or perish.

Thirdly, there are three gates which we should strive to *enter*.

Escaped from the kingdom of sin and Satan and the world, whither are we to fly? Is there no other kingdom in which we may find refuge? Indeed, there is; a happy, peaceful, glorious kingdom; "the kingdom of God's dear Son" (Col. i. 13). It is the nursery of the "inheritance of the saints in light." And the appointed gates into it are repentance, faith, obedience. These have to be gone through, however strait and narrow they may be, however disagreeable to these proud hearts of ours. But if the finest dressed lady in England wishes to get into the Great Exhibition, she will have to go through a small door and a turn-stile; she can't sail in in her barouche, or be dropped down in it from a balloon; and if the Emperor himself would get into the Mammoth cave in Kentucky, he will have to crouch and crawl in like an Indian, for a hundred yards.

Repentance is a *low* gate; sorrow for selfishness and coldness towards God, and obstinacy and the angry temper, and the lying lips. But Christ requires it of us. We feel that it is proper and necessary. And when we have gone through that gate, what joy springs of our tears!

Faith is a *difficult* gate; to renounce utterly our hope of delivering ourselves from God's justice, and intrust our case to Him who says, "I will give you rest." Yes, it is hard to believe that God's favour is a free gift; that no money or price can obtain it; that it is to be had simply for "His name's sake." But without this faith in His finished redemption, we have yet to go through the principal gate into the kingdom of God.

Obedience is a *painful* gate; painful to flesh and blood. For they demand to be consulted, and they cannot bear being mortified. But God's precepts are plain, and written down for us, and "they are not grievous." Soon we perceive that they are full of gentleness and reward, and intended to promote our welfare. As we form the habit of obedience, its yoke is easy; and instead of toi'ing under it as the ox does under his load, we glide through it as a laden sloop glides down the river with a fair wind and tide.

Shall we not seek to "go through, go through" these blessed "gates"?

Lastly, there are two gates which *shut us in for Eternity!*

This is an awful thought. Once go through them and we are shut in irrevocably. No skill, no perseverance, no pleading will unfold them! They resemble those iron gates which we have in London. They will let you in, but not out; you may push and rush at them as you will. They let you in as softly as a mother's arms, they resist your exit as a wall of adamant would.

There is the gate of Hell. You can go through it without trouble. Stop your ears to our warnings, listen to the devil's whispering, yield to temptations, and you will go through it as readily as a straw goes into a whirlpool, or a feather into a lion's den. But be sure of this, that having gone through it, it closes upon you! You will go through it no more! Your portion and society thenceforth are whatever lies within it.

But there is the gate of heaven! My young friends, I beseech you, set your faces as flints towards this gate. Jesus is the "way" to it. Embrace Him, and cleave to Him, and without doubt you shall go through it. Within it is Jesus Himself, waiting to receive you. Within it are the precious relatives who died in Jesus, and whose entreaties that you would meet them were sealed with their parting kiss. Within are the spirits of the just, from Abel to Martha and Mary. Within it are fountains of living waters. Within it are crowns, and harps, and white robes. Within it you are beyond the reach of sighs and suffering and fears. No medicines, no weary watchings, no tolling bells, no separations, no graves there! These are "without" that gate, with "dogs, and sorcerers, and idolators" (Rev. xxii. 15). The pearly gates which exclude these from it for ever, will encircle you for ever in all this bliss.

Thrice welcome hour which shall bear us the summons, "Go through, go through the gates, into the joy of thy Lord!"

J. B.

XXXII. The Fading Leaf. Isa. lxiv. 6. "*We all do fade as a leaf: and our iniquities, like the wind, have taken us away.*"

You have all been familiar, in the autumn months, with the leaves gradually losing their fresh green, becoming yellow with spots of decay, and at last falling! lying for a little at the foot of the tree, then whirled away, leaving the leafless branches gaunt and bare against the grey sky.

We are like those leaves, and sin has made us so. The text tells us three things about sin.

I. *Sin is deadly.*—It is not, "We shall fade as a leaf," but "we fade." The fading is a present thing. Of course it is true that on some future day, near or far off, we shall die and be buried; but this is a present thing! "In *the day* that thou eatest thereof thou shalt surely die." When you sin, you are killing yourself; sin is suicide: "He that sinneth against Me wrongeth his own soul." Whenever you commit a sin you separate yourself further and further from the Great Fountain of Life. When you sin you wrong God, you wrong your friends,—but you *kill* your own soul. Holiness is life and peace; sin is death.

II. *Sin is hateful.*—The fading yellow of the leaves did not seem to the prophet to be beautiful, but hateful, hideous, so he took them as a type of sin. Now, sin is a thing that mars beauty, just as some loathsome disease might. Perhaps you have seen some one all marked and scarred who was once beautiful, but never can be so again. That is what sin makes of us. Of some sins you can see the outward traces. Temper wrinkles the face, and makes it unlovely. Drunkenness leaves foul and unmistakable marks. But we have very dim eyes, and are apt to deceive ourselves, and often what is loathsome in God's sight looks well enough in ours. Only remember He is never deceived, and to Him there is just one ugly thing in the world, and that is sin! just one beautiful thing, and that is goodness.

III. *Sin is strong.*—It is like the wind which sweeps the leaves away. And we are like the leaves—very weak before the wind. You know how one sin brings another. If you speak an angry word, and a quarrel begins, you go on from bad words to worse, and perhaps say and do things you will repent all your life. You never meant it. No! but your iniquities, like the wind, carried you away; Peter denied Christ once, then twice, then a third time. He was taken away by his iniquity. You tell one lie, and then another to hide it, and another and another, till you wonder how you could be so base. Sin is strong! and it has, like the wind, taken you away.

This is a dark picture. But Jesus Christ throws a bright light on it. He died for the faded leaves, that they might become green again. And He is the living Vine, and the leaves in that strong tree are safe, however the winds may sweep. Dear children, are you trusting Him! His blood washes away the stain, and His strength keeps us; and if we are in Him, death is not death any more, but the entrance into life. "There is but a step between me and death," said an old minister, "and that step is the Lord Jesus Christ."

W. R. N.

XXXIII. A Bunch of Grapes. Isa. lxv. 8. *"Destroy it not; for a blessing is in it."*

This is said of a bunch of grapes. What a beautiful, yet what a fragile thing it is! How easily it is "destroyed"! For instance, wild animals might destroy it. "Take us the foxes, the little foxes, that spoil the vines;" or thieves, in clambering over the walls on which they grow, might tear and crush them; or boys might throw stones at them in pure mischief when they were out of reach. Hence vineyards are fenced in and watched, and traps are set, and trespassers are warned off. It is to prevent their being "destroyed."

And why not destroy them? Because "a blessing" is in them. Frail as they are, there is that in them which should make them precious in our eyes.

Here we have four lessons taught us by a bunch of grapes.

I. That great good may be stored in little things.

II. That God alone puts it into them.

III. That they should be spared for this though they are little.

IV. That if it is lacking in them, they will be undone for ever.

I. We learn from our text that great good may be stored in little things. A bunch of grapes is a little thing, and yet there is a "blessing" in it. Its juice is most cheering. What would people do in hot countries without it? A bee is a little thing, and yet we owe the delicious honey, with its curious honeycomb, to it. An egg is a little thing; but there is meat enough packed up in it to save your life for days. An acorn is a little thing, and yet there lies in it the future giant oak.

The infant Moses, and the boy Joseph, and the lad David, and the Hebrew maid, were little in comparison with the princes and captains of their age; but what mighty good was stored in them! The Holy Babe, wrapt in swaddling clothes, and lying in a manger at Bethlehem, was little; but in Him was the light which lighteth every man that cometh into the world. And what a blessing has flowed out of little books, little tracts, little hymns, little prayers, little words of reproof or encouragement spoken in season! A child may be a missionary to the ignorant children in her or his neighbourhood, a ministre to a careless father or mother, a model to sisters or brothers. With a heart given to Jesus, a child is a sun which cannot but shine, a fountain which cannot but send out streams, a flower which cannot but fill the air with sweetness.

That is the best of blessings. A heart in which Christ reigns, in which His Spirit dwells, which wears His image and is zealous for His kingdom, such a heart is richer than the "cluster with new wine" in it. It has in it the new wine of God's grace.

II. God alone puts the blessing into little things.

We should remember this lest we be proud and self-conceited.

Does a watch insert its own wheels and chains? Does a piano contrive its own keys and strings? And who but God imparts to the medicinal herbs their virtue to heal our diseases, or to the grain of wheat its power to throw up the tall stalk with the golden ear on it?

And who but God can break our hard hearts and exchange them for hearts of flesh—pure and tender and lowly hearts?

Herein He displays His wisdom. Who but an all-wise God could fill little things, "earthen vessels," with the excellent treasure, and glorify Himself out of the mouths of sucklings? We must have large things to work with; God works with coral insects, and drops of rain, and grains of sand.

Herein also He displays His omnipotence. He enshrines a jewel in what is weak and exposed, and yet shields it. The Queen's regalia in the Tower has to be guarded by iron bars and soldiers. But God entrusts that priceless thing, a soul, to you; and then, if He so pleases, the invisible angels protect it—it is secure against the "gates of hell."

Herein He displays His condescension and compassion. Is it not marvellous that He should deign to use worms of the dust in His service? This is His delight. He passes by the tempest, and waters the fields and gardens with the imperceptible dew. He chooses the humblest instruments.

And so, though but a child, He will stoop to you and endue you with heavenly gifts, as He did Samuel, and Solomon, and Josiah, and Timothy; and cause you to be a fruitful bough, it may be in exceedingly dry places.

III. Little things are to be spared for this blessing in them. "Destroy it not, for a blessing is in it." We have seen that the blessing in the cluster is the new wine. Not that vile, adulterated stuff, half water, half fire, which can be bought in England; not that "rare old wine," which people buy at a guinea a bottle, to redden their noses with; but the new wine as God created it, straight from the berry. Destroy not the cluster for that blessing's sake.

Everything, however little, which has a blessing in it should be spared. Therefore we cry out against the wanton destruction of robins' and linnets' and larks' nests. What glad songs for wintry mornings are suddenly quenched when they are torn to pieces.

The Lord Himself would not even have the broken bread and meat after dinner wasted, because a blessing was in it. "Gather up the fragments," He said.

How frequently God has spared offending cities and families because a blessing was in them! He would have spared Sodom itself if there had been but ten righteous in it.

Are there not plenty of little things which you are apt to despise because they are little? There are your vows and resolutions. You formed them when you were in trouble or under impression. Don't let them seem trifles to you now.

There are your habits. These are invaluable—habits of obedience, truthfulness, diligence, self-denial.

There is your character. Your fair fame once sullied or suspected becomes like a negro's skin; it is black and you cannot soap and wash it off.

And there is your interest in the poor heathen. What a blessing there is in that, both for yourself and for them! Destroy it not by coldness or forgetfulness; but fan it to a brighter flame, until you are aglow with it from head to foot.

IV. If the blessing is lacking in them, they will be undone for ever. "Destroy it not, for a blessing is in it"; as if it were said, if there were no blessing in it, then it might be destroyed. Who begs mercy for a parcel of nettles, which do nothing but sting? Who begs mercy for wasps and hornets? No; we say there is no blessing in them, let them be swept away. This is pictured forth to us in the withering of the fig-tree by the roadside. It was cursed because it was barren.

Saul had no blessing in him, Judas had none, and they were destroyed. It was the blessing in them which preserved Lot and Peter, although they yielded to temptation.

If there is no blessing in us, we are doomed. The unprofitable servant hid his talent in the napkin; but he could not hide himself from his master's indignation. God plants us in His heritage, He digs about us, He trains and defends us. If, notwithstanding this culture, we are conscious of no active blessing in us, no gratitude to Him, no desire to do His will, no sorrow that we have grieved Him, no yearnings towards Him who shed His blood for us on Calvary, what can we expect? What can be before us but the axe and the terrible order "Cut it down, why cumbereth it the ground?"

Implore God for this blessing. Plead for it for Himself, that you may be a noble cluster to His praise. For those around you, that they may partake of your happiness, feel your influence, and thank God for you. And for yourself, that instead of awaiting the wrath of God, you may be assured of His favour, and filled with joy and peace. May we all have such a blessing in us, and then we shall have no fear of the sentence, "Destroy it." God Himself will say, as of the new wine in the cluster, "Destroy it not, for a blessing is in it." And who shall destroy what He champions?   J. B.

XXXIV. Bad Habits. JER. xiii. 13. "*Accustomed to do evil.*"

I. *Bad habits and how they are formed.*—Some things are natural to us. We never needed to learn them. We are made with them, *e.g.* breathing, moving, crying, eating, drinking. But there are some things which seem as natural as these, which we can as little help doing. Once we could not do them. They were painful to do at first, but by doing them over and over again we got into the way of doing them, and they are now habits. For a habit is just something we have got accustomed to do. We are made up of *habits*. Almost anything may be made a habit if it is just done often enough or long enough. Bad habits are generally most easy to be got at because we have a bad heart to begin with, but some are painful and unpleasant to acquire. Almost all our habits are acquired in youth, and when we become men and women it is hardly possible to get quit of them. The great inducement to what is evil is that it is "just for once." Doing a thing once does not make a habit. "One swallow does not make a summer," but it is on the way to it. And doing a thing once makes it easy to do it again and again, till it becomes a habit.

Take a few specimens of bad habits :—

(1) In the matter of *reading*.—Well-trained children know how to discriminate between what is good and bad reading. A book was sent by the author to a friend. The next time they met he asked if he had read it. He replied, "No, it is a bad book." "How do you know, if you have not read it?" "We do not need to eat all the meat at table to know whether it is good or bad, if we find one bite tainted we order it away." We should so deal with bad books. Reading sensational novels keeps many from being saved.

(2) In the matter of *speaking*.—Slang words; coarse and low expressions; vulgarity; half untruths; half oaths; disrespectful words to parents, teachers, masters, or mistresses; things we think smart or witty; speaking against, or telling tales about people—all these become habits. Then there is the habit of exaggeration, making everything appear greater than it really is, which makes young people grow up liars.

(3) In the matter of *food*.—We should not live to eat, for that puts us on a level with the beasts. Then there is over indulgence in sweetmeats, and learning to smoke and drink wine and other intoxicating drinks. These are all bad habits.

(4) *Carelessness and slovenliness*.—Untidiness in dress, awkwardness in manner at table, etc.; doing things in a wrong or defective way to save trouble and effort; doing

things with the left hand that should be done with the right; want of steadiness in keeping at anything.

(5) *Procrastination.*—Putting off till to-morrow what ought to be done to-day. Being late for school, church, etc. These bad habits have a bearing on higher things, for there is a tendency to put off the soul's salvation.

II. *The power these habits get over us, and the difficulty of their cure.*—They hold us in their grasp. You have seen ivy clinging to an old wall; if you try to take it away the wall comes with it. Or you have seen a little boy on a horse; he has such a control over it with the bridle that he can make it go where he likes. These are pictures of our habits. One of our Edinburgh ministers was in Africa, and a little negro boy, who had never seen a white man before, put his fingers to his lips and began to rub his hand, expecting the white to come off. God says if you can make a black man white, or get the spots off a leopard, then you who have been in the habit of doing what is bad may be brought to do what is good. A man was once walking along the shore when his foot was caught in a link of a chain. He could not pull it out. He called for help, but it was unavailing, and the sea came in and he was drowned. That is what bad habits may do. They hold you fast, and unless there is help from God there will be death at the end.

III. *The possibility of their cure.*—In order to the cure of bad habits there must be:
(1) A new heart.
(2) Earnest prayer.
(3) Constant watchfulness; and,
(4) Resolute and self-denying effort.

J. H. W.

XXXV. Pride. JER. xiii. 15. "*Be not proud.*"

AN old grandfather once quoted this short text at the family breakfast table. All present said that they had never heard it before, and they did not believe that it was in the Bible. He declared that it was, and he gave them a week to find it in, and promised the finder half a sovereign. But at the end of the week nobody claimed the ten shillings.

They had ransacked both Testaments in vain, and the

old grandfather had to show it them. And so, many a precious gem lies hid in this vast mine till a light is struck over it, and lo! it glitters.

These words teach a very complete and very important life lesson to us all. We all of us know what pride is. We feel it in ourselves. We are quick to observe it in others. It is one of those hateful little snakes which crept out of the serpent's mouth when he said to Eve, " Eat of the tree, and ye shall be as gods," and unfortunately Eve let it creep into her heart through her ear, and ever since it has been born in all her posterity. It is exceedingly deceitful, so that it escapes punishment often by passing itself off for what is excellent It changes its colour as the chameleon does—amongst the grass it will be green, in the sun it will be golden, in the flower-bed it will be pink; and yet its true colour is black, for always and everywhere it is sin. The worst charge that we have to bring against it is enmity to God, setting up idols where He alone should reign, and breeding in us envies, strifes, malice, things worthy of death.

Its varieties are endless—let us think of four of the chief.

I. There is *race pride*—pride in our ancestors. It is a blessed thing to have pious parents, it is certainly an honour to have progenitors who have distinguished themselves. But what is there to boast of? Did we help to make them what they were? and are we doing as they did? Is not the recollection of them enough to humble us, because of our shortcomings? As for pride in descent from those who were rich or titled, and yet did not serve God, if we could have a glimpse of them now as they are now, mayhap we should never again refer to them. The Jews were race proud. "We have Abraham to our father."

But God heaps contempt on their pride! "God is able of these stones to raise up children unto Abraham."

II. There is *face pride*—pride in one's outward appearance. Lovely or manly features are not to be despised. They are said to be a "fortune" in themselves. It is astonishing how much favour they obtain, how many bolted doors they open, how much ice they melt. A handsome child will be sure to learn that it is handsome! and then is pride's opportunity. It feeds and fans the spark till it is a flame, and the flame till it is a consuming fire. And then beauty is no longer beauty—we associate it with mirrors, coxcombry, self-worship, self-conceit, and prefer the plainest countenance which has the ornament of a meek and quiet spirit. You cannot prevent the report of your mirror or the remarks of foolish visitors, but you can prevent these from being nourished and cherished by brooding over them. David was "ruddy and fair" but he reckoned it as nothing compared with right doing. Absalom cared nothing for right-doing, but everything for his long beautiful hair—yet his hair proved to be a halter to hang him!

Beware, lest some fondly doted on prettiness of yours proves a snare to you.

III. There is *place pride*—pride in your position in society.

You may live in a fine house, and flatter yourself that you are better than those who live in cottages. You may live in town and flatter yourself that you are better than those who live in the country. You may have talents upon which you gallop into popularity, and you may flatter yourself that you are better than your jogtrot neighbours.

But do any of these things render you actually better? that is wiser, holier, nobler? From whom did you receive them? And if you received them "without money and without price" from God, why should you be haughty about them?

IV. There is *grace pride*—pride in godliness.

This is the worst sort of pride, and it is the most subtle and difficult to root out. It is more an evil odour or a poisonous insect which hovers around the buds and blossoms of our piety than a bud or blossom itself.

But it cannot be denied that there is such a thing, and that it mingles occasionally with our prayers and praises, our charities, and even with our repentances and tears. We are puffed up! we congratulate ourselves, we weigh our devotions, or services, or emotions in the sanctuary balance, and then, when we ascertain that they are satisfactory, we offer incense to self instead of to God.

We have to be on our guard here, or grace pride will corrupt all our grace, as a drop of vinegar will corrupt a pan of milk, or a spoonful of yeast a trough of dough. Its mere breath upon anything infects it. "Be not proud," for we have nothing to be proud of. We are poor, weak, dependent creatures. If, like the vine, we have ripening clusters on us, it is because the heavenly Husbandman has planted, and trained, and watered us. And if, like the barren fig-tree which our Lord sought fruit on, we have only leaves, then, instead of being proud, we ought to be sitting in sackcloth and ashes.

"Be not proud" because it is abhorrent to God.

Do you desire His presence and approval and blessing? You cannot have it if you indulge pride. "The proud He knoweth afar off." "God resisteth the proud." It is so wicked in His sight. Debtors to Him for each beat of their pulses—proud!

"Be not proud" because it is so unlike Christ.

He is our model, and where was pride in Him? He had none of it. He knew everything, and possessed everything, and could do everything; but He laid all His honours at His Father's feet; He chose fishermen for His companions, and welcomed babes to His arms, and condescended to men of low estate.

He requires that His disciples now be as He was in the world. You cannot be Christlike if you are proud. What! Proud, and yet like Him who bore the bason and towel round that supper chamber! and who yielded Himself to spitting and scourging and crucifixion for guilty sinners!

"Be not proud," because it is ruinous. "Pride goeth before destruction." It is like leprosy, which, though a mere spot at first, at last spreads over the entire body. Pride is a crime as well as a malady. God is angry with it and must punish it; it will bring on us that terrific sentence "Depart ye cursed."

Some children are very proud. He who loves them, and seeks their eternal welfare and who never commands without a purpose, says to them "Be not proud." If strong in their self-will, they say, "Nay, but it is nice, and we will be." Then let us cry for them, "Father, forgive them."

Some children are proud occasionally. They have fits of it, and then they will be again modest and humble. We should watch against those sudden outbreaks. They, too, defile and damage us, as Moses and Hezekiah and Peter all discovered to their cost.

Some children are bravely struggling with pride to subdue it; God prosper them! Naturally it is powerful in them, but they perceive its loathsomeness, and are determined that it shall not have the mastery. They are checking and starving it. They long to be conformed to Jesus. Such children are to be envied. The kingdom is theirs and they are apparelled for it already.

J. B.

XXXVI. The Storms of Life. NAHUM i. 3. "*The Lord hath His way in the whirlwind and in the storm, and the clouds are the dust of His feet.*"

You know, my young friends, that when our Lord was teaching on earth, He would often point to the things around Him—to the birds, flowers, or flocks—to everything the people could see, and tell them there was some lesson they could learn from them. I suppose when we hear a storm, and think of it at sea, our first thought is, "Why are there such things as storms?" We do not feel it so much in the middle of the city; but out on the sea, there the storm is a terrible thing, and men may well ask, "Is there anything that a storm can teach us."

This is what the storm can tell us, what the prophet told the people hundreds and hundreds years ago—that the Lord has His way in the storm as well as in the peaceful summer. Storm and tempest fulfil His work.

What is a storm? There is nothing new in a storm. The winds were there before—but now the winds come sweeping in one way. They can thus destroy noble and mighty vessels, and tear up majestic trees; and all through the Bible a storm is compared to something that happens to us in life, and there is One who is called our Refuge from the storm. What do we mean by a storm in life? Just as all these winds sweeping in one direction cause a storm, so a storm in life is not one little temptation or anxiety, but it is when the troubles come on thick and the difficulties and temptations come on in crowds. Look at Job—one sorrow and then another, then one trial and then another. And then he bowed down to the very earth till the storm had swept over him. That is what we mean by a storm in life. I suppose, boys and girls, you think there is no such thing, for you are in safety. In bed this morning you did not think much of danger, for the storm was without and you were within. But the day will come when you will have to go out. You are like a ship that will have to face the tempest. In the dock it is in safety, and for months and months it goes on building, and adding on planks and riveting them together so that the water shall not get between them. And then the machinery and fittings are added, and it all goes on and there is no danger. Then the ship goes out into the harbour, and then upon the water to see whether she is watertight. Only after all that she goes out and is able to defy the tempests and storms.

And this is the way, my dear little friends, that you are being built up by parents and those who have the care of you, or pastors whom God has sent—all are trying to join your life together and make you strong; but the day must come when you will have to go out and face the storm.

Oh, that you could remember this—all the loving hands that now surround you must loose their grasp. You leave the nursery, and the whirlwind will try you. Oh, if you think there is little danger of your life being swamped, take care. You have seen a harbour perhaps. Down at Dover, or wherever it may be, there is the harbour—a great arm, as if the land held out its arm and said, "I will direct you." The small boats even lie there safe, for they are within that mighty arm.

That is how most of you are now waiting to go on the voyage of life, and there is the strong arm of a father's or mother's love carrying you safely across those temptations, but the day must come when you must go alone.

There are two things that you will need then—you do not need them so much now. First, you must be strong-made, that is, your character must be, as it were, drawn all together—not going one way and then another as chance may direct. You must feel, "Here I am, God has sent me into life as if there were no other, I am not to be drawn to the right or left owing to the choice of others. Soon I must go into the storm and rely upon God."

Do not neglect this while your character is being built. One ship looks as good as another, but the storm tries them. If you walk across the park this afternoon, the trees all look the same. They all look the same in the sunshine; but when the storm bursts, and rushes through the branches, then you know what branches and trees are sound and what are not.

So it will be with you when you pass through the storm of life.

Another thing you must have. Not only are you to be built in devotion and love and grace and truth and purity, but you must have One to steer you on the course. Remember a ship is no good if it stops still—it must go from one place to another. Your voyage is from this world to Heaven; and so you must be strong, otherwise any little turning to the right or to the left, any little untruth, any little falseness, any little impurity may be dangerous. Always it should be, "I am making for that point; and there is One abroad whom I can trust. He knows the way."

You know who will steer you. Your Master is Jesus, and the Bible is your guide.

Remember, many a ship has been well-built, and steered well for a time, and then there came some storm. Some tremendous sorrow comes upon you, and the greatest sorrow that can come upon a father or mother is, that one of their children should grow bad and become a wandering sheep. Think always of that; the greatest sorrow that can be brought upon your father or mother, is the sorrow that you can bring upon them. There are great griefs and great trials against which no vessel seems strong enough, but even then there is One who is a refuge against the worst storms of life.

A ship was coming across the Atlantic, but a terrible storm came on as they neared the English coast. And as day after day passed, and the storm still raged, the captain said, "All hope is over." And those on board looked with white and fearful faces at one another, and one man cried, "I see the coast;" and then there came a wild shout from another, "I see the lifeboat!" And, bounding like a living saviour over the livid waves, came the life-boat, and the crew were rescued and the brave men saved.

And so in the worst storm of life, when your whole frame and faith seem broken by the tempest, there is the hope of rescue by Jesus Christ, who is the same to-day, yesterday and for ever.

T. T. S.

XXXVII. The Centurion. MATT. viii. 5-14.

ON which side of the garden wall, children, would you expect to get the finest fruit—on the inside, where the gardener has carefully tended the fruit, or on the other side, where the seed has accidentally dropped and grown up by itself? On the inside, would not you say? And if you found on the other side more order and better fruit than inside, you would be very much astonished. So was Jesus when He found this heathen man with such a beautiful trust and character as He had not met with among His own people—the sons of Abraham. The Old Testament tells us that the people of Israel were set in the earth like a vineyard, of which God took great care, and whom He made as good as He could by sending His own servants to them; but instead of bringing forth fruit, as He might have expected, Jesus found a people full of sin, who would not accept Him, who persecuted Him, and who at last were so angry with Him, that they put Him to death.

When you go home this afternoon, children, it will do you good if you will try to find out how many heathen people in the New Testament were praised for their faith. This man was a Roman soldier, and you might find how many heathen soldiers were mentioned in the New Testament, as being useful and good men, who were near the Kingdom of Heaven before they got into it. You will find a good deal of instruction in this. This man was a soldier, a Roman soldier—that is a soldier in the Roman army. All that he said to Jesus was suggested to him by his experience as a soldier. Everything in military work depends upon discipline and unquestioning obedience, upon the strict carrying out of orders whether the eye of the commander is upon the soldier or not. He is no use in an army who will only do his duty when he is watched by his superior officer, and who cannot be trusted to carry out his orders when nobody is watching him. This centurion knew this. He knew that the word of authority carried power with it, and brought about what was needed in absence as well as in presence; and so when Jesus said He would go to the centurion's house and cure the boy, he said, "There is no need for that, for you can give command to disease as I command my men. You need only speak the word, and the disease will obey you."

And so it was. Jesus could utter the word, and the word could fulfil itself though He were not there. Do you not see how this centurion, being a soldier, and being accustomed to strict discipline in the army, enabled him to understand the position of Jesus with relation to the unseen world? He understood Jesus Christ's control over the forces of nature better than the Jews did; so that our Lord said, "This man has grasped the proper idea of My place and power better than any Jew whom I have met."

Let us, children, try to understand this view of the Roman centurion with regard to Jesus and His power. If our Lord's word were only effective in His presence it would be a bad thing for us, for we have not His presence. Whatever the emperor of this centurion commanded had to be done, though the emperor himself were far away. Jesus Christ is our Emperor; and though He is far from us—farther than this man's emperor was—He yet rules upon the earth. The word emperor is taken from imperator, which is a word of command. It signified the head man over the people. Jesus Christ is Imperator and Commander. The forces of nature are His soldiers, and He sways all hearts. And when we ask Him to bless and pardon us, let us remember that He is our Emperor, and that His word runneth very swiftly, and fulfils itself in Heaven and in earth.

J. O. D.

XXXVIII. Hospital Sunday. MATT. ix. 12, 13. "*I came not to call the righteous, but sinners to repentance. They that are whole need not a physician, but they that are sick.*"

NOW, I do not know whether it has ever struck you, but it has often perplexed my mind to think what a number of ills and aches and pains and troubles there are in this world of ours and amongst our human kind. I daresay a good many of you young people have already, young as you are, had your share of pain and suffering.

I daresay some of you boys and girls have had measles and whooping-cough, and a lot of those other juvenile ailments; perhaps scarlet fever or small-pox. And I daresay some of the older people here have had their share of rheumatism, and heart disease, and various other weaknesses to which they tell us our flesh is heir.

Now, what a blessing it is to think that while there is such an amount of suffering, and so much pain, that comes, somehow or other, to most of us; and comes more or less to all—what a blessing it is that there are so many means of relieving distress and pain and suffering. Why, we have our doctors, trained nurses, dispensaries, infirmaries, hospitals, where the very best skill and kindest nursing that are to be found in the land are at the service of the poor, and those who can provide least for themselves. And I do not know any Sunday that ought more to draw out the sympathy and the kindness of a human heart or a community, than the Sunday when Christians, young and old, are called upon to give their small contribution to the maintenance of those noble hospitals that are doing so much good amongst the poor and suffering in this great city and throughout our land.

Now, when we think of the very great number of ailments that there are, and when we think that by any one or other of these, or by accident, by a broken limb, by a fall or a bruise, any one of us may die, it is enough to make us really afraid to look at that great list, and think that each one which attacks us is taking out a pin of this earthly tabernacle, and helping to bring down to the ground this house of clay in which each one of us lodges and accommodates an immortal spirit. But then this very spirit itself, that has its lodgment in this tabernacle of clay, of human flesh, is subject to a terrible ailment, an ailment that is universal, that nobody escapes; the queen on the throne suffers from it, the meanest beggar on the highway has it; a boy that is playing at school, or a little girl lying on a sick bed at the hospital, all of us here, I in the pulpit and you in the pews, are infected by this terrible disease.

I wonder if one boy or girl here will speak up and tell me the disease in one word. ("*Sin.*") Sin! Of course. That is the disease from which we all suffer, and it is a terrible disease, for in a certain sense there is no cure for it. It is one of the saddest things which I have to see in my visiting at sick beds, to see one of the very worst diseases that can come to a human body, and that is a cancer. For it there is no cure when it gets beyond a certain stage, and the poor sufferer can only suffer more intensely day by day, with the dark and lonesome grave as the only prospect of relief.

Well, but here is sin, born with us, strengthening with our strength, growing with our growth, unless we take the one and only means which is provided to counteract sin. We cannot get rid of it except in a certain way, and unless we adopt that remedy it will bring us at last to death. It is spoken of in Scripture as a leprosy, as a wound, as bruises, as putrefying sores, as death. "You hath he quickened who were dead in trespasses and in sins," says the Apostle Paul.

Now, I have told you about sin and about everybody in the world having it, whether old or young, strong or weak, active or feeble; whether we have the flush of life that lightens up so glowingly some of your cheeks, or whether we are pale and worn; it is a disease we all have and one for which there is only one remedy provided in all God's word, the only remedy against sin. I wonder if, in a word, any of you can give me its Name. ("*Jesus.*") Yes! That is the only Remedy; sin is the disease, Jesus is the Remedy. Now, just for a little while I am going to speak about Jesus as the one and only Remedy; as able to save the very worst cases, that is my second point; and the third one is, He gives His services without money and without price; and, last of all, He is waiting to save and to heal the children.

First, then, I am going to speak of Jesus as the one and only Remedy. Now there are a great many symptoms of this terrible disease of sin, and I would like very much to ask you of the names of some of them. Why, the symptoms are legion, they are manifold; any little boy or girl who is cross and angry, unkind or disobedient to parents, or to brothers and sisters or playmates, is showing the symptoms of sin. A boy who swears or uses bad language ; a girl who speaks lies ; all who are dishonest, who are in any way regardless of God and the things of God, they are all showing the symptoms of the foul disease of sin. We see the symptoms on the street, in men and women rolling along the worse for drink ; in the Police Court, in the crime that comes there, and in the crime that shows itself throughout the world in a thousand ways.

It is a disease that has its stronghold in the human heart, and all the while is infecting and spreading itself over all the elements of human activity ; sin is in many creatures, and there is one remedy against it, whether in the human heart or in its manifestations in the world. Some people think that education will put a stop to it ; some other people think that if everybody could be brought to don the "blue ribbon" it would put a stop to it ; some think that if police regulations were strict enough it would put a stop to it. But we know that there is only one way of getting at the root of this disease ; by dealing with it in the heart and conscience, and bringing the person who is suffering from it to the Lord Jesus, who can give pardon and cleansing, and a new heart. Jesus is the only One who can take away the heart of stone and give us a heart of flesh ; He alone can cleanse us from the stains of evil that we have contracted all our lives.

Now, I have spoken to you about Jesus as the only true Remedy for sin ; but it is only when we come to trust in Him, and get a new heart and a cleansed life, it enables us to overcome sin.

But now I want you to remember that Jesus heals and saves in the very worst cases. The most skilful doctor is often quite unable to effect a cure in a person who is suffering from trouble or disease. I once heard a very pretty story from a friend of mine who visited sometimes the hospitals. And there, in one of the beds at the hospital, there was a little boy. He had been brought into the city from the country, and his mother had stayed with him some little time in order to accustom him to be alone in that big place amongst strangers. But now she had gone away when my friend visited the hospital. And as he came from bed to bed, he came at last to this little boy, and he went and made inquiries about his circumstances and found he was suffering from a bad leg; and the doctors had given it as their opinion that the leg would have to be taken off, as that was the only chance of saving his life, and perhaps even that might not be successful. And so when my friend found out this, he spoke very kindly and tenderly to him; told him of the operation that must be performed some day soon, and bade him keep up a good heart. He said the doctor would be there, and he was a kind man; the nurses too would be there; and you do not need to be afraid or lonely, because very likely it will be the means of saving your life. And when my friend had finished speaking, the little boy says: "Yes! and let Jesus be there too!" Some few days afterwards, when the operation had taken place, he went to see him, and came to the crib where the boy had been, and found it empty. He looked at the nurse, she shook her head. And then he knew well what had happened; he knew that the little boy had gone home! Jesus had been there, along with the doctors and the nurses, and He had taken the little lamb to His bosom and carried it away to a better country, where the inhabitants shall say no more: "I am sick," and the people that dwell therein are forgiven their iniquity. Children, what a grand thing it will be for you and me to say when we are laid on the bed of sickness or death, we can count on Jesus being with us, able to keep us, and fold us in His everlasting arms and bring us to the blessedness of His own kingdom.

So you see, when the earthly doctor's skill fails, and he can go no further, what a grand thing it is to have the Great Physician to heal all the woes of the immortal spirit, and bring His people to that land where they will be happy in blessedness for ever.

This is all, perhaps, a long way from the point; but never mind, it may impress some truth on your hearts, and the great truth I want you to realize is this: Jesus is able to save to the uttermost all who come to God by Him. It does not matter how sinful we have been, if only we come to Him for the forgiveness and grace to make us happy in His presence.

And then I said, Jesus gave His services for nothing. He gives them without money and without price. Nobody can buy His medicine, anybody that wants it can have it for asking. All the wealth of the Indies, all the gold mines in the world, can buy not even a little bit of His grace. It must come to us freely from God; it cannot be got for money. And He gives it without money and without price to every little child that comes into His presence and asks for pardon. The little child will get all his sins forgiven; the little girl that kneels in her room and asks Jesus for a new heart, Jesus will surely give it to her freely and for nothing.

We cannot purchase these great gifts of Jesus, but we may have them for the taking, and if we take them to our hearts it will make us happy, now and eternally.

But then I said that Jesus is waiting to heal the children. Yes! Jesus was ever the children's Friend. You boys and girls here; your hearts are young now and tender, not yet have they grown hard like the stone pavement outside there. When you are older they will grow harder; and it is just now, at this time of your life, that you may best learn of Jesus, to love Him and give yourself to Him, to love and serve Him as your best Friend, and then He will make you happy hereafter. Don't imagine that there will be time for you, or that it will be better for you, to think about all this when you grow up into men and women. You have just as much need to be saved as the grown-up people, and you have just as much need to be made good and pure and true as they have. There is a beautiful hymn which represents the Man at the Gate in the Pilgrim's Progress, receiving all sorts of people when they come to enter in at the Way of Life. The man says: "I am willing with all my heart," and a little child comes :—

> "I am only a little child, dear Lord,
> And my feet already are stained with sin,
> But they said He had sent the children word
> To come to the Gate, and enter in.
> And the Man at the Gate looked down and smiled,
> A goodly smile and fair to see ;
> And spoke as He looked at the trembling child,
> 'I am willing with all my heart,' said He."

Jesus was the Man at the Gate, and He it was who

said: "Suffer the little children to come unto Me, and forbid them not, for of such is the Kingdom of Heaven."

Will you try, dear children, to remember the things we have spoken about this afternoon? How sin is the deadly ailment that we are all suffering from. How the one and only Remedy is Jesus Christ. How Jesus can save the very worst cases; and can do His willing work just when the doctor's work ends and he can do no more. And Jesus gives the healing without money and without price. And remember this too, your Friend the Lord Jesus is waiting to give His healing touch to the children, to make them happy in His love and His salvation.

T. N.

XXXIX. On the Sea. MATT. xiv. 22-36.

PROBABLY not all of the boys and girls who have heard me read this beautiful section of the Gospel have ever seen the great sea. Certainly few or none of you have sailed upon it; and it would be a very difficult thing for some of you to imagine or know the beauty and terribleness of the sea. In the Book of Job it is said that God alone dwelleth on the waves of the sea; that is to say, He who made it has all might over its great waters, and even over those unknown depths that are beneath its surface.

And to us men the sea is a thing we have reason to fear, because it swallows up in its grave so much of the treasures that men possess, its bottom being strewn all over with the riches it has stolen from men. And more because it has stolen many of the precious lives of men. So that all we can do cannot save us from the attacks which the sea makes upon us year after year. But let us learn this lesson, which Jesus certainly wanted to teach His people—that He had power not only over the land but over that great and terrible sea. It is His, and as God, He travels over it. So that if you behold the sea and you fear it, knowing that you cannot battle with the storm, you must try to remember, boys and girls, that there is not a billow of the sea which is not in His hand—in the hand of Him who is your dear Friend and Lord, and to whom you say prayer before you lay your head down on the pillow at night.

And not one dear precious life will be swept away by the sea unless by the will of Him who walked on the waves. The sea is an emblem to us of care and trouble from which we cannot save ourselves. So that we can learn this lesson from it: that Jesus is master of all great troublous things.

He has power over the things of nature and of the world, and He uses His power for the good of His friends. And this is wonderful too, that He can make His friends as strong on the sea as Himself; for it seems to me that His making Peter walk over the sea is a more wonderful thing than that He, Himself, who is Lord of the sea, should walk upon it.

In all our troubles, therefore, let us remember that the secret of safety and deliverance is confidence in Christ; is to have our eyes firmly fixed on His strong face and firm hand. So long as Peter kept his eye on the great calm eye of Jesus, and remembered that His dear Lord had all might over the waters, so long was Peter strong, and so long he was drawing strength from Jesus. The moment he allowed his eyes to drop from Jesus' eye, and looked at the waves, that moment his soul began to quake within him, and he began to be weak.

That is the secret of courage and spiritual strength for us. Let it be a lesson for the youngest of us, not to fear, and let it be a lesson for the oldest of us, to trust. May God add His blessing.

J. O. D.

XL. Witnessing Children. Matt. xxi. 15. "*The children crying in the temple.*"

THIS is very beautiful. It is one of the most beautiful things noticed concerning the great day of Jesus' entrance into Jerusalem. You recollect the story: how the Lord sent two of His disciples to the village on the slope of Olivet, charging them to bring the ass and the colt, which they would find at a particular place; how He seated Himself on the ass, and slowly rode towards the holy city, followed by an immense crowd of people; how multitudes on hearing of His approach, streamed out of Jerusalem, and met Him, and then turning round preceded Him, strewing His path with their clothes and with branches; how the air was rent with hosannahs which became louder and louder as the procession neared the Temple, glittering with gold and marble. Indeed a wonderful sight, a wonderful hour! All the city is moved. Strangers, of whom there were then tens of thousands, ask, Who is this? Priests and scribes do not need to ask; they know that it is Jesus of Nazareth; but they are angry. We can see them, as the cavalcade sweeps past into the courts of Jehovah's sanctuary, scoffing, scowling, their brows knit, filled partly with fear and partly with fury. But they say nothing until—the children cry. The children are waiting for their King; and as He enters the Temple, they form in rank around Him, shouting in gladsome chorus—a chorus renewed and ever renewed, as the eyes of some one hitherto blind are touched, and the blind one sees; or the lame, obedient to the Almighty word, starts up to leap and walk. Oh yes! they are sore displeased, these bigoted priests and scribes; and they force their way to Christ, and with ill-concealed sneers, they demand, "Hearest thou what these say?"

We are going to linger for a little over the picture of the children crying in the Temple. Because it is not only affecting, as a feature of Jesus' triumph; it is the sign of something true in all times. Remember *where* the children were. They were in the Temple. They had their place in the house of God. They had a right to be there, as well as their parents, for God's covenant embraced them too. They had received the seal of that covenant; and so they had been "planted in the house of the Lord." Now you, young people, are also in God's Temple. You are a part of His congregation. God is your Father. Jesus is your Saviour. The Holy Ghost is your Sanctifier. You have not been left outside the place of privilege and blessing. You have been taken inside. The promise to the fathers is a promise to the children also. Therefore we think that you should not be left in the cold; that all the prayers, and the praises, and the teachings in church should not go to the older folk; nor that all the writing in magazines meant for religious instruction should be addressed to those of riper years.

There are three thoughts suggested by the picture now before us:—

I. *The children see, whilst others are blind.*
II. *The children sing, although others are silent.*
III. *The children receive the blessing which others lose.*

I. They see what priest and scribe, with all their learning, see not—*the Son of David.* They read in His presence and the wonderful things which He does, the title and the patents of His royalty. No doubt have these sweet children, What prevents the faith of others—pride, seeking honour one of another, the evil heart which is the seat of unbelief—does not hinder their sight. The eye is single, and the whole body is full of light. And so whilst many around are in thick darkness, because of the veil that is over their face, they have found the great secret, "*Hosannah to the Son of David!*"

There is a special fitness between the mind of youth and the truth as it is in Jesus. Some people think that you should not be taken to church, should not be taught to pray, should not be told about God and Jesus and heaven until you are older, and thus are more able to understand these high and holy things. We do not agree with such. We believe that you have a power of seeing these things, of feeling these things in their simple force and reality, which many older persons do not possess. Their souls are heavily freighted with care, "and custom lies upon them with a weight heavy as frost, and deep almost as life." None, as I take it, can understand Jesus Christ's heart better than the young. So it was proved in the Temple hundreds of years ago; so it has often been proved since. The child sees the childlike; and the heart of Christ is the heart of the most childlike. "Learn of me, for I am meek and lowly." Have you seen Him? Others ask, Who is He? Have you not got *your* answer ready?— "Hosannah to the Son of David."

II. Then the children sing, although others are silent. There is something, you know, very discouraging in frowns and rebukes; but frown as the priest and the scribe may, the children will sing. They cannot help it; out the song must burst, the soul is so full of joy. That day the word about the Church was fulfilled, "A little child shall lead them."

We read of many lands where the men and women are silent, sunk in superstition or indifference. Their hope lies in the school and the teaching their children get there about Christ the Saviour. There are many instances in which the hymns of the children influence their parents for good. So the "crying of the children" is breaking on the silence and even hatred to Christ of the parents. May we not hope that the song of the children will, ere long, overcome the silence of the parents, and that as the voice of many waters the song will sound through the whole world, "Hosannah to the Son of David." The word is "cry." It is the lifting up of the voice with strength; a bold, full, hearty song, which Christ declared the very perfection of praise.

There was no shade of selfish feeling in it. The whole heart went out with it. That is the best sort of music! The music of which Luther spoke, when he said that Satan was its bitter enemy! the music which invigorates one's own soul whilst it inspires the souls of others. Children, it should be the music of our lives. First, it goes straight to Christ. He is the one and the all. And then it goes boldly out for Christ. Let all hear; let all know on whose side we are.

We have a place in the temple that we may there witness for Him together with all true souls who have washed their robes and made them white in the blood of the Lamb. O boys, be strong for Jesus! In school, at play, at home, in work, wherever you are, stand up, "cry," for the true and right. Let your hand always have hold of your sword. the Word of God. Girls, live for Jesus! Blend your cry, the testimony of your sweet gentleness and patience, your readiness to help and comfort and minister to others in Christ's dear name, with the praise which waits for God in Zion.

III. The children receive the blessing which others lose. The King's smile, the assurance that to Him their cry is sweetest praise. "Hearest thou?" ask the priests. "Yea," is the answer: "have ye never read, out of the mouth of babes and sucklings Thou hast perfected praise." This reply opens up to us Christ's mind and way towards children. He delights in the children's songs of praise, and opens wide His arms to them. "Suffer them to come to Me."

There are flowers that last all through the summer and autumn! there are others that bloom and die in May and June. Thus too you find many graves in the cemetery very short, with little stones over them, telling of early deaths. Early deaths are early takings home. And oh, what a welcome, as the golden gates lift their heads, and Jesus receives His own! To be with Christ is far better.

But the welcome is given whenever you come. The moment you receive Him as your Saviour, He takes you and sets you as a seal on His heart, and rests in His love, and rejoices over you with singing. And a wonderfully blessed thing it is to go through life, with all its changes and trials, and know that it is so; that you can always count on the Friend that sticketh closer than a brother; that, every day, you can come anew with your sinful heart, and be washed and cleansed anew from sin, and go and serve Him with gladness. I feel that there is no higher honour which Christ can put on any one, that He can give no surer sign of His welcome, than opening the way and opportunity of being useful, and helping us to be useful, with a bright and loving spirit. And such honour is often put on the children. It is scarcely possible to say how very, very useful a truly good and happy child can be. I heard a French pastor, who has done much work for Christ, illustrate this. A little girl had learned to read the Bible. She used to read portions to her mother. "I wish I could read," said the mother; "but it is too late to learn!" "No mother," was the answer: "I will teach you." And she sat patiently every day and taught her mother. And some of the neighbours, when they heard, wished to be taught too. And so a class of older women gathered around the little girl. "There I found her," said the pastor, "going over the Primer, all listening to her, and following her; and then, when the lesson was over, she read them a part of the Bible." Is not that very fine, the child surrounded by mother and her neighbours, whom she teaches and guides! Christ's welcome was overflowing from her to them. The rill that had been opened in her own soul was in her a well of water springing up to everlasting life.

Yes, the welcome which the children crying in the Temple receive cannot be pent up in their own bosoms. It issues from the soul which it blesses in rivers of living water. Christ's welcome is a light in the eye, a thrill in the voice, a swiftness in the foot that speeds on his errands, a new life and light and power. Well-come is fulfilled in "Well-done, good and faithful servant."

J. M. L.

XLI. The Waste of Time. MATT. xxvi. 8. *"To what purpose is this waste?"*

WHAT would you think if you were to see a man—who, by working hard day after day, was able to earn a wage of twelve shillings a-week—going down each evening, after he returned from his work, to a neighbouring harbour, and throwing into the sea a shilling of his hard-won money, while his rent was running on unpaid, and his clothes were getting worn-out, and himself was half-starved? What would you think of him thus throwing away a full half of his wages every week—by his folly preparing for himself a prison or a grave? I am sure you would say the man was mad; and most other people would say the same.

But there are other precious things in the world besides shillings and pounds. There is *time!* You may have heard a saying, "Time is money." For instance, if you were interrupting at his work a mason who is paid by the hour, or one of the young women in a factory who is paid by the piece, they might say to you, "Time is money; every quarter of an hour that you take up is the loss of so much wage to us." But I go farther than that, and say, time is *more* than money, more costly and precious far; money cannot buy it—you cannot tell its value in gold. And God has given to none, young or old, more of this costly article than each needs. He has measured out to each just his needful portion, in which to do his work, and to prepare for eternity. What, then, are we to think of him who should do with his time what we supposed the workman to do with his wages— throw the one-half uselessly away?

Now, dear children, have not you been doing this? Let us just look at one of your ordinary days, and see how you spend it. Suppose you rise at eight in the morning, and go to bed at nine o'clock at night, as many of you do : There is a day of thirteen hours for you. What have you

K

made of it? How much have you used aright, and turned to some good purpose? and how much have you *lost*? And if so many as six or seven hours of a day have been wasted, what a loss that comes to in a month or a year! —what a tremendous loss in the course of a lifetime! Surely you will not wonder at me sadly asking the question, " To what purpose is this waste?"

The time of youth, above all precious, is most of all wasted; and the waste can never be made up. There is a boy at school—how does he employ his school time? Whenever his master's back is turned, he is drawing figures on his book or slate, or *talking* when he should be *learning;* or when a neighbour comes in at night, and his mother's attention is diverted, his book is laid aside and he slips out to his play, till it is time for bed. And that can never be made up for in all his after-life. When he grows up to be a lad he feels the want of it. He might get advancement in his shop, but he has not education enough. He goes to night-schools, but the difficulty and drudgery of learning then are too much for him.

There is no time like that of youth for storing the mind with useful knowledge. There is no time like youth for treasuring up what is good in the memory, as I myself can testify. Chapters of the Bible which I learned when a boy, are fresh on the mind as when first I learned them.

What shall I say of the waste of Sabbath time, given to you by God to prepare for a fast-coming eternity? What shall I say of the excuses of some for neglecting the Bible and prayer? How is it that some, when their mothers would have them daily read a portion of the Holy Scriptures, say they have no time? Why, where the form of prayer is kept up, is it so hurried over by many young people, that you would think they have hardly had time to repeat ten words, before they are up from their knees again? They say they have *no time*. If we did not waste so much of our time, we might have plenty of it for reading God's word and for prayer. Could you not save a little from your *play?* Could you not save a little from your *sleep?* I have heard of servants and washer-women, who had to be at work very early, still finding time to worship God.

By-and-by you will think that I have not dwelt on this

too much. Some, ere long, when their time is all but spent, and eternity is close upon them, will bitterly bewail that they did not sooner consider and take warning from this question.

I have seen boys and girls like yourselves giving themselves up to Christ, and getting from Him pardon, and peace, and joy of no common kind. How anxious and earnest one and all of us should be! Every day is precious! To-day there is opportunity! Is it to pass unimproved? are you to continue unblessed?

J. H. W.

XLII. The Blood of Christ. MATT. xxvii. 25. "*His blood be on us and on our children.*"

ON this day 1850 years ago a strange procession might have been seen passing from out the gates of an Eastern city. As the procession passed by there was an outer crowd looking on merely from curiosity; some nearer were taking an interest in the scene itself, and above the cries of "Crucify Him, crucify Him," might have been heard the sobs of a certain woman. In the centre of that strange procession, surrounded by Roman soldiers, there was a poor man bearing a cross. On His head there was a crown composed of thorns, from beneath which the blood was pouring; in His hand He carried a reed which had been put there in jest; and his face was so shamefully treated that one scarcely likes to mention what it was—for that rude mob had spitten upon him; and but for the purple robe they had in scorn thrown around his shoulders, you would have seen that they were marked with the lash with which He had been beaten. And if some one on the outskirts of that crowd 1850 years ago had asked who He was, the answer would have been, "A carpenter from Nazareth, whose name is Jesus, the son of Mary," and that He was going forth to be crucified. But if you ask me to-day who was that, we have to tell you that to-day that brow is crowned above that of any earthly king, for He is the King to-day above all kings. That hand which bore the reed, to-day carries in heaven the sceptre over all the kings of the whole universe. That face which was so shamefully treated, is adored to-day by angels and archangels. He sits to-day upon a throne that is high above all kings, and around it there gather in praise and adoration all the hosts of heaven, all the cherubim and seraphim who laud, and millions and millions who have loved and died for Him, whose sins have been washed in the blood that fell in Jerusalem that day. And from this myriad host there goes up the glad shout, "Worthy is the Lamb that was slain."

Oh, what a difference between that first day and this! And yet it must be always remembered that what put Jesus to death, and what caused these men to use him so, is here even to-day—sin. And wherever sin is, the sin which you think, the sin which you do, the sin which you speak; whatever is untrue, whatever is false, whatever is cowardly, remember that is sin, and it was sin which crucified Christ. False priests gave Him up to die, cowardly friends forsook Him, weak Pilate was afraid to deliver Him; and wherever, boys and girls, cowardice, weakness, and false friends are, remember that these were the things that crucified Christ. He answered nothing.

Now I want you to notice one point. There was only one thing that could make Jesus turn round that day, only one thing that moved Him. What was that? One of His own friends said, "I know not the man." "Jesus turned and looked." It must have been a look full of wondrous rebuke and pity. It seemed to say "*You*, to whom I have been so good; you, whom I have so loved; My own friend, deny Me!" On that terrible day remember that this was the only thing that moved Christ.

That is just what boys and girls and men and women may do to-day. We whom He has loved, we for whom He has died, we who call ourselves by His name as Christians—if we ever act as if we know Him not, He will be pained. Let us not join with those other rebels, who cried, "His blood be on us and on our children."

But how strange that after all, that cry of brutal execration, "His blood be on us and on our children," we may say to-day. And, O fathers and mothers, what better could you say for yourselves and little ones than that cry which 1850 years ago Christ heard before His crucifixion, "His blood be on us and on our children?"

T. T. S.

XLIII. Lent. MARK i. 13. *"And He was there in the wilderness forty days, tempted of Satan; and was with the wild beasts; and the angels ministered unto Him."*

I WISH this afternoon, my young friends, to speak to you about Lent. This consists of forty days which are called the season of Lent. Suppose you were walking down a street, and you saw at the door of a house an avenue of canvas, and the servants and others wearing wedding favours, you would know that there was a wedding; but suppose you saw every one had mourning bands on their hats, and were dressed in black, you would say, "There must be a funeral." And so you know what the state of the case is, by the dress and general appearance of the people. If they all look happy and joyous, you think it must be a wedding; but if they look sad and in sorrow, you think it is a funeral. You see there are different kinds of times in life, times of happiness and sorrow, and times of gladness and joy.

And so it is in what we call the Christian Year. There is Easter, when our Blessed Lord rose from the dead; and Christmas, when our Blessed Lord was born; these are times of joy. This is a time of sorrow. This season is called Lent, because of the old word Lentum, meaning Spring. So this is a time of the year when we should think not of the glory of our Saviour's birth or resurrection, but of the one sad theme. What is that? Sin. There is nothing else need make us really sad, nothing but sin. What is sin?

Now sin is any boy or girl or man or woman saying, "I will do just what I like." That is sin. Yes, boys and girls, all the sorrows, all the misery, all the wretchedness you see around you in life, all comes from people saying, "I will do just what I like." I think there are boys and girls here who have said that sometimes. Have you said that? It is the root of sin.

What is a root? It is what you put in the ground, and is perfectly different from the flower which grows up, and you are surprised to think how that flower comes from that root. But it does. When I say sin comes from the boy or girl saying, "I will do just what I like," you see the flower is not like the root. The thing that grows up is not the thing that is in the ground, but it comes from it. What is the harm, you think, in saying, "I will do just what I like"? Because you ought to say, and pray to God to be able to say, "I will try to do what God likes." What does God like? God likes everything that is pure, everything that is true, everything that is unselfish, everything that is right. You do things that are impure, that are untrue, that are selfish, that are not right, instead of trying to do what God likes. That is sin. For you often, very often, and I also—for I often do wrong things—like our own way. What we must strive to do, is what God wants.

Now Lent is just the time of year when the Church and we clergymen ask you to fight the battle of what is right. You have got an enemy; you must fight him. Your enemy is the devil. Now, whenever you have an evil thought, whenever your father or mother say, "Do this," and you think you can do better than what they have told you to do, that is the work of the devil. Whenever you do a thing that is not quite right, that is the devil. And so I would ask you for the next few weeks to try and put this enemy, the devil, to flight. Feel that you have got him to fight, that everything that is wrong in you comes from him. How can people fight him? You remember that Oliver Cromwell had a great many enemies in this country, and he always wore armour under his coat. He put on armour to defend himself against his enemies. You have got this enemy, and you must try at this time of the year—for of all times this is the special time of the year set apart for this—to put on your armour against the devil.

What is this putting on armour? I mean a little more praying, a little more thinking before you do anything, a little more attention at night to God when you say your prayers. I suppose you all say your prayers. I want you to begin to-night to carry it on with a little more earnestness and reality. Do not think of anything else; for half-a-minute or a minute think of yourself and God. Think of anything you have said unkind or disobedient, and think of nothing else for the moment, but say, "O Father, forgive me that for Jesus' sake, and, O God, give me a little more strength for to-morrow, not to do it again." That will be quite enough; do not try to say long prayers, but try to think of your own heart.

Now, boys and girls, if you will do this during the next four weeks it will do you good. I should like to see every boy and girl not only praying more earnestly, but doing some acts of self-sacrifice. Some little pleasure you are going to have, say "I am going to give up that." But there is no use in giving up a pleasure except for some purpose; unless your self-sacrifice is for something good. I do not mean the money you give here for the poor children, but so as to manage at the end of Lent—that is Good Friday morning—you may say, "I have got so much extra, what shall I do with it?" Now never do anything, whether you are young, or if you live to be a hundred years of age, without asking God. Ask Him to guide you and help you, and He will, for He has promised you. Ask God, then, what He would have you to do. One little boy or girl who has been reading about the heathen children, poor little souls, who have never heard about the Lord Jesus Christ says, "I will send it to a Missionary Society." Another will say, "I remember the poor ones at the East end of London. I will send it for them." And that will be a little sacrifice, something more than you are doing during the other days of the year. During the next few weeks every little boy or girl will not have a birthday, but some will, and you are going to have a present. Well, ask your father or mother to give you the money instead, and say, "I will give that this year to God." That is what we call sacrifice. This, and everything else, must be done through Jesus Christ.

This, of course, will not make you a good boy or girl; but give it because you feel the Lord Jesus Christ came down from heaven and died to save you. Say, "For His dear sake, for the sake of Jesus Christ who loved me, and whom I am trying to love, even ever so little, for His dear sake I will give up something." Give it up to help His Kingdom.

Now do try and think of these things during this season. The time we commemorate is the time when the Lord fought the devil for forty days. Ask your father, or mother, or friend to help you. And when you go home, teach your brothers and sisters and young friends that Jesus Christ loved them, and died for them; and try to live that life which He desires us to live, and we shall have the eternal life which He has obtained for us, of joy in heaven.

T. T. S.

XLIV. Christ in the Storm. Mark iv. 35-41.

I WOULD like the children to think for a moment why it was that our Lord Jesus was so fearless in the storm. I do not know whether any of you were ever at sea in a storm ; but you can easily understand that it is one of those times when the courage of most people turns into terror. The boatmen who were with Jesus, and who were much more accustomed to the water than He, were afraid and stricken with terror. Yet Jesus was perfectly fearless. Not only was He able to speak calmly, but when He was awakened suddenly, with the voice of terror in His ear, He did not lose His composure. He was without fear.

Now, children, why did Jesus have this fearlessness? He answers this in the fortieth verse ; " And He said unto them, Why are ye so fearful, how is it that ye have no faith ? " He means that if they had trust in God they would not be so fearful, and that He was not afraid because He trusted in God. Then the next difficulty is, Yes, He was without fear; the storm could not strike terror into His heart because there was no fear for Him, inasmuch as He commanded the sea. But our Lord did not use His power to save Himself only. He did not turn the stones into bread. He did not use His power with the Roman soldiers for His protection. He never did His miracles except by faith and trust in His Father. It was by faith He lived and moved and had His being and did His purposes.

But, you say, we cannot do wonders like that if we were in a storm. No, that is true ; but if we are about our duty, we may be quite sure that God will protect us until our work is done just as much as if we were in the boat with Jesus. All Christians are in the hands of God, and under the protection of God, as these men in the boat were. The fact that Jesus is not with us in body, makes no difference. He is with us still, and He protects us still ; only it is for God's glory if we are to die or suffer ; and when that time comes we shall not fear to die if we trust God. We shall not be afraid to meet the storm, even though the storm should wreck our body. We are in God's arms. It does not matter whether we die in the sea, or in our beds, for all places are alike really safe to him who is in God's keeping. That is the true feeling of fearlessness. Our true life is hid with Christ in God. Here or there, awake or asleep, on the battle field or in our bed, living or dying, all is alike if we are hidden with Christ in God, if we are His children, and are always with Him. If we live, we live unto the Lord ; if we die, we die unto the Lord. Living or dying we are the Lord's. Where is the place for fear? Why are ye so fearful? May God bless the reading of His Word.

J. O. D.

XLV. Evil Spirits. Mark v. 1–20.

Only a few words on this passage for the sake of the boys and girls. You know that Holy Scripture teaches us that there are many persons in the world whom we do not see. Besides men and women, and boys and girls, who are human, there are other persons who are not human. And we call them "spirits," by which we mean we do not see them, we do not know when they come, and we do not know when they go away. But we know from God's word that they are not very far from us. There are good spirits, and they are called angels ; and we are told in Scripture that these are sent as messengers from God to warn good people against sin and temptation, in ways we do not know, simply because we do not see. And on the other hand, there are bad spirits, who are called devils, or demons, or fiends. And they, too, are not far from us. They seem to have some power, to be permitted by God to harm us sometimes, and to put bad thoughts and desires into our minds. And this man about whom I have just read, is a terrible example of how these spirits can torment a man. They had made a madman of him—that is, a man out of his mind, who was in utter wretchedness, who could not live among his fellow-men, and who could not be taken because he was, as the Gospel says, like a wild beast. It shows what would become of men if these spirits had their own way—that is, if we had not some one to protect us, and who keeps our minds and bodies safe from every wicked power.

Now the great lesson of this passage is, that our dear Lord and Saviour Jesus Christ, who was born of Mary for our salvation, is a strong helper, is stronger than the evil spirits round about us. It is great thing for you and I who know so little of this unseen part of the world, that if we know that there are spirits trying to do us harm, we also know that there is One who is their Master. If we did not know this we should be afraid of what would happen to us some day. We should be afraid of dying, for we should not know but that we should fall into their power. But it is a comfort to know that there walks upon the earth the dear Lord who was much stronger than a whole regiment, that is what the word "legion" means, for a whole regiment was put to flight by the bare word, "go." They were His creatures, His servants; He could speak and scatter them with a breath. He is our Friend, and uses this power for the good of man. Let us not fear, therefore, let us be strong and brave to resist these evil spirits when they come to us and try to make us bad; whether they come speaking by the lips of bad men, or in whatever form they come, let us not be afraid; but let us remember that our Friend, Jesus, is far stronger than they, and that those who do His will, and act right, are quite safe from all spirits, seen and unseen, in this world and the next. God be praised for this. Now children, let us pray.

Blessed Lord and Saviour, Jesus Christ, unto Thee and unto Thy Father's keeping we commit ourselves and all those we love. Let us be saved from all evil, let no wicked spirits have power to harm us. Deliver us from wicked thoughts. Make us good and strong and pure, free from pain and wickedness, and unkind and impure desires, Oh, our Lord Jesus Christ, who art King over both this world and the next, the seen and the unseen, be Thou our King and Shield, the Captain of our salvation, and our Great Deliverer. And we beseech Thee, oh, our Lord Jesus Christ that Thou wilt fight against evil thoughts, and evil words in this wicked world of ours, until victory is on Thy side. And let us stand with Thee. We pray Thee, Lord, that Thou wilt make us holy and humble and gentle; may we put our whole trust and confidence in Thee. Do Thou be pleased to give us the spirit of endurance and earnestness. Do Thou spread abroad such wonderful trophies of Thy great power that there shall be no room left for mistrust. Keep Thy Holy Church, keeping it from the intrusions of the world's spirit. Bless the children; have mercy upon all mankind. Let the children learn Thy love and goodness and power, and become as the children of Jesus Christ our King. Tear down all wickedness, and let the light of the Gospel flood the hearts of all men. Answer us, Lord. Let our cry come unto Thee with power, for Thy Name's sake. Amen.

J. O. D.

XLVI. The Demoniac of Gadara. MARK v. 15.

"*And they come to Jesus, and see him that was possessed with the devil, and had the legion, sitting, and clothed, and in his right mind: and they were afraid.*"

JESUS spent thirty-three years on earth, and all the while He went about going good. He delighted to do it. He would sacrifice needful rest or food to do it. He would go out of his road to do it. He would do it for the vilest.

In this chapter we have a memorable example of this.

He was occupied in teaching and healing the multitude who flocked to Him in Capernaum; but he suddenly wanted to be landed on the other side of the Sea of Galilee. His soul was yearning towards a lost sheep there. So He entered a ship and started. When Jesus left the boat, He walked towards the lost sheep whose rescue and salvation had brought Him over. Where is he? Yelling and with threatening arms behold him advancing to meet Jesus. What a lost sheep! Utterly lost to any but Jesus, but not to Him.

I. *The misery of the man.*—He was a notorious character—a desperate maniac. There was a whole host of fiends in him, so that he had the horrors of hell in his own bosom. Does it astonish you that he was "exceeding fierce," so that none dared approach him? And was it for such an one that the Son of God undertook this voyage, and was it on his deliverance that He was now bent?

And can He recover him out of the grasp of the tyrant? Yes, verily, and that in the space of a few minutes.

II. *The majesty of Christ.*—As soon as the fanatic man caught sight of Jesus he rushed to attack Him. He supposed that He was a mere man; but Jesus put forth a secret influence, which awed him, as it did the soldiers in Gethsemane. Instead of springing on Him in a fury, he fell down on the ground and worshipped Him, for Jesus had commanded the unclean spirits to come out of him.

That command awed him and he cried, "What have I to do with thee, Jesus, thou Son of the most high God. I adjure Thee by God that Thou torment me not." At His majestic word the devils obey and withdraw, as a beaten garrison does from a beleaguered castle, crest-fallen, conquered; and the man crept up to the feet of his Saviour, received with gratitude the garments which were offered him, and began to speak lovingly and gently as an angel.

What a display of Christ's majesty was this!

III. *The mischief of the devils.*—This was shown in their violence when in the man. They turned him into a tiger —the terror of his neighbourhood. But it was further shown in what they did when they had left. They begged permission to go into an immense herd of swine feeding hard by. Jesus suffered them. No sooner were they in their new entertainers, than the whole herd ran down a steep place into the lake and were choked. What became of the devils? It would appear that they scrambled out of the swine and entered into the Gadarenes. The Gadarenes, we are told, assembled round Jesus and "entreated Him to depart out of their coasts." Was not this another instance of their determined mischief?

In conclusion, devils are abroad in England as in Gadara. If they do not rule us, they have access to us. None of us but have heard their evil whispers. Satan would, if he could, drive you, as he did this poor man, from those who love you, and strip you of the white robes of purity, and make you a curse instead of a blessing.

Now Jesus promises to aid us against him. Are you putting yourself under His daily protection? Does He hear you morning and evening crying "Deliver us from evil?" Keep close to the Lord Jesus and you will escape all the snares of the Wicked One.

So, doubtless, as the boat pushed off from Gadara's shores, the freed captive would say with tears, "I will keep near to Him in all holy conversation, and then I shall be sure that He will keep near to me, till I meet Him in His heavenly kingdom."

J. B.

XLVII. Jairus' Daughter. MARK v. 38-42.

THIS is very much a story for boys and girls, this story about the little girl of some twelve years of age, this Jewish damsel, who was so wonderfully brought back by our blessed Lord from the state of the dead. If you had been living then it might have been your case. She was the only child of her father and mother, and you can easily understand how deep their grief and distress were when her father hurried from her chamber to seek the help of the strongest he could find, the One who was most likely to save his little girl's life. But let us pass from this.

While Jesus was on his way with the father, Jairus, a woman insisted upon being cured of her disease, and while Jesus was yet speaking to her, messengers came to Jairus saying, "Thy daughter is dead; why troublest thou the Master any further." So they thought it was too late; they were not aware that no time is too late for the power of Jesus. Then Jesus came unto the poor father and strengthened his hope and said, "Fear not; go on trusting, trusting in Me." Jesus took the charge of the house as soon as he got there, and the charge of the bedchamber too. The house was full of grief and confusion, as houses are apt to be at such seasons. But Jesus took charge of it, and the first thing he did was to make peace. He quieted the house where the women were beating their breasts and crying; and when he had thus reduced that tumultuous dwelling to peace and order, then He proceeded to do His great and awful work of fighting with death.

We have seen His power since we began these readings. Do you remember one story we read since we commenced these Sunday morning readings, in which Jesus brought back the dead to life? We have here another, that our Lord Jesus Christ, who is our Friend, is Lord of both parts of the world—the part to which we belong, the living; and the part yonder, among the spirits of the departed whom we call dead, where we cannot go just now, but where we shall go at death. You have had friends who have passed away and whose bodies are in the cold graveyard. Their spirits are in the unseen world, and we cannot go to them. But there is One, and only One, who has dominion over both worlds. Both worlds are in His hands, one in His right and the other in His left hand, and He binds them both in one because He is Lord of both. He is the Lord of the living, and He is the Lord of the dead.

And do you notice how the Lord of the living and the dead speaks about dying? He will not have the word "dying" used. He puts it aside; there is no such thing as we call death. "Why make this ado and weep?" He asks, "the damsel is not dead, but sleepeth." He says this, because dying, to Him, is only a temporary falling asleep to waken again. We think if it is a sleep, it is a long sleep. But then a thousand years are but as a day to the Lord; and whether the sleep lasts, as did this girl's, for a few moments or for a thousand years, it is all one to Him to whom a thousand years are a day. He calls it a sleep. Try, boys and girls, to think of your departed friends as asleep. Just think of them as does our Lord Jesus; and when you and I have fallen on our long sleep we shall still be in His care who is the Lord of the living and the dead.

And just remember, that when Jesus allows death to knock at your door, and to come in, it is not because death is stronger than He. It is because He has a good reason for permitting it. He is so completely the Master of death that He makes it His messenger to do His bidding; and when death comes to our dwelling and takes away one we love, let us bear in mind that death is not Jesus' enemy but His messenger. He is like an angel; he takes away our friend in his bosom. He has no power at all over us without Jesus.

These things take away the sting of death, and the Apostle tells us they take away the fear of death from the good man's heart. Let all the good boys and girls in my congregation not fear death. Fear very much to displease your Saviour, fear very much to live an ungodly life, fear very much to be away from Him who is our friend, and death's enemy; but do not fear death, it cannot hurt you. Jesus has conquered death long ago once and for all, and it is now His servant.

Whether living or dead (or asleep, as Jesus calls it) we are quite safe in the hands and in the gracious care of Him who is Master of death and who loves His people, blessed be His name for ever.

T. T. S.

XLVIII. Herodias' Daughter. MARK vi. 25. "*And she came in straightway with haste unto the king, and asked, saying, I will that thou give me, by and by in a charger, the head of John the Baptist.*"

GOD teaches us by bad examples as well as by good ones. The good are like those little tug-boats which guide ships into a harbour, the bad are like black and shattered wrecks on a sand-bar, which say, "keep far away from here." The Hebrew maid, and Ruth and Rhoda, are shining stars for ever and ever! Herodias' daughter is a burnt out fire-work; it was bright for a moment, but now it is ashes!

And yet the Holy Spirit was ready to do for her what He did for them; but they chose wisdom's ways, which are ways of pleasantness and peace, whilst she chose the broad road which ends in destruction. She lived as a butterfly does, for mere pleasure. They were content to toil, as the bees do, to lay up treasure in heaven.

We learn from Josephus that her name was Salome. Of her early history, however, we know nothing. But we can see that from her infancy she had this great disadvantage—her relations were altogether worldly. Her father, Philip, was a poor degraded creature. Her mother, Herodias, was a very wicked woman, with two husbands,—proud, malicious, a hater of truth and righteousness. Her uncle, in whose palace she and her mother were now at home, was a match for her in everything, perhaps, but in her courage and determination. The Gospels set him before us as an open adulterer—as a coward—afraid of John the Baptist, trying to pacify his conscience by doing many things which John preached, yet willing to please Herodias by shutting John up in prison, and consenting at last to kill him for the sake of keeping a drunken oath.

"He added this above all to all the evils which he had done." With such friends we should expect that Salome would be no model. She might have been, by grace, the daughter of worldly parents, and in the midst of ungodly companions—she might have worn "white robes and a crown," but it is generally otherwise. Children follow their families; if they lead them unto Vanity Fair, into Vanity Fair they go; if they lead them toward the Celestial City, to the Celestial City they turn.

I. Salome was a shameless girl.

This appears in her permitting herself to dance her best in the midst of a company of sensual revellers. How could any modest girl have done it? But she liked it, it fell in with her depraved tastes.

Can a dove be happy in a den of lions? Cultivate retirement and purity of mind. They will save you from a thousand snares. Boldness is a ladder which it is easy to climb, but before you think it, it trips you over, and you get a broken bone if not a broken heart. What are beauty, intelligence, accomplishments, without the bloom of innocence on them, or the veil of diffidence over them? We have seen them without that bloom, without that veil, and thought of what Solomon says about a "fair jewel in a swine's snout."

II. Salome was unprincipled.

This usually accompanies shamelessness. With no principle the vessel has no rudder, and so, of course, is the sport of the tides. She may drift amongst pirates, or icebergs, or whirlpools. Principle is a settled purpose to do right, because you are clear that it is right. It never changes or yields. It is the compass always pointing north, not the weathercock varying north, south, east, or west, with every wind.

If Salome had had any principle she would have refused to take advantage of her uncle's rash vow. He uttered it when flushed with wine, not knowing what he said. But she pocketed her scruples, and hushed her inward monitor, and greedy of gain she only said to herself, "What a chance! What shall I ask?"

Children are often tempted to do wrong. The path looks inviting. Soft voices cry, "Come." You can if you will. It merely requires a shutting your eyes to the truth, to your convictions of duty, to the lessons of your teachers. It is a slight thing to leap a hedge, or break a pane of glass, and then the thing coveted is yours. Then you have what you desired—your Sunday afternoon's truancy, or your playfellows' cheers, or your employer's property. But consider, that hedge is of God's planting there, that pane of glass is God's putting there! On this side you are prosperous, on that side you are ruined!

Pray for real, deep-rooted principle. "The still small voice" is what you have to listen to. It will protect you and direct you as an angel would.

There is a pretty old saying, "He who snatches shall be covered with scratches."

III. Salome was a hardened girl.

When her mother said, "Ask for the head of John the Baptist," she should have cried out with horror, "Mother, you are mad! That would be murder!" But she did not hesitate for one instant; "she came in straightway with haste unto the king." She agreed to this conspiracy; she felt as her mother did about it; she would forego "half the kingdom" to satiate their revenge.

Why, her love for her mother alone should have induced her to refuse, to preserve her from such dreadful guilt. But Salome was hardened; she did not fear God or the judgment day; she had no pity, it had been drowned like a half-fledged bird in the torrent of her passion.

And she went through with it with the same brutality. The executioner was immediately dispatched to the blessed man's dungeon, and speedily brought back the precious head, and gave it in a charger to the damsel, and the damsel carried it to her mother. What a burden for a maiden! A pale, livid head! A blood-stained head! Salome could bear that head, severed at her request, to her mother, as she would a dish of food.

God deliver us from such hardness, and from everything which produces it!

Children must guard against this. We say now, "I never could do what she did." But we might creep along to it by degrees. The boy who begins by spinning cockchafers and tormenting cats, gradually gets on to delight in cruelty to his fellows, and at last is a hero in all but his power to cause suffering.

L

There was a lad who was strolling through the fields with his sister. They found a nest of rabbits; the sister was charmed with the nest itself, so snug and warm, and lined with down, and with the tiny occupants. But the lad seized them, mimicking their squeaks and their struggles. In vain his sister wept and entreated; he flung them up into the air, and shouted as each fell dead on the stones. "Confound your tears," he said, "you should hire yourself to an undertaker." Ten years after, that sister sat weeping again by that lad's side. He was in chains, sentenced to be hung for shooting a farmer whilst poaching. "Sister," he said, "do you remember the nest of rabbits, ten years ago, how you prayed and I ridiculed? I verily believe that from that day God forsook me and left me to follow my own inclinations. If I had yielded to your tears then, you and I would not be weeping these bitter tears now."

We do not pretend to reckon up all the mischief which is wrought at fashionable balls, or at the gay saloons to which the young men and women of our large cities are allured. But we take this as a specimen of what was brought about in a banqueting hall. The devil played the music at that feast, as he does at too many, and the next morning there was a funeral, a sorrowing band shouldering a headless corpse to the tomb! That is not the only funeral, those are not the only lamentations, which have been begotten of a dance for the praise of men.

We may have a "fiery dart" shot into one at church, or in our closets; but if we go to balls and saloons we open our bosoms to them, and it will be strange indeed if Satan does not drive them in by the dozen.

J. B.

XLIX. Refreshment Sunday. St. Mark viii. 1–8.

This Sunday in Lent is called "Refreshment Sunday." It occurs in the very middle of Lent, that is the forty days before Easter. It is a kind of pause or halt in the journey. When a traveller passes over a long journey, and after passing over the desert comes to a green spot, that is a place of refreshment. And this is a day of refreshment, and it is called Refreshment Sunday, because there is in the Lesson and the Gospel for the day something about food.

The Lesson for the day in the Old Testament is about a great famine, and the Gospel for the day is about our Lord feeding the multitude. I want to tell you that story, and help you to understand what it means.

It was getting to the end of the day, and there was a great crowd around our Lord. Now He had been teaching all the day, and so wise and beautiful were His words that the people remained all day doing nothing but listen to the great Teacher. I sometimes think of boys and girls, and men and women, who get tired if one speaks for a quarter or half-an-hour, and I think what a wonderful Teacher the Master must have been for the people to have listened to Him all the day.

Now the evening was come, and nearly all the people had travelled from some distance, and the disciples, that is our Lord's immediate friends, said to Jesus, "What shall we do with all this great crowd of people? They will starve. It would require a great deal of money, which we have not got, to go to the villages and buy food." Our Lord said, "Give them something to eat." The disciples said, "We cannot; we have nothing but a little bread and a few fishes. Here are thousands of people—how can we feed them." I suppose the fishes they had got from the Sea of Galilee, because, as you remember, some of them were fishermen. "Make them sit down in groups in order," said our Lord, for He liked order. And St. Mark tells us when they were all sitting down it was a beautiful sight. In the East they wear bright colours. They wear coloured garments on the head and shoulders, and so as they sat down they looked like flowers and plants over the mountain side. Fancy that beautiful sight—the people with their coloured garments, who had been listening to Jesus's teaching all day. They were weary, but Jesus tells them to sit down.

What happens? The disciples came to Jesus with the bread, and He broke the loaves and blessed them, and as His disciples took them they multiplied, and all those thousands of people are fed by Jesus with a few loaves and fishes. And when they had eaten enough our Lord says, "Gather up the fragments," and they gather several basketsful of what was over and above. What a wonderfu miracle; what a glorious day for those people.

Now all this teaches us something more than merely that Jesus fed the multitude. You know if you saw a shadow on the ground that there must be something behind, or reflecting that shadow. You would be quite sure if you saw the shadow of a horse that there would be a horse, and so on. And so these miracles are shadows. They tell us of something that is behind them; and the shadow of this miracle is, that just as our Lord fed the bodies of these men, so He can feed our souls.

First, this miracle teaches us a lesson about waste. They gathered up the fragments that were left. Children, never waste anything. I know some children who are very wasteful, who think that when a pencil is worn down half way it should be thrown aside. If you are careful you will take care of all fragments. You will show in little things what you are in great things. Do not be careless about your books. Do you think that is a strange thing to talk to you about in church. You must remember that our blessed Lord was Himself so careful about these pieces of bread. It was *He* that was careful.

Then another lesson is that we are all to make use of what we have. Our Lord could have fed the multitude without these loaves. You have all got certain things which God has given you. Just as Jesus said, " Bring these loaves and I will make them of use to you," so He says to you, little boy and girl, " You have a good memory; you have a taste for learning languages; you have a taste for music." Whatever you have, Christ says, " Bring it here to me." It seems a small thing to you, but, O boys and girls, if we would bring to Jesus all our things and say, " Lord, bless this and bless me in my lessons to-day," what a glorious thing it would be. I wonder how often you ask Christ to be with you in your lessons. Everything we do should be brought to Jesus. He loves boys and girls. It is only those who love Christ who can be really happy. You should bring to Christ on your knees every morning your lessons, saying " Lord Jesus, bless me this day," and in the evening say, " I thank Thee, O Lord, for having blessed me this day." If we did this what a joyous and happy life we might live.

Above all, He will feed your souls. He will feed us with Himself; with His own self; feed us so that we shall live with Him for ever. Feed us with the words of the Bible; feed us in answer to our prayers, morning and night. Feed us by what He teaches us in church on Sunday; feed us in our public prayers; feed us in the hymns we sing. Feed us afterwards, as we grow old and take the bread and wine, which are the type of the blessed body and the blood which He gave for every one of us on the cross.   T. T. S.

L. "**He took them up in His arms.**"   MARK x. 16.
"He took them up in His arms, put His hands upon them, and blessed them."

A LITTLE child once said, "When I am well I like to be carried by my father, but when I am ill I like my mother to carry me." When asked the reason, he said, "When I am well, my father carries me on his back, and it is great fun; but when I am ill, my mother carries me in her arms, and it makes me feel well." That little boy did not know that he was helping to preach the gospel. Jesus was like his good mother. "He took them up in His arms, put His hands on them, and blessed them."

I. *The arms of Jesus are "stretched out" arms* (Ps. cxxxvi. 12).—This shows that the children are welcome to Jesus; that He is ready to receive them; that He bids them come to Him; that He longs to embrace them. You have seen a mother teaching her baby to walk. She puts her child against a chair, goes back a little, stretches out her arms, and says "Come." The eye of the little one brightens as he sees the mother's encouraging smile and the safe landing of the outstretched arms, the little limbs begin to move, the first voyage of life is taken, and its end and reward are the mother's embrace and the mother's kiss. I would ask all the children of the Church to make their first venture in life a venture into the outstretched loving arms of Jesus. One of the sweetest songs that any of us can sing is, "Safe in the arms of Jesus."

II. *The arms of Jesus are holy arms* (Isa. iii. 10).—This means that Jesus is holy, the holy Son of God. But it also means that those who flee to the arms of Jesus are made holy. When a little child was taken away from a wicked, drunken home, with a bad father and mother, and placed with other children under the care of a good woman, who was a wise mother to them all, the child said to the matron one day, " I wish my father was here, for I think I would love him good." This is what Jesus does with all the children that come to his arms. He loves them good. When they are in His arms, bad tempers and sinful thoughts, and pride and untruthfulness, and all inward evil are cast out, and they are made by Him pure in character and useful in life.

III. *The arms of Jesus are strong arms* (Isa. lxii. 8).— Some time ago there was a shipwreck on the coast of Africa. There was a little child on board, who was a great favourite with all, and the special pet of a strong sailor. The ship struck on a rock not far from the shore, and was sinking in a fearful storm. The strong sailor rushed into the cabin, took the little child out of its weeping mother's arms, wrapped his oilskin coat round it, folded it to his bosom, and jumped into the raging sea. All on board perished, and the people on the shore, on rushing down to the sea, saw nothing but a man lying with a bundle in his arms. The man had a wound on his head, and was quite dead. He had been dashed against a stone and killed, but his bundle contained a living child. The child was saved by the strong arms of the sailor, though the sailor lost his own life. Jesus laid down His life to save His children, but He rose again from the dead, and now holds them in arms so strong that they are out of all danger from sin and sinful enemies.

IV. *The arms of Jesus are everlasting arms* (Deut. xxxiii. 37).—Not long ago I was visiting a dying mother. She was leaving six children, and they were all young. After reading God's word to her, and speaking to her, and hearing from her that she was dying in peace and hope through the grace of Jesus, I asked permission to kneel down and pray with her. She said, "Oh yes, but give me my baby in my arms." I took her baby from a neighbour who was in the house, and laid it in her arms. I then kneeled down and prayed, and when I was done she kissed her baby and gave it back to me. She died that night, and now that child is left without the comfort of a kind mother's arms. But the arms of Jesus are not like the weak arms of flesh that fall away in death from the children they embrace.

His arms are round His children all through life, and through the raging flood of death, and He keeps them after death happy and blessed in His own eternal home.

Now the children of the Church must remember that Jesus takes up in His arms *willing* children. If they refuse to come to Him and are not willing to be cared for by Him, He will let them alone. And when left to themselves they will fall into sin and ruin and be lost. And they must remember that He also wants the children He takes to His arms to *trust* Him. He knows what is best for them, where they are to live, how long they are to live, and what they are to do. He makes all the children who trust Him good and useful in this life, and happy and blessed in that which is to come. But I think I hear some manly boy saying, "I do not like to be carried; I want to walk alone." We like manly boys; but what is manliness? The Bible tells us that it is leaning on God, trusting God, receiving grace to do the will of God. To live without God, to despise His grace, to refuse His guidance, to flee from His loving arms, is to be unmanly and unsuccessful in life. The two great lessons we all need to learn confirm the truth of the text that stands at the head of this page. The first is from the lips of Jesus, "Without Me ye can do nothing"; the second is from the pen of St. Paul, "I can do all things through Christ, which strengtheneth me."

G. W.

LI. An Easter Message. MARK xvi. 7. "*But go your way, tell His disciples and Peter that He goeth before you into Galilee: there shall ye see Him, as He said unto you.*"

·THAT was the mystic statement made by the angel from the empty grave of Christ on the first Easter Day; and what I want you to notice in it is that the only one person mentioned by name is Peter. Peter was one of our Lord's disciples, so that the message "Go, tell His disciples," included Peter among the rest. Yet strange to say the message was—"tell His disciples *and* Peter." But as Peter was one of the disciples, why was his name mentioned? To-day you know is Easter Day. You know to-day was the day when our blessed Lord rose from the dead, and on this day the message was sent, " Go, tell His disciples and Peter."

Why was Peter thus mentioned? It would seem strange if I were, when speaking of my congregation, to say, "Go, tell all the children," and then mention one by name. There was, however, a special reason for Peter's name being mentioned. You remember what Peter had done three days before. You remember how Peter went into the hall where Christ was being tried, and where He was sentenced to death, and when a woman said, " Surely you are one of His friends," Peter said, like a coward, as he was at the moment, "I know not the man." And a second time he was asked, as I reminded you last Friday, and he again said he knew not Jesus. You remember a third time, when it became more dangerous to be known as a companion of Jesus, a man said, " I saw you in the garden ;" he was afraid they would know he was the man who had drawn the sword for Christ, and Peter cursed and said he had not known Jesus. You see people are brave for a moment, and then become cowards when they have to suffer.

And now Christ had risen from the dead how Peter must have felt. What would you have felt if you had done this to your kind friend? Peter had heard of His death and burial, and how He had come up a living Lord, having conquered death. He hated himself. If you had done this to an earthly friend, you would be afraid to meet him. I daresay your friend would say, " I will not have anything more to do with that coward who deserted me in my need." And Peter must have feared that this would be Christ's feeling on Easter Day. I daresay Peter must have felt so bitterly sad, so angry with himself, and I suppose the blessed Lord, who is always so full of pity and always so full of mercy to those who treat Him ill—I suppose He thought, "If I send a message merely to the disciples, Peter will think I do not include him. Poor fellow! he is almost broken-hearted for his sin, and bad as he has been to me, I cannot be cruel to him." So Jesus at the moment of His resurrection, when He came forth from the grave, remembered that poor sorrowful, sinful man ; and the only name that was mentioned that first Easter Day was the name of the cowardly Peter

Now, boys and girls, try to understand that, and get it into your hearts, and learn a lesson from it. You know the day of joy it was. You know that all Jesus had said about His being the one to judge the world was proved true by His rising from the dead. That makes Easter Day a day of such joy. It is the joy of having a friend who is proved to have been true. Everything He said about Himself, every promise He made to others, is proved to be true because He rose from the dead. You know we have been all cowards. Boys and girls and men and women, brave as we have been in other things, we have been cowards very often about Christ. Wherever there has been any danger about losing some pleasure in following Christ, we have preferred our pleasure to His will. This is like Peter denying Christ. Yet the most cowardly can draw near to Jesus, because Christ sent that message to Peter, and He sends it to every one who has sinned, and to every one who has sorrowed for sin.

So that though we may have been cruel to Him, though we have been ungrateful to Him, yet on this Easter morning the message comes from Christ to every one of us, "Go, tell my disciples—above all tell that boy, tell that girl, tell that man or woman, or whoever it may be who has been most cowardly, who has denied me simply because there might be danger—tell them that if they are truly sorry for their sin, and believe that I overcame death and despoiled the power of the grave by My death and resurrection and ascension—tell them that they shall see Me, and that their sins shall be forgiven."

That is the glorious message of Easter for every one baptized with the name of Christ, and who earnestly, by prayer, endeavour to live a pure, holy, true, and brave life, in the spirit of Jesus Christ our Lord.

T. T. S.

LII. What shall we do? Luke iii. 10-15.

THE words I have specially selected for our text this afternoon are those contained in the question, "What shall we do?"

There were three distinct classes of people who asked the same question—What shall we do? The time and occasion when this question was asked was when John the Baptist was preaching and baptising in the wilderness about Judea. And the event is recorded by St. Luke. It shows us how John applied his doctrine of repentance to various classes.

In the first place, let us consider these three classes or orders. We read "And the *people* asked him." The "people" are separated from the other classes, and we may infer that the people here referred to were of the rich class, those most able to give, and this class in the Jewish nation was greatly wanting in charity; and this was a generally besetting sin among the rich classes of the Jews, this want of charity. He puts, as it were, his finger upon the black spot in their character immediately. He answered, "He that hath two coats, let him impart to him that hath none; and he that hath meat let him do likewise."

Now, dear children, this want of charity among the Jews does not exist amongst us in this district, and is certainly not the case in this church of ours. There have been many instances of want in this district; but I am thankful to say that there are found here noble and kind friends who have relieved them immediately. And you, dear children, who come to this church Sunday after Sunday, through the kindness of your friends, and perhaps through self-denial on your part, are able to give your little gifts Sunday after Sunday, which in the end amount to a large sum, and provide for six cots for sick children and for poor children.

Next came the publicans to be baptized, asking "What shall we do?" These publicans were not what we call publicans in the present day. They were a class of tax-gatherer, generally of a low order; and in collecting the taxes they often cheated the people. You remember the words of Zaccheus—a chief publican—"If I have done any wrong to any man," he tells our Lord, "I will restore it fourfold." You see he was conscious of wrong. John answered the publicans, "Exact no more than that which is appointed you." Observe he does not tell them to leave their calling, but simply to conquer the great temptation of their calling. He tells them to do their duty.

A third class came and put the same question. These were soldiers—Roman soldiers—going down to fight the

King of Arabia. John first tells them to do violence to no man. They were apt to be violent so as to extort money. And he then tells them not to falsely accuse any man. Soldiers often did this in those days. Again he says, " Be content with your wages," or rather, " Be satisfied with your allowance." Be content with your wages! Good advice and especially needed by servants. And again let us carry this spirit of content still further. However we may be placed, whether rich or poor, whether we have much or little, let us be content in our station. There have I know in past times charges been brought against our soldiers of cruel and violent conduct; but, dear children, if they have one characteristic it is bravery. Again, if there be another characteristic of the British soldier, is it not gentleness, mercy, and lovingkindness? We have had cases lately in Egypt of mercy and lovingkindness on the part of our troops. How can such kindness go without bravery?

Such, then, were the three classes of people who came to St. John, asking the question, " What shall we do ? "

Now, dear children, I want you to ask yourself this question, " What shall we do ? " There is but one answer to that—Do your duty. Do you remember that the greatest admiral England ever had—Admiral Nelson—just before the battle gave the signal throughout the fleet, " England expects that every man this day will do his duty." England did her duty on that day, and the gallant admiral his duty full well. He fell while fighting for his country and his king. Do your duty, dear children, towards God and man.

Our duty towards God is contained in the first four commandments. Christ said, " Thou shalt love God ; and the second commandment is like unto it, Thou shalt love thy neighbour as thyself." St. Paul says, " Love is the fulfilling of the law." Therefore, dear children, in answer to the question, " What shall we do ? " I will give you now three little duties.

First of all, and this is the greatest, Love God. The second is, Love your parents, or relations, or friends. The third is, Love one another. And whilst doing these duties, consider also, dear children, your besetting sin. There is some sin which clings to us more than any other, and this special sin we call the "besetting" sin. In the case of the rich Jewish people it was a want of charity; in the case of the publican it was extortion; and in the case of the soldiers it was violence and cruel conduct. So that each of us have our besetting sin, and let us try to get rid of it altogether. Let the rich break off from the rich man's sin, let the poor break off from the poor man's sin, let the old man give up the sins of age, and let the young man give up the sins of his youth. Dear children, do not have unkind thoughts of one another, do not envy another, and avoid disobedience. You remember the well-known hymn in which these words occur—

"Let not your angry passions rise,"

and remember you should be obedient to those who rule you, and be kind and loving to one another.

Thus, dear children, you will dwell in brotherly love and fulfil the law of Christ; and if, boys, you are spared through God's mercy to grow up and to become husbands and fathers and soldiers and statesmen—do your duty. If, girls, you are spared through God's mercy to grow up to become mothers—be kind and content, loving one another. Thus will you one day, one and all, hear these gracious words spoken to each and every one of you, "Well done, good and faithful servant, thy duties are done, thy works are ended, enter thou into the joy of thy Lord."

J. W.

LIII. One thing. LUKE x. 42. "*One thing is needful.*"

OUR subject is the way to heaven, and we shall consider five texts.

FIRST TEXT—"*One thing is needful.*" Let us go to that high hill so often mentioned in God's word—Mount Olivet. We walk up a short way, then turn round, and we see at about two miles west that marvellous city, Jerusalem. We climb to the top of the mount, and almost beside us, on the eastern slope of the hill, we see a village. It is Bethany, described by John, and known, doubtless, in heaven, as the town of Lazarus and Martha and Mary. We see the Saviour enter into their house—He often went to lodge with that family after His day's labour in teaching, preaching, and working miracles in the great city on the other side of the hill. Jesus enters the house. Martha, who it is presumed was the elder sister, sets herself to tidy the room, and attend to the personal comfort of the Divine Visitor. Mary sits at His feet, according to the Eastern custom, as a scholar, lovingly looking to Jesus, and listening to the gracious words of Him who spake as never man spake. To both sisters He said, as He says now to you and me in His Gospel according to Luke, "One thing is needful"—that is, you cannot be really happy unless you be on the way to heaven, through believing on Him, who is the Way, because "He that believeth on the Son *hath* everlasting life;" and that is heaven begun.

SECOND TEXT—"*One thing thou lackest.*" Once, while Jesus was passing through a multitude, a young man of pleasing appearance came forward and said to Him, " Good Master, what good thing must I do to inherit eternal life?" To which the answer was given—not to do certain things, and he replied, "All these things have I kept hitherto, what lack I yet?" But Jesus knew everything about him perfectly, as He knows everything about each of us, and He said to the man, "One thing thou lackest; go, sell whatsoever thou hast and give to the poor, and come, take up the cross, and follow Me." The young man wanted the heart to part with what of the world he did not need, and to give it to the poor; and so he parted with Christ at the very door of conversion, turned his back on the way of eternal life, and went away sorrowful—Jesus was sorry too.

THIRD TEXT—"*One thing I know*, that, whereas I was blind, now I see." Jesus was again passing through a crowd, and saw a man who had been born blind, when He, the Almighty Physician, spat on the ground, made clay of the spittle, anointed with it the blind man's eyes, and bade him go and wash in the pool of Siloam.. Without hesitation he went and washed, and received his eyesight. It was not because the clay was put on the blind man's eyes, and that they were washed, that sight was got; but because the man believed in the power of Jesus, and so did as Jesus bade him. The time for such wonders is long past indeed, but Jesus by His Spirit works greater wonders still. He opens the blind eyes of the soul, and that is the greatest miracle of all. And when you undergo this change you can say, One thing I do know, that, whereas I was blind, now I see. I formerly was fond of sin; I did not care for holiness or the way to heaven, nor did I know the Saviour —my soul was blind. Now, what a change! I see sin to be that which God hates, and I hate it. I see holiness to be beautiful. I love the way to heaven, and I see Jesus to be altogether lovely.

FOURTH TEXT—"*This one thing I do*, forgetting those things which are behind, I press toward the mark for the prize." So said the Apostle Paul—as says every child of God. Like Peter, when on the water by Christ's invitation. He planted his feet as firmly on the top of the waves as if he had been walking on a rock. He was forgetting the fury of the sea and of the winds; he had Christ in full view, and he was drawn to his Divine Master by an invisible cord of belief and love. But the cord slackens; he listens to the roaring waves, takes his eyes evidently from Christ, and thinks of the helplessness of poor Peter himself, and so begins to sink,—till again, looking to Jesus, he is safe. Let your motto ever be, "Onwards, upwards, heavenwards, looking (away from ourselves, weak and helpless) unto Jesus." Then are we without doubt on the way to Heaven.

FIFTH TEXT—"*One thing have I desired of the Lord.*" You say, I trust I have got the one thing needful—Lord, I believe, help my unbelief; hence you say, as the Psalmist did nearly three thousand years ago, and God's people have done ever since.

"One thing I of the Lord desired,
    And will seek to obtain,
That all days of my life I may
    Within God's house remain:"

the meaning of which is beautifully brought out in these words of that grand poet for the young, Isaac Watts:—

"Lord, how delightful 'tis to see
    A whole assembly worship Thee!
At once they sing, at once they pray;
    They hear of heaven, they learn the way.
I have been there and still would go,
    'Tis like a little heaven below."

R. F. F.

LV. Knocking. Luke xi. 9. "*Knock and it shall be opened unto you.*"

ANY morning, in a great city like London or Edinburgh, there are hundreds of thousands knocks at doors. The postman knocks with the letters, the milkmaids with the milk, the tradespeople for orders; doctors knock at their patients' doors, friends at their friend's. And all these hundreds of thousands of doors will be opened; some by servants, whose business it is; some by the owners of the houses, who have no servants; and some by little children, who are very fond of running to see who is there, and what good things may be coming in. And yet I suppose there is not one of these hundreds of thousands of doors which has this written over it, "Knock, and it *shall* be opened unto you." There are the names on brass plates of the people who live within; and now and then there is "knock and ring," and the knocker itself seems to say, "I'll call them for you;" but there is no "*shall* be opened" to be seen there, it is always a venture. Nay, the bolts and bars and locks within are right against the "*shall* be opened," for they are to prevent the opening for at least eight hours out of every twenty-four. And then there are doors—such as trap doors in ancient castles, or vault doors in old cathedrals—which cannot be opened. They are nailed or walled up for ever! The hinges are rust, the handles dust. You might knock at them night and day as hard as a sledge hammer and they would turn a deaf ear to you.

I. What door is this then on which is inscribed, "Knock and it *shall* be opened unto you"? This is our first question.

What is the "*door*" here spoken of? I think it means the ear and heart of God our heavenly Father. And as it is through Jesus that we can speak to Him, and as it is through Jesus that His love replies to us, so Jesus is *His ear and His heart* to us. "I am the door," he said. He listens to our sin-defiled prayers and presents them to God; and He is the fountain of grace, from which flow God's answers of peace. Our petitions *go in* to God through Him and *return from God to us* through Him. Does God hear us? It is for Christ's sake. I delight in that thought that Jesus is our *door* in to God, that He is our heavenly Father's ear and heart to us. In Him God draws near to us, and listens to us. We reach His almighty ear. In Him God looks tenderly upon us, and feels tenderly towards us; we reach His almighty heart. I would not have another door if I could; an angel door, or saint door, a Mary or Joseph door; I am satisfied with my Jesus door.

What a difference it makes who the door-keeper is, whether it is a rough sentinel with a bayonet, or a feeble infant who cannot move the key, or an angry beadle who growls at your troubling him. I remember in a large French church there were several wooden boxes with small holes in them. Those who came in fell down on their knees at these holes, and began to whisper. Within the box was a Romish priest, to whom they told their sins and secrets, and then he assured them of God's forgiveness. They dropped a shilling in through the hole. I felt much more inclined to thrust in a sharp-pointed umbrella. And yet this is the right idea, but it is foolishly and wickedly perverted. It is right to approach God through another that is holier and higher than ourselves; and we are to expect God's favours through him. But then who is that higher and holier person? Certainly not a mere creature, who is as guilty and needy as ourselves; but Jesus, whom God has appointed for that purpose—who is as divine as He is human—who is as truly one with God as He is one with us—who

> "Knows what strong temptations are,
> For He has felt the same;"

and yet has from eternity been the centre of God's smiles. They were withdrawn from Him but for a single moment in His whole existence. It was when He was expiring on the cross for us. You recollect how He cried out, "My God, My God, why hast Thou forsaken Me?" But presently they rested on Him again, and then they rested on Him *for us* as well as Himself. So now we need not fear to press close to God in Him. "Boldly" is the word which the Apostle chooses for it, "or in full assurance of faith." For it is a brother door, a mother door. It is not a door of boards, but a door of "bowels of mercies." It is not a cold, hard, dumb door, but soft, sympathizing, alive. It is our dear Immanuel, the ear and the heart of our God, who Himself said this: " Knock, and it shall be opened unto you."

II. What is it to "*knock*" at it? Is it not to pray? Is not this just what Jesus was discoursing about? The disciples had said to Him, " Lord, teach us to pray ; " and He was teaching them to pray. He taught them by a model prayer—the Lord's Prayer. When then a minute afterwards He speaks to them of " knocking," they would be sure to understand Him as referring to praying. But you will notice that, before He uses this strong term for it, He has passed on from prayer generally to a particular kind of prayer—*earnest* prayer. By a simple parable He has shown them the power and certainty of such prayer as that. If you went at midnight to a neighbour and begged three loaves of bread of him—though he would be vexed at being disturbed, and slow to rise from his warm bed, and reluctant to go down to the kitchen ; though he would positively refuse to do it at the beginning, nevertheless, if you persisted and entreated (as you would if you were aware of his *kindness*, and if you really *wanted* the loaves), then because of your "importunity" you would succeed— your neighbour would open the door. And so, depend upon it, says our Lord, if you thus pray—if you pray from your soul—your heavenly Father will grant you the Holy Spirit. " I say unto you, *knock*, and it shall be opened unto you."

To knock, then, is to pray fervently. The passengers in a ship may be in the habit of praying ; but when there is peril—when the storm is bellowing, when the masts are falling overboard, when the captain is hopeless—then they meet together in the cabin and *knock* at the door of God's omnipotence. A parent may be in the habit of praying for her babe regularly, ere she lies down to sleep ; but if she is suddenly summoned to see it gasping in its crib, and fixing its unconscious eyes upon her, she betakes herself to *knocking* at the door of God's compassion. Jesus Himself, whilst He was constantly praying, may be said to have added knocking to praying in the garden of Gethsemane, when He thrice repeated His prayer, and with fresh energy each time. The Syro-Phœnician woman in the Gospels

M

is a beautiful illustration of this knocking. She could not be daunted. She would not be put off. "Yea, Lord, yet the dogs eat of the crumbs which drop from the master's table." That was a loud and vigorous *knock*. David, too, as many of his Psalms prove, was wont to knock. Read the 142nd and 143rd as specimens.

Earnest prayer is the prayer which honours God; which attains its object; which opens the door. That is why your prayers are so fruitless; they lack earnestness. You present yourselves at the door, but you do not knock; you do not "find," because you do not "seek." You walk about in the field where the treasure is, but where is the searching and digging for it? You sail about over the pearls, but where is the stripping and diving for them? What can you expect from a few dry sentences mumbled at a chair, without the slightest affiance in God, without the feeblest lifting of your desires to God, without the weakest stretching out of your hand to knock? But when you have learned to knock in your prayers—when sorrow or danger compel you to it—then you will be ashamed of these lazinesses. Meanwhile, let us recollect that it is not said, "Repeat a form of prayer," or "Drop by your bedside and bow your head," but "*Knock*, and it shall be opened unto you."

III. What is the *opening?* Is it not this, that God will be attentive to your prayer? It is a *solemn promise* of that; not that He will fulfil your prayer—that is another thing—but that it shall reach Him. His wisdom and kindness may decide that it had best not be fulfilled, or that the fulfilment had best be delayed. Will you not leave that to His wisdom and kindness? But there must be *no doubt* that the prayer is lodged in His ear and heart. If there is doubt about that there is no encouragement. It is a risk, a chance, a "may be," not a "*shall be.*" But no, it is a "*shall be.*" We may be confident of that. It is settled, sealed. God is bound by it. "Knock, and it *shall be* opened unto you." That is the important thing, that we shall have an *audience*. We have but to supplicate and on this we may rely, that those arrows of supplication, though shot from a trembling bow, shall pierce the skies, shall not stop short of God's throne, and God will gather them up and the message which they bore thither.

Try Buckingham Palace door, if that will be opened to your knocking. You would probably be arrested and fined for your presumption. Kings and queens cannot mount this motto on their doors, because it would expose them to endless annoyance and impoverishment. Soon they would have to say, "The door must be fastened, we are worn out;" or "we have no more left." But not so with God, for He has inexhaustible supplies for us. Though He enriches millions, hour by hour, He is no poorer, it is but a million of thimbles dipped in the ocean, or a million of ants stealing grains of earth from a mountain. My son or daughter says to me, "Let me have a kiss." I am pleased and not robbed. A kiss is sweet to them, but it would cost me nothing if I let them have them by myriads. And God has "*good and perfect gifts*" to bestow on His sons and daughters, as freely and bountifully. It is His joy to load us with them, and to have us thoroughly happy in the abundance of His pardon, and strength, and peace, and protection. Can we not believe this?

When Jesus was here did He not open the door to those who knocked? Who were refused? Who could say, "He would not do it for me?" The leper, vile as he was, did but knock thus, "Lord, if thou wilt," and the door was opened to him. Blind Bartimeus knocked impatiently, but it was opened to him. Nicodemus and Zaccheus knocked timidly, but it was opened to them. She who wept over His feet at Simon's feast, and wiped them with her hair, she knocked without a sound, and yet it was opened to her. Those who assembled to pray for Peter's deliverance from execution, knocked and knocked on till the execution was awfully near; but long before, the door had been opened to them, as they saw when Peter stood before them. Of course it was, for God has said it, and it cannot be altered, "Knock, and it *shall be opened* unto you."

And I trust that you who are now perusing this page can add your testimony to the truth of it. You can say, "Yes, I knocked and it was opened to me, I never knock but it is opened unto me."

In conclusion I have two exhortations.

Knock *perseveringly*. Do not be frightened by unbelief, or by Satan's suggestion that it is useless. He will do what he can to dishearten you—but persevere! Would you be driven from a door by a cat mewing, or because it was necessary to repeat the knock? To flesh and blood it is a strange thing to pray where there is nobody visible; but here you have what is quite as solid, the pledge of God from the lips of Jesus that He will open to you. Therefore knock perseveringly.

Knock *modestly*. Not with that familiarity which is so shocking, as if God was your equal; as if you could demand what you require! He is Jehovah, you are a grasshopper before Him. Be careful of your speech, therefore. Lie low; imitate, not the noisy fellows who spring down from carriages and batter our doors in with their rude violence, but the hungry or thirsty animals—the cow or the sheep—which *plead* with moans and tears for what they claim of us.

A lady visitor climbed a flight of stairs to what she conceived to be a forlorn attic. She was prepared to behold squalor, poverty, wretchedness. Fancy her surprise when a nice, neatly dressed boy bade her welcome to a room, the walls of which were covered with capital prints, and the floor with piles of books. The furniture also was sufficient and suitable, and there was a cupboard which had sundry articles of crockery and food in it. He told her his story. He was an orphan, and a member of the Shoeblack Brigade. He had obtained, he said, these things by "*knocking at the door.*" When his work was slack he applied himself to studying odd bits of newspaper, and as the gentry and merchants resident around cheered him on with pennies, he "guessed" he would knock at their doors and ask for such pictures and books as they did not value, for he was fond of them. They would not let him be rebuffed; they willingly contributed what was nothing to them, but a fortune to him. What he had duplicates of, he sold, and bought furniture, crockery, and food with, and "what was curious," he said, clothes nearly always accompanied the presents of pictures and books, so that he was seriously contemplating a rag and bone shop of his own. And it was "knocking at the door" which had done it.

May we so knock at that celestial door, knock at it so faithfully and frequently, that we may have as goodly a heritage to show for it as this enterprising boy had for his knocking at the doors of oak and pine.

J. B.

LV. The Barren Fig-tree. LUKE xiii.

THIS is the parable of the unfruitful fig-tree, and I have read you the other verses because they tell us why the Lord spake this parable. There was great excitement in Jerusalem. Just before this, people had come from Galilee and stirred up what we should call a rebellion, and Pilate had very properly put them to death ; and when our Lord came—He was from Galilee also—they fancied that He was going to stir up another revolt, and they thought He had a better chance. They told Him that Pilate had slain the others and mingled their blood with the sacrifice upon the altar. Then our Lord told them this parable. He said that a man once had a fig-tree in his garden, and he came year after year—he was evidently a very patient man—and still he found no fruit. Then he said to his vineyard man, " Behold, these three years I come seeking fruit on this fig-tree and find none ; cut it down, why cumbereth it the ground ?" Then the dresser of the vineyard pleaded that the tree might be spared. Give it one more year ; but after that, if it bears not fruit, let it be cut down.

The first thing this parable teaches is, that the Jews were God's own people, God's chosen people, who were to bear fruit among all nations, that by showing other nations how true and devout they were they would be won over to serve God. But they did not do this, and God cut them down. Forty years after these words were spoken the temple was burnt.

But the lesson I want to tell you about is about yourselves. We are fig-trees planted in the Lord's garden ; we have Him coming year after year looking for fruit and finding none, and at last the Master will be compelled to say, " Cut it down ; why cumbereth it the ground." "Cumbereth" means taking the place of others, taking the nourishment from other plants. But the keeper of the vineyard, even the Lord Jesus Christ Himself, says, " Let it stay another year. I will water it, I will manure the ground, and then if it bears no fruit, cut it down. Now the reason I want to speak to you is—You are all little trees planted in the garden of the Lord. He does all He can to make you fruitful trees in the garden; but the time may come when the loving Master Himself will have to say, "Cut it down; why cumbereth it the ground?"

Then the keeper of the garden, the Lord Jesus, says "Spare it for another year. Up to this day it has borne no fruit; but spare it one more year." You have been planted, boys and girls. God has watered your life with His blessings. He has shone upon you the sunshine of His love. He has sent pastors and teachers to dig around your roots, so that all blessings may be yours; and still the Master of the vineyard comes and finds no fruit. You may have felt things, you may have learnt things; but the one thing is this—Have you lived better, nobler, truer, purer lives? Have you considered before resting for the night whether you have done one bad thing; have you uttered one disobedient word to your father or mother, have you said one unkind thing to your brother or sister— have you been sorry for so doing before saying, "Our Father which art in heaven"?

Now, when you kneel down to pray, just think, "Am I bearing any fruit to God? He has spared me while others have been cut down." He comes to seek fruit to-day, after these months of our teaching and praying together. He seeks fruit in your hearts, the fruits of kindness, meekness, purity and love. Oh, does He find any here of whom He will at last, after long and patient waiting, have to say, "Cut it down; why cumbereth it the ground?"

Surely the thought of Him coming to this earth and living and dying for us—is not that enough to melt our hearts and make us resolved to lead nobler and more fruitful lives? It is an awful thought, that the Master comes to-day to each of us, seeking fruit. May the great God grant in His great mercy that He may not come to any one of us and find no fruit.

T. T. S.

LVI. Excuses. LUKE xiv. 18. "*And they all with one consent began to make excuse.*"

A PARABLE is a short story or history which our blessed Lord used to illustrate or impress upon His hearers some great and precious truth. There are many parables which our blessed Lord delivered, most of which are familiar to you. There is the parable of the Sower, of the Tares and Wheat, of the Sheep and Goats, and many others; and I want to call your attention to-day for a short time to the parable of the Great Supper.

Let us consider the occasion when it was delivered and where it was delivered. Christ was in a Pharisee's house, and it was the Sabbath day; and there came to Him a man suffering from the dropsy. It was the day on which the Pharisees would not have done any act of mercy like this. But our blessed Lord at once heals this man. He then teaches humility, and He then shows who are our best guests. I have gone back thus because this affects the incident. He says, "When thou makest a feast, call the poor, the maimed, the lame, and the blind"; and then He begins to deliver the parable of the Great Supper.

He does not begin this parable as usual with the words, "The Kingdom of Heaven." He was seated among the Pharisees, who rejected the Kingdom of Heaven. He tells them that a certain man—that is, God Himself—made a great supper. The great supper was the offer of salvation through the gospel; and servants who were to bid men come into the supper were of old the prophets and apostles, and now ministers, and they said, "Come, for all things are now ready." And we find that everybody with one consent began to make excuse. There were three excuses. The first was, "I have bought a piece of ground, and I must needs go and see it." That, children, seems to me a poor excuse. Would not a man see a piece of ground before he bought it? The next said, "I have bought five yoke of oxen, and I must go and prove them." Now, would a man buy these without first trying them? The third said, "I have married a wife, and therefore I cannot come." These three excuses were simply feeble evasions. All these people refused the offer of salvation; they put the world first of all.

We read then, that when our Lord heard these refusals He was angry. He said, "Go out into the streets and lanes of the city. Bring in here the poor, the maimed, the halt, and the blind"—that is, bring in the publicans and sinners. You know our blessed Lord said, "I came not to call the righteous but sinners to repentance." So our Lord gives this order, to call the poor, the maimed, the halt, and the blind. They accepted the invitation. Then our Lord said, "Go out into the highways and hedges and compel them to come in, that My house may be filled. For I say unto you, that none of those men which were bidden shall taste of My supper." It was the Gentiles who accepted the invitation.

Children, here is a great supper; here is a general invitation, first to the Jews, because they were God's chosen people; and, when they refused to receive the gospel, you remember it was preached afterwards to the Gentiles. The Apostle Philip preached to the people of Samaria, and Peter baptized the centurion, and Paul preached to the Gentiles.

Specially would I call your attention to the words, "And they all with one consent began to make excuse." Now, children, how frequently in this world people make excuses. When some people are asked to do anything they say "I cannot" when they can, or they will say "Not at this moment, but to-morrow." They put off a great deal from day to day, and perhaps it is never done.

Remember, children, if a thing is to be done in your schoolroom, or wherever it is, do it at once—any duty of any kind, any act of love or kindness—do it at once, and do not put it off. Procrastination is the thief of time. What is procrastination? It is the putting off of anything from day to day. Dear children, make no excuses for not doing any good thing. Make no excuses for not coming to church. Make no excuses for not attending God's house; but go whenever it is possible to join in the service of prayer and praise.

One more word and I have finished. The great thing is to do the right thing at the right time. A person may be in sorrow or trouble, and how a word spoken in sympathy in due season goes to the heart of the sufferer. You remember that at the great battle of Waterloo, when the

French lines were seen to waver, the commander-in-chief of our army gave his order to the Guards, and in a few moments those lines were broken and dispersed. In the late Egyptian war there was a great march in the night, and our troops burst on the Egyptians at the break of dawn. That was doing the right thing at the right time. Do whatever you do with all your heart and soul and strength, and use the opportunity, take the present time; and above all, do works of mercy, lovingkindness, and goodness. Never, dear children, make an excuse for deferring *them*. Never make an excuse as you grow up for doing those things well pleasing to your heavenly Father. And may God support you for many a long day and year to attend His worship and join in His praise.

J. W.

LVII. The Joy over one Penitent. LUKE xv. 10.

"*There is joy in the presence of the angels of God over one sinner that repenteth.*"

AFTER the parables of the Lost Sheep, and the Lost Coin, and before the parable of the Prodigal Son, our Saviour puts these words (Luke xv. 10): "Likewise, I say unto you, there is joy in the presence of the angels of God over"—what? Something man calls glorious? battles? the discoveries of science? the fall of kingdoms? No. "Over one sinner that repenteth." Man's *great* is very small with God; and nothing on earth is so great as the conversion of a sinner.

Let us try to understand this joy. Like the joy of the shepherd and of the woman, *it is heightened by the loss, the long search, and the many dangers.* Elihu Burritt tells that some boys once visited the Natural Bridge of Virginia. The soft limestone rocks there are deeply carved at the bottom with the names of visitors, and one of the boys resolved to carve his name—Jim Voe—above all the rest. He did so, and then found that he could not get down! He tried to reach the top, but soon lost heart. The news spread like wildfire, and hundreds flocked to the spot—his father and mother among them. After many hairbreadth escapes and hours of fear, he was landed safely on the top.

And then what a scene of joy! The heavenly ones look down on all the sinner's dangers, and so are the more filled with joy when the lost is found.

And joy in heaven over the penitent is *universal*. The friends and neighbours of the Shepherd in heaven are the saints and the angels, who bear a great good-will to man. As all under the roof joined in the song of the prodigal's father, so all in heaven share the joy over the penitent. As great grief is solitary, so great joy is social, and grows by the number who share and express it. No grumbling elder brother puts a jarring note into heaven's song.

This joy is also *in the bosom of God*, for it is "in the presence of the angels of God." All the angels look God-wards, and so God only is in their presence. What! the return of a sinner increasing joy in the abodes of everlasting joy, in the bosom of the Father? Yes, the text says so. A toy brings joy to a child, but not to a man; common things gladden common men, but not great men; the joys of the greatest of men are probably beneath the angels, but what must it take to add to the joy of the ever-blessed God? The return of one sinner does it; for *all this joy is over one sinner, one outcast*, any one, no matter how mean, if he only repents: it is not in honour of a king, or of a genius, who repents. Do not think that you are lost in the crowd, that you would never be missed, that you are just like a leaf falling in the forest, or a drop sinking in the ocean. You greatly err, not knowing the Saviour's heart, for not one escapes His eye; He follows you as if there were only one world, and you its only inhabitant. And all in heaven think of you: "Rejoice with me; for I have found my sheep which was lost" (ver. 6). He needs to say no more, as they all knew perfectly what one sheep He meant, and had eagerly watched His search for it.

Before we part, let me mention the lessons you should learn here:—

I. *The value of one lost soul.*—God counts it worth all that searching, and the saving of it worth all that joy. "Honour all men," then. The most worthless being you ever met is worth more than all earth's gold. Beneath a beggar's rags lies a jewel more valuable than all that ever flashed on the brow of royalty.

II. *The sinner's grand encouragement.*—Some gentlemen preach the gospel to the poor in London theatres, and one of them told me that they had to make it a printed rule of their society that no preacher should take his text from the fifteenth chapter of Luke. Every one of them, wishing to give great encouragement to great sinners, was somehow drawn to this chapter; and the people smiled as preacher after preacher began by reading the same verses. Here is the very marrow of the gospel. You do not need to make Christ willing. He is as willing to save you as the shepherd was to find his lost sheep, or the woman her lost coin. Your loss is His loss. It is His chosen work, His joy, to find you. Will He deny Himself this great joy? Can He wish you to perish? Why, then, do you stand afar off in doubt and trembling? It is His joy and glory that He "receiveth sinners." It is as natural for Him to do it as it is for the shepherd to seek his lost sheep.

III. *The mark of heavenliness.*—It is to sympathize with those who seek the lost, and to rejoice with them when the lost are found. God give you this spirit.

J. We.

LVIII. Why children should come to Jesus.

Luke xviii. 16. "*But Jesus called them unto Him, and said, Suffer little children to come unto Me, and forbid them not; for of such is the kingdom of God.*"

The people who saw Jesus did not all love Him. Many loved Him, and those who were much with Him found Him more wonderful than any person that ever walked the earth. What things He said to them, speaking of heavenly things so simply, a child could understand!

He talked of the little birds flitting by one day, and His words turned every chirping sparrow into a witness of God's care for us all. He talked of the flowers sprinkling the grass near where He sat, and His words made the lowliest of them blossoms of Paradise, silently teaching us all that we may reach beauty and glory by simple trust in the Lord. He spoke of the forgiveness of sins, and made it seem no small thing to ask God to forgive us. At the same time Jesus showed God so ready to forgive that He is like a shepherd going after a lost sheep, or a father watching for a returning son.

While always talking of such serious things, Jesus in some way made children like to be near Him. The picture of the text is not filled out by the image of reluctant children urged on by their parents. We are right in thinking of some infants carried in their mothers' arms and stretching out their hands toward the Saviour, while older ones of various ages ran before their parents to come the sooner to Him whose person won their hearts before He spoke and said: "*Suffer the little children to come unto Me.*"

Jesus still calls. He wants the children of this generation to trust Him and obey Him while they are in this world, and to be with Him in the better world, where He has prepared a place for all that love Him.

I. The children of to-day should come to Jesus *because they need such a Teacher, Saviour, and Friend.*

I remember a company of blind children from an asylum waiting at the door of a church for some one from within to lead them to their place. Parents and teachers can lead a child to the door of a good life, but Jesus only can lead into goodness and heaven.

Neither child, woman, or man is wise enough, or strong enough, to go through life safely alone. The largest company gathered anywhere in church or Sabbath school is like David's flock. There came a lion and a bear and took a lamb out of the flock. Who could defend them? They had no power to help one another against a lion and a bear. Then David, who was the shepherd, ran to their help. He risked his life for that lamb. He met the lion and slew him and the bear also. He brought back the lamb alive and safe. Were not the flock glad? Did they not from that time run to David whenever danger came near?

The great tempter of souls is like a lion, and no one but Jesus is strong enough to meet him. Let every child, when tempted to do wrong, run unto Jesus, who has met this lion and risked His life for us and gained a great victory.

Children need Jesus, too, as a Saviour from wicked things they have already done. Some of you boys have been known to swear and to cheat on the playground, and some of the girls have cheated the teacher on examination days, and talked spitefully about one another. You did not suppose the minister knew it. Very likely you would have kept back the word or the deed if you had known that he heard or saw you. Dear child, remember that God has heard every word and seen every act. Will He forgive these sins? Do you forgive and forget it when some one calls you bad names? Do you easily overlook it if some one gets above you or wins a game by cheating?

How can any one who has done such things take the least comfort in saying "*Our Father, which art in heaven,*" until he has first come to Jesus to be forgiven?

Without going into particulars about honouring father and mother, speaking the truth, loving others as yourselves, it is enough to say that God knows every wish, thought, and feeling, and sees in children's hearts many wrong things that are hidden from their parents and teachers. Children should come to Jesus because they need forgiveness, which He alone can give. Every wrong deed, every bad wish, every pang of a troubled conscience is a fresh reason for coming to Jesus.

II. Another very different reason why children, and little children, should come to Jesus is, that *they are not so far from Him as those who have grown old in sin.* We may say that every child is born close to heaven's gate. How innocent and almost angel-like every infant looks when sleeping in its cradle or cooing on its mother's lap! If a little child will take the hand of Jesus, it seems but a step into holiness and heaven. But every day of sin is a journey away and down from heaven's gate. Some who are yet children have sinned so much already that it is for them a great way back to a good life. How much farther it will be for any of you if you do not come to Jesus now, but go on sinning another year!

Children's consciences are tender. Children's hearts have fresh affections that turn to Jesus almost as readily as climbing plants in June wind about their proper support. If those plants lie along the ground till August, they can hardly be made to climb at all so late in their life. Childhood is the time for the heart to begin clinging to Jesus. Those that come to Him then will entwine themselves closer and closer about Him to the end of life.

III. Another reason for children coming to Jesus is *His special love for them.* There never was a shepherd boy that did not think more of the lambs than of the sheep. There never was a little girl who did not care more for her kitten than for the full-grown cat. The young animals are always the centre of interest in the farmer's barn or field. And Jesus has a peculiar love for children. How many miracles He wrought for children! He healed a nobleman's son with a word, and cast out an evil spirit from the young daughter of a despised Syro-Phœnician woman. He came down from talking with Moses and Elijah on the Mount of Transfiguration to cure a lunatic boy. He raised from the dead the son of a widow at Nain, and brought back to life the daughter of Jairus.

He gave also other marks of peculiar love for children. He once set a child in the midst of His disciples, and said to them: "*Except ye be converted and become as little children, ye shall not enter into the kingdom of heaven.*" He said of little children that "*their angels do always behold the face of the Father in heaven.*" Most beautiful of all is the story of the text. Jesus not only spoke the words, but He took the children in His arms, laid His hands on them and blessed them.

Some one may ask at what age a child should come to Jesus. The word for little children is used of John the Baptist when He was an infant, and of the daughter of Jairus when she was twelve years old. So Jesus tells us not to forbid or hinder children of any age coming to Him. Josiah began to seek the God of David when eight years old. Timothy is said to have known the Holy Scriptures from infancy. And to-day many of the best Christian people cannot remember when they became Christians.

Are you five years old? Jesus says you may come to Him. He will not turn you away to wait till you are older. Are you ten years old? You ought to have begun to love Jesus long ago. Are you fifteen, and have not yet given Jesus your heart? How many years you have lived without the happiness you might have had in the love of Jesus!

Have you not more than once been very much afraid

when some stranger was coming to the house, from whom you thought you would rather hide yourself? Did it not sometimes turn out that the stranger was so kind and good and took such pains to give you pleasure, that you lost all fear and made friends with him, and danced with pleasure whenever you heard he was coming again? Do not be afraid of Jesus, but come to Him. He is strong to help you, and He is all kindness and goodness. He loves children with a special love. He will pardon all your sins and give you peace of conscience. He will be your very best friend for ever.

W. C. W.

LIX. The Lost Sinner and the Seeking Saviour.

LUKE xix. 10. "*For the Son of Man is come to seek and to save that which was lost.*"

THE great mirror God makes use of is the Bible. It is like a looking-glass in the dark till God's good Spirit shines on it, and then we see ourselves as we never saw ourselves before. The word "lost" in this text is a truthful description of many of you.

I. A SINNER LOST.—Many of you have seen a little card with three prayers on it: "Lord, show me myself. Lord, show me Thyself. Give me Thy Holy Spirit." How do you expect to get an answer to the first? It will be by such a text as this, and the prayer is answered when you have discovered that you are a lost sinner. What is involved in being lost?

(1) *It is to be without God.*—I do not mean that you do not know about God. You all know God made you, and yet many of you have no God, and it would be all one to you if you were told there was no God. You would not feel, speak, or act differently than you now do. It is a sad thing to be an orphan, or to have no friends or no money, but it is far worse to have no God. In the fifteenth chapter of Luke we have a parable about a lost sheep. That is a picture of those who have no God. There is a God. There is no doubt about that. But is He yours? Can you go out at night when the stars begin to shine, and look up and say, "*My* God?" Would you dare do that? Any boy or girl who has no God is a lost child?

(2) *It is to be without hope.*—What a bright and beautiful thing hope is. Hope is like the cork jackets sailors put on when going out in a life-boat. It keeps people's spirits from sinking, and their hearts from breaking. A boy at the foot of his class does not break his heart about it. He hopes to be up to-morrow. A young Frenchman is taken away to be a soldier, and he is bright and happy, for, he says, he hopes to be one day a marshal. A child is ill and weak, but smilingly says, "The doctor says I will be better soon, and I hope in a day or two to be well again." I have seen people very ill who were blithe and cheery and genial. They were dying, but they had a hope, and knew that when their bodies were laid in their graves their souls would be in glory.

> "For hope will sing with courage bold,
> There's glory on the morrow."

But if when you are ill the doctor comes and examines you, and in answer to your mother's inquiry, shakes his head, that is enough for you. You say "I am afraid he has no hope." A lost sinner has no hope. He has no hope of heaven, no hope of being with Jesus, no hope of joining his friends who are "not lost but gone before."

(3) *It is to be in a state of bondage or slavery.*—You know what a slave is. You have read about slavery in America. Sometimes we get into a state of bondage, and know it. A boy climbed a ladder and felt his way about in a dark loft, when suddenly there was a click, and his hand was fast in a rat trap. He cried out, and his friends came and found the little captive. Some of us are like that. We do something very bad, and in a moment conscience says, "You are caught; you are a slave." But sometimes we do not know it. You have seen boys snaring birds on the snow in winter. It is only when they try to get away that they find they are captives. Many of us are like that. We think we are free and can do as we like, but our evil dispositions, our bad tempers, or our bad habits have got a hold of us and we only find it out when we try to get away from them. If any of you would allow me to twist a bit of silk thread round your hands, you would be my prisoner in a few minutes. That would be a picture of some of you who indulge your bad tempers, and give way

to untruthfulness, and are prayerless and careless, and associate with bad companions, and are disobedient to your parents. What you could easily have burst asunder at the beginning now holds you like a vice; you are a slave. Slaves are lost children.

(4) *It is to be under condemnation.*—" He that believeth not is condemned." God says those who have not believed in the Lord Jesus and taken His way of salvation are condemned already. They are lying under sentence and only waiting the executioner.

(5) *It is to be dead.*—I met a lady in a cemetery, and she said to me, " I have lost my little daughter." She meant she was dead. The two words are often used for each other. That is God's description of a lost sinner. " This my son was dead . . . he was lost." While you are unsaved you are dead in trespasses and sins. Dead people do not run away from danger. Your parents may have prayed with you, wept over you, pled with you, but all in vain; you are dead. I would God's Holy Spirit would quicken you, and give you a look into this wonderful mirror, so that you might know what it is to be lost.

II. THE SEEKING SAVIOUR.—He is here called by a very precious name, the Son of Man. He is God's Son, but man's Son as well, loving, sympathising, patient, persevering, all that is good. He *seeks* the lost sinner. Sometimes it is through a sermon, or a text, or family worship, or some book you are reading quietly, or a companion becoming anxious, or a friend taking ill or dying, or God's hand laid on yourself. The Lord Jesus, the Good Shepherd, the children's Friend, is always seeking lost children, every day in the week and every week in the year, and, what is better, He is always finding lost children. That should be good news to some who have made the great discovery that they are lost.

III. A SINNER SAVED.—When a lost sinner is saved, he has found a God; he has a hope for time and for eternity; he has been pardoned and is no longer under condemnation; he has liberty, the glorious liberty of the sons of God; and he has life—" This my son was dead and is alive again."

J. H. W.

LX. Abide with us. LUKE xxiv. 29. "*But they constrained him, saying, Abide with us; for it is toward evening, and the day is far spent.*"

THIS portion of Scripture records one of the eleven distinct appearances of our Lord after His resurrection. This is only alluded to in one verse by Mark. Let us glance at some of the leading points of this narrative and conclude with one or two lessons which it suggests.

We read that on the day of the Resurrection, the great Easter Day, two of our Lord's disciples were going to a little village called Emmaus. The name of one, Cleopas, is given. Of him we do not know anything more than his name. Some think that the other was Nathanael, others, Peter, and many believe it was Luke. This last view seems most probable because I do not think that that last disciple could be the Apostle, because we are told that on their return they found the eleven Apostles gathered together. Therefore I think it most probable that this disciple was Luke.

These two were journeying along the road to a little village about seven and a half miles from Jerusalem. These two disciples are as it were taking a quiet country walk; they are leaving a place where a great event has just occurred; and they are full of sorrow. They are speaking doubtless of our Lord's suffering, crucifixion and death. You know perhaps, my dear children, what a comfort it is sometimes in times of sorrow or joy to open one's heart to those whom we love. What a comfort it is, children, when we have a great joy to tell it to others; and what a comfort it is when we have a sorrow. And we are born to sorrow as the sparks fly upward. These two disciples had a great sorrow. They had seen their Lord and Master crucified; as yet they knew not that He had risen. While they are thus communing together our blessed Lord joins them. They did not know Him, Mark says, "He appeared in another form." Christ asks them the subject of their conversation and they tell Him, and they wonder at Him, who has been at Jerusalem, where the facts of our Lord's death were so widely known, that He should ask them what these things were. And when they had told Him their sorrow, our blessed Lord shows them that the very things which shook their faith that our Lord was the Messiah were the very things which proved that the Lord was the true Christ. And He began expounding to them, beginning at Moses and the Prophets. Doubtless, children, our Lord began with the first book of the Bible—Genesis—where we have a prophecy how the Seed of the woman should overcome the serpent. And again He spoke of the paschal lamb, which was the type of the great Lamb of God; and then perhaps He spoke of the Good Shepherd and the Lamb that was led to the slaughter. And perhaps He spoke of Himself as the Lord of Righteousness and the Son of Man. You see that our Lord took all His thoughts from the Holy Scriptures, because that would impress these people, for they believed the Old Testament and would therefore believe this was the Christ.

They came to the end of the journey and our Lord made as though He would go further on His way. They begged Him, they constrained—that is, urged—Him to abide with them, for, said they, "It is toward evening and the day is far spent." And Christ tarried with them, and sat at meat with them, and He took bread and blessed it, and brake it before them. And there was, I think, something significant in the way in which He broke that bread, something perhaps which reminded them of that very great miracle, the feeding of the five thousand; for we read that as soon as He had done this their eyes were opened, that is, they knew Him. Perhaps they had seen the print of the nails on His hands as He uplifted them to break the bread. Then He vanished out of their sight.

Such is a short history of the journey of the disciples to Emmaus, and I want to bring home to you to-day, in the few moments left to me, just two lessons for you to think over.

First of all, I would dwell for a moment upon that expression, " They *constrained* Him." These two disciples pressed our Lord not to go on His journey—they constrained Him. Our Lord likes to be entreated by His people. He wanted to see perhaps if these disciples were weary of Him. In Old Testament history we read that

Abraham said, "Pass not away, I *pray thee*, from my sight; and we read that Gideon said to the angel, "Depart not hence, I pray thee." Now these words, "I pray thee," show that God loves to be entreated by His people; that those who would have much must ask much.

Again, notice that we see in our text that our Lord loves to try our faith. He made as though He would go further, to see if they would press Him. And they constrained Him. In Old Testament history we see that God dwelt with Jacob when He would not let God go until He blessed him. You remember the Canaanitish mother, who got through the crowd, and it was not until a third time that Christ answered her request. Again, He dealt so with the man at Capernaum; and this proves that Christ loves to be entreated.

Remember this in your prayers—Christ loves to be entreated, Christ loves to be entreated. Let us not be like the Jewish king of old, who smote three times on the ground and then stopped. Pray, in the words of our text, "Abide with us." Does not this remind us of that hymn,—

"Abide with me, fast falls the eventide,
The darkness deepens, Lord, with me abide."

Dear children, may all of you in your young age pray to Christ, "Abide with me;" and if it pleases God to spare you to grow up, let that still be your prayer; and when you get to old age you can look back and say, "In life as this has been my prayer, may it be also in death—'O Lord, abide with me.'"

J. W.

LXI. Behold the Lamb of God. JOHN i. 29.

"*Behold the Lamb of God, who taketh away the sins of the world.*"

IF any of you are expecting to find happiness in the things of a present world, you are mistaken. You will never find happiness till you know the Lamb of God. If you are trying to be happy in any other way, you may try on, but you will be disappointed. There is a story about an Indian nurse who came home with a lady to this country. One morning she looked out of the window, and the snow had been falling till it covered all the branches of a tree opposite the window, and she said, "Oh, how beautiful it is!" and then, "Oh, how soft it is! I will take some of this home to my own country, and show this beautiful thing to my friends at Calcutta." So she gathered some of the branches, and put what she had gathered into her trunk. You smile at this, because you know that it would be all gone before night. Well, that is just like the happiness you expect from the things of this present world. It looks very fine and beautiful, but just wait awhile, and where is it? You will never be happy till you know the Lamb of God.

And then, if any of you are trying to get the better of your bad temper and sins without having first come to Christ, it will be a total failure. You may resolve, but you will break your resolutions; you may promise, but you will break your promises. The great preacher, Mr. Spurgeon, says he was once reading a book at a window. He saw a fly on the window, and he tried to sweep it away with his hand, but the fly was there still. He made another attempt, did the same thing over again, and the fly was just where it was; and he then found that the fly was on the other side of the pane. Now, if you try to wipe away sin out of your heart—if you try to get the better of your corruptions in your own strength, without first coming to the Lamb of God—you are trying on the wrong side, it will be an utter failure. You can neither be happy nor holy till you come to the Lamb of God.

I want to speak to you first of all about *the preacher* mentioned in the text—this man John; then I want to tell you about *the crowds that came to hear him;* and then I want to tell you about *his famous sermon.*

First, about *the preacher.* His name was John. His father's name was Zacharias, and his mother's name Elisabeth,—two of the best people that lived in Judea in those days. In after days he was called John the Baptist, to distinguish him from another John—John the Apostle. How he got that curious name was this: God revealed to him, in a way not mentioned to us, that this was to be his employment when he grew up to a certain age—he was to go and preach, and, along with his preaching, he was to baptize people with water. Well, with this in prospect, you can easily understand that he would be trying to get an education that would fit him for that. But he never went to school or college. He was the son of a priest, but he did not go to the Levites to be taught. He was in the deserts till the day of his showing unto Israel. The deserts were places where there were no rows of houses. There might be a cottage here and there; but there were miles of pasture ground where the sheep fed, but where there were no villages and no clusters of people. There he lived, going up and down there; and often you would have found him under some shady fig-tree, reading the five books of Moses, the books of the Prophets, and singing the Book of Psalms very likely, and the Song of Solomon. No doubt you would find him singing there with all his heart. He was brought up in the study of God's word, and under that fig-tree you would find him in prayer. It is told in the history of the Covenanters, that one of the young martyrs, Hugh Mackail, before he became a preacher, expecting terrible days of persecution, used to go to the sheep-farms and live among the shepherds for weeks at a time, praying and reading the word of God, to fit him for the storm that was coming. And so young John the Baptist was fitted for all his difficult work in the way I have told you of.

In the countries where there are priests, they wear a dress of their own, different from other people. But when John the Baptist came to preach, he wore a garment of camel's hair,—a very lasting kind of garment, but with no beauty in it, and rather coarse. About his waist he had a girdle. In the East you will see some splendid girdles; people that have plenty of money make them glitter with silver, and sometimes with gold. John the Baptist was content with a plain girdle of leather. And what about his food? Some of you are far more particular about your food than he was. He made no grumble about poor fare. He gathered locusts, took off their wings, kneaded them into a sort of cake, and ate them. And he gathered wild honey from the places where the bees deposited it,—sometimes in the trunk of a tree, sometimes in the crevice of a rock. He was not caring about meat and drink and dress. What took away his anxiety about this? It was this,—he had a consuming desire to glorify God and to win souls to Christ; and, full of this, he forgot everything else.

A very extraordinary thing about him was, that though great crowds gathered round him, he never preached in towns. We like to go where there are plenty of people. But John the Baptist went to the pasturing grounds where the shepherds were. He began to preach to the shepherds. He preached to a few at first, and they told others that they had heard an extraordinary young man; and then all the shepherds and their wives and their children came, and a little crowd gathered round him in the desert. And then when the shepherds went to the markets, they told the people in Bethlehem and Hebron and Jerusalem, and more people came to hear him. He never went to Jerusalem or to any great town, but he stood in the desert and the people came to him. The Holy Spirit was poured upon the people, and they went out of their houses with an extraordinary desire to hear what he was preaching about.

And another thing about him is this, that there was never a preacher who did so much work in so short a time. Constantly you find something in the Gospels about the Baptist, and yet he only preached six months, and then was cast into prison. But in that six months' time he had shaken the whole country. When God's Spirit is poured out, a short time is enough to accomplish a great work.

Another striking thing is that John was more than a year in prison, and he died a very sudden death. You know the terrible story, how the daughter of Herodias danced and pleased Herod, and what came of her dancing, and how the mother rejoiced over the head of the Baptist because that tongue that reproved her sins was now silent in death.

But yet Jesus says, that of all the prophets born of woman there never was a greater than John the Baptist. We must learn that it does not greatly matter what kind of death we die—it is the life we live that concerns us. John Newton was once talking to a friend who told him of the death of some one, and another friend said, " How did he die ? " " There is a more important question than that," said Newton ; " How did he live ? " John had very large congregations—all Jerusalem went out to hear him.

There were were simple shepherds and learned Pharisees and Sadducees and Levites, and there were Herod's soldiers asking him questions. But while there were many hearers, there was just one way of salvation for them all. "Behold the Lamb of God, that taketh away the sin of the world." This was John's sermon. It was always in his mouth now that Christ had come among them.

Some say John was a terrible preacher. He did sometimes preach terrible sermons, and every minister that preaches all God's truth sometimes preaches terrible sermons. But John's work was to be a forerunner and to point to Christ; and this sermon, "Behold the Lamb of God!" really describes the strain of John's preaching. And when he preached such things to the Pharisees, speaking of them as a generation of vipers, it was just in order that he might send them to the Saviour. A lamb is a very gentle creature; but that is not the real meaning of "The Lamb of God." A lamb is one thing; the Lamb of God is another. God's Lamb means the Lamb of God's sacrifice. For 1500 years among the people of Israel, except a short gap in their history, every morning about nine o'clock, and every afternoon before the sun set, a lamb was slain upon the altar. Only think how many were slain, when twice a day, and on Sabbath a great deal oftener, a lamb was slain; and at other times I cannot tell how much oftener. All this was to be a picture of Him that was to come,—a picture of the Lamb of God, Jesus Christ, of whom the paschal lamb spoke, of whom Isaiah spoke. With all this before him, John says, "There is the Lamb of God;" when Christ came in sight, he said to his hearers, "There is the Lamb of God, the real sacrifice for sin; come and behold Him." Now we point out Christ to you in this way. Here is the true sacrifice for sin, the only sacrifice for sin. God sent Him, and God accepts Him. He taketh away the sin of the world. Now you are not to make the mistake of some people, who say He *has taken away* the sin of the world. The text does not say that; it says, He *takes* it away. Never believe people that tell you that He has taken away the world's sins. He has not done that. Do not believe people that say He has paid the world's debt. He has not paid it; but He does pay the debt of all that come to Him. The meaning of the "taketh away the sin of the world" is, that it is His office and employment to take away sin. Every sinner, young and old, that comes, is sure to find Him ready to take away their sin, for it is His very work. Good Thomas Boston says: "He is like the physician in a regiment. He does not give physic to all the regiment,—perhaps they are not ill,—but he is the one to do it; he is the one they are to come to if they are sick, and there is no other." So Jesus is our Physician, our Saviour, whose office it is to take away the sin of the world. Will you come, and, like Abel in early days, lay your hand on this Lamb of God, and look up to the Father and say, "Accept me in Jesus"? Is it not a fine hymn, that—

"Gentle, holy Jesus, without a spot or stain,
By wicked hands was taken, and crucified and slain.
Look, look, if you can bear it, look at your dying Lord;
Stand near the cross and watch Him,—Behold the Lamb of God!

"He has become our Surety, and what we could not pay
On the cross He paid it for us, on that great and dreadful day.
Oh, wonderful redemption! God's remedy for sin,
The door of heaven is opened, and you may enter in."

"Behold the Lamb!" That time mentioned in the thirty-fifth verse, when John the Baptist preached this sermon over again, two of his disciples followed Jesus. One of the two that night got well acquainted with Jesus Christ, and became the man that lay upon Christ's bosom—John the Apostle. And John the Apostle is so fond of speaking about the Lamb of God, that about thirty times in the Book of the Revelation he speaks of Him by that name; he seems to be never tired of the name by which he first knew Him.

We have no way but one of escaping from the wrath to come; not a man, woman, or child can enter into heaven but by being washed in the blood of the Lamb. Are you washed? Have you accepted the Lamb of God, who is the Saviour of all sinners?

A. A. B.

LXII. Nathanael. John i. 48. "*When thou wast under the fig tree, I saw thee.*"

"Even a child is known by his doings." If children pray we know that they are Christian children. If they do not pray, we know that they are living "without God in the world." The beating of the pulse is the best and surest sign of life, it settles the matter without a coroner's inquest; and so the desire to pray is the best and surest sign that our souls are alive. Those who never pray are like swans which have let their legs be tied and their wings be cut,. and then drift helplessly down the river towards the Channel. Still they might be rescued if they would but cry out; but no, they float along, dumb as the fish beneath them, and they will continue to do so till the sharks drag them under and they perish.

But now, what is it to pray? for the heathen and Papists pray, after a fashion, and if earnestness and endless repetitions went for anything, their prayers sometimes would be models, for they will sit repeating them by the hour, and that often with the most affecting lamentations. Our missionaries say that there are few things more touching than to see the Jews praying "at the place of wailing," before a part of the old wall of Solomon's Temple in Jerusalem. If vehemence of grief could obtain them a hearing, God would not turn a deaf ear to them.

It may be that in studying the text we shall get to understand what it is to pray effectually. There we are shown a man named Nathanael, "an Israelite indeed, in whom was no guile," sheltered from the sun's heat and from human gaze beneath the spreading foliage of a fig-tree. And what is he doing there? We cannot doubt that he was holding communion with God,—praying over the promises of that Blessed One "of whom Moses and the prophets did write,"—asking God to fulfil them now, and show him "His salvation." And what happened? His prayer was granted. His friend Philip was sent to say to him, "we have found Him, He is here with us, Jesus of Nazareth, the son of Joseph." Nathanael hesitated, for Nazareth was a notoriously wicked city; but Philip persuaded him. They went together to Christ. Christ received him graciously, described his character, reminded him of the fig-tree, assured him of still greater privileges, and made him an Apostle.

O sacred fig-tree, where in silence seeds were sown which soon produced such a golden sheaf! But let us observe from it :—

I. *That God is present everywhere.*

We are apt to confine him to heaven, or to our churches and chapels. But this is a mistake; His presence fills space. There is not a corner so obscure that the worker of iniquity can hide himself from Him. He is at the side of each little coral insect in the ocean's bed, to keep it in health and activity; and of each little sparrow that chirps on our eaves, to feed it and mark its fall. He saw Nathanael under the fig-tree as plainly as He would have seen him in the Temple. He saw Adam and Eve when they sought to conceal themselves amongst the trees of Eden. He saw Abraham on the mount, so that, at the exact moment when he was about to dart down the knife and bury it in Isaac's breast, He stopped him. He saw Hagar in the wilderness when she kissed Ishmael and laid him down to die, and the poor lad moaned aloud in his agony of thirst. Then the Lord opened her eyes and she saw a well of water. He saw Elijah in the lonely cave, and startled him with the question, "What dost thou here Elijah?" He saw Peter asleep in the inner dungeon, and Paul tossing about in the awful darkness and confusion of that tempest in which he was wrecked off the coast of Malta, and visited both of them. That was the *proof* that He saw them. Whither, then, shall we flee from Him? Echo answers, Whither? By His Spirit He is as truly with us as He is with the glorified saints. A general-in-chief need not be visible with a dozen armies which he directs. By means of telegraph wires connecting his head-quarters with them he is virtually with them, though absent in the flesh. We have thousands of nerves in our bodies, but they so report whatever they feel to the brain, that the brain is in intimate union with the whole frame. But God Himself is *really* close by us; in Him we live, and move, and have our being. We sleep under His shadow; we eat and drink before Him; we draw our breath out of His hand; our thoughts no less than our acts are naked and open to His sight.

This is to be remembered—and when we remember it, shall we not *fear the Lord, and rejoice before Him with trembling?*

II. *God especially watches us when we are on our knees.*

This was what He would convince Nathanael of,—that as he was engaged in prayer under the fig-tree, of course He had beheld him. To pray is to seek God's face; and when will that face be turned beamingly upon us if not then? Mark how He had noticed that new thing in the converted Saul of Tarsus,—" *Behold he prayeth.*" He may seem not to attend to us for a while, as He tried the faith of the Syro-Phœnician woman. There she was, supplicating, but He made as though He saw her not; she might as well have been at the feet of a wooden idol. But it was only for a while; then He looked lovingly at her, and praised her, and bid her have what she would. Daniel was entreating God to tell Him when the Babylonish captivity would end and his nation be restored. How soon *he* was satisfied that God saw him there! suddenly, ere he had left off pleading, Gabriel stood shining before him straight from God with the wished-for message.

If we recollect these and other similar instances, they will encourage us in our prayers. We do not speak to ourselves when we pray, or whisper to a God who may be absent, "pursuing, or on a journey, or must be awakened from his slumbers;" we address ourselves to Him who is certainly bending over us, who certainly is aware of our errand, who certainly will be conscious of our faults if we are hurried, or drowsy, or hypocritical, and who certainly will be conscious of our endeavours, if we resolutely fight against these, and press through to His throne. An African lad was laughed at for his solemnity when he prayed. What did he say? "I was talking to Him who shed His precious blood for me on the cross! I felt that He was searching me through, and I could not trifle."

III. *We should have a particular spot where we can resort for prayer.*

Nathanael's was a fig-tree; Jacob's was an altar, which he set up wherever he journeyed; our Lord's was either a mountain or the garden of Gethsemane. He withdrew Himself from the multitudes, and retired there as to His closet. Therefore He says to us, "Enter into thy *closet,* and shut the door, and pray to thy Father which is in *secret*." The thrushes in our fields have a chosen branch on which they continually perch for their morning and evening songs. It is said of Washington that, when encamped in the woods, he always reserved to himself a thicket where he could have his devotions undisturbed. And Bishop Leighton frequented a grove in a public park in Ireland, and at last it was left entirely to him as if it was his own property. You may have read the story of the "Path to the Bush;" the beaten track through the forest to the "praying huts" of the native converts, and the faithful girl hinting to her sister that the *grass was growing* in her path to the bush.

Ah! have not some of us particular spots hallowed by such associations? They may now be far back in the distance of years, but we don't forget them. We may be removed from them hundreds of miles, but there they are, green and fresh in memory,—the scented arbour, the quiet lane, the leafy forest, the old ruin, the ship cabin. Secure to yourself a "sanctuary." It may be difficult to obtain it in a small and busy dwelling, but there must be opportunities despite disadvantages, where the "*will*" will hit upon the "*way*." The starling will discover a hole for her nest when the nesting season arrives, or will bore it for herself if she can't; and the timid hare will discover a lair for herself on the barest common, or scratch it for herself if she can't.

Lastly, God will honour those who do thus pray to Him.

Nathanael prayed to Him under the fig-tree. Jesus rewarded him before his fellow-disciples. He put, as it were, a crown of pure gold upon his head. He declared that he should be a witness of His glory in His kingdom.

The pearl is formed in an oyster at the bottom of the ocean amongst crabs and bleached bones, but its beauty causes it to be dived for and fetched up, and set in a royal diadem. So those who have fellowship with God in solitude are adorned and prepared for God's service, and by-and-by He will call them to it. Esau could not have guessed how it was that his brother conquered him with kindness so easily. He had not seen him wrestling with God by the brook the night before. Nehemiah wanted Artaxerxes to grant him a favour; before he commenced his request, as he was offering him the wine-cup, he lifted up his heart in prayer to God, and at once the monarch was melted, and he ordered Nehemiah to do whatever he chose. We have a glimpse of Jesus praying at His transfiguration, and it was "*as He prayed*" that His countenance became radiant with celestial lustre. That penitent who crept into Simon's banquet-hall to the Lord, and used her tears for a bath and her hair for a towel in her adoration of Him, she did it "under the fig-tree," saying nothing, nothing said to her; but presently the "honour" was bestowed on her to Simon's shame, and then followed the "Go in peace, thou art forgiven."

A soldier as he was carried wounded from a battle, said so frequently, "Thank God, thank God," that his companions enquired what he meant: he replied, "Why, before I went into action I prayed that I might do my duty, and not be afraid of death; and God upheld me so that I bore the flag bravely, and I *thank* Him for it." Have you never had your prayers turned into comforts in hours of trouble,—into pillows when you were sick, into staffs when you were weary, into manna when you were hungry, into music when you were sad?

And it would be singular if it were not so, for prayer is just putting yourself into connection with God's bounty and tenderness; and then it will be administered to us according to our "several necessities." If you plant a vine by a southern wall in a rich ground, you expect that it will thrive, for God undertakes the rest,—the nourishing and cherishing it, the supplying it with dew and showers, and what its roots can absorb.

Now, *be cheered on to pray.*—Much in prayer, you are as Noah within the ark. The flood may surround you but it shall not harm you, and on it you shall ride triumphantly over all the temptations and trials which beset us here, till it land you in the home in the skies.

Be warned against neglecting prayer.—You cannot do it and escape; for then you wander about exposed to every fiery dart, you have no armour on yourself, no Divine shield covering you. It will be marvellous if you can continue to "restrain prayer" and not suffer for it, for to pray is a command, and those who do not pray pour contempt upon it, and "they that despise Me shall be lightly esteemed."

There is the " fig-tree " waiting for you ; hasten under it, and nothing in heaven will be sweeter to you than that word of the Lord " When thou wast under the fig-tree *I saw thee.*"

J. B.

LXIII. The Pool of Bethesda. JOHN v. 1-16.

I WOULD like to notice just the real facts about this pool. It seems that through some cause at certain, or rather uncertain, periods there was some bubbling up of the waters—probably by some subterranean fissure or escape of gas—and at these times the pool was thought to have power to cure various forms of disease. This belief was very prevalent, and exists to this day. Some of the things in nature, which we consider are brought about by natural causes, such, for instance, as the medical virtues of this water, were accounted for by a messenger from God, an angel, who caused a commotion in the water. There was a marginal note in John which some one thought was in the original, and thus it came to be inserted in our Bible. In the Revised Version you will see these words are left out, because they had got in accidentally. We read in the New Version, " Now there is in Jerusalem by the sheep gate a pool, which is called in Hebrew Bethesda, having five porches. In these lay a multitude of them that were sick, blind, halt, withered." Then there is a marginal note about the angel of the Lord troubling the water. But these words are struck out of the text, and are only used to explain the belief of the Jews as to the supposed virtues of the pool.

Well, our Lord was always going about seeking to do good, and it was a natural place for Him to be found here. This man mentioned by John demanded special pity. You know, children, there are to be found in every great town—in London, for instance—people who have not been out of their beds for a great many years more than you have been in the world altogether. These poor invalids have been sick and confined to their beds for many years. Sometimes these poor people have been kept in their beds, by God's providence, for twenty, thirty, or forty years. The man spoken of in the text was not confined to the house, because out of doors the air was warm and balmy, and he could lie on his mat.

There was something almost touching in the great hopefulness with which this man year after year lay where he thought some day he could get to the water; and our Lord knew—as He knows the troubles and hopes and fears of all men—the hope deferred which makes the heart sick of that poor man, and had pity on him, and undertook to cure him, if he had confidence to expect a cure. And the words, "Wilt thou be made whole?" uttered by Jesus, seem to suggest to the man that he should look rather to the speaker than to the medicinal waters for help. He was a true angel indeed, though not the angel of the Lord expected by the people to trouble the water.

But you will observe that the importance of this story, and the reason for which John has told it, is not the cure of the man—for this was not more wonderful than many others Christ did—but to show the hatred it brought against the Lord by the Jewish priests. The complaint brought by the priests against our Saviour was that He had broken the Sabbath; and this led to the persecution against Him, not only in the capital city of Jerusalem, but in the whole province of Judea. This is very important, because it was the beginning of the persecution which culminated in our Lord's crucifixion.

And our Lord gives us the true idea of that holy day, for He says it was given for the good of man, to be a benefit to the body and soul of all men—but to their bodies and souls alike; and whatever benefits the bodies and souls of men is not breaking the Sabbath. The Sabbath is to be kept in spirit, and for the purposes for which it was given. Works simply for personal gain, for the prosecution of our secular business—these are to be done as little as possible. But there are some kinds of work which must go on on the Sabbath—but works of personal gain are to be done as little as possible on that holy day. The works of charity, works of kindness, works which do good to the bodies and souls of men—these are to be done as much as possible. Instead of complaining and finding fault with them, as these captious and troublesome Jews did, Jesus teaches us that we are to do them as much as possible, and never to be weary in good works. May He give us the wisdom and power that we may both know and do them.

J. O. D.

LXIV. The Lad and the Hungry Multitude. JOHN vi. 9. *" There is a lad here which hath five barley loaves and two fishes, but what are they among so many ? "*

As we read over the story of the way Jesus fed the five thousand, we cannot help wondering how this little boy came to be in the great company. Here was a crowd of people who had left their homes and sought out the Saviour that they might hear more of His gracious words. And yet, without much forethought, they had, it seems, brought no lunch or food with them ; so that the question arose, How shall they be fed ? Two hundred pennyworth of bread (about six pounds five shillings' worth), says Philip, one of Christ's disciples, would not be sufficient. Another disciple, Andrew by name, ventured the rather strange suggestion that there was a lad present who had five loaves of coarse barley bread, such as the poor people in that country used to eat, and two small fishes, probably caught in the lake near by. He evidently thought it was a circumstance hardly worth mentioning, for he immediately adds, "but what are they among so many ? " Well, Andrew was wiser than he seemed, for, as the narrative tells us, this little which the lad had, as blest and used by Jesus, was sufficient to feed five thousand people. So, as a matter of fact, it was what this unknown boy had which really furnished the dinner for this hungry multitude. From this little bit of Gospel history we may learn :

I. *The interest a boy can have in Jesus.*—This lad was undoubtedly desirous of hearing and seeing Christ. He may have heard his parents or acquaintances tell about the wonderful things the Saviour did, and, boy-like, he probably made up his mind that, when an opportunity came, he would go where He was, and look and listen. There was evidently something about Jesus that interested little people. We know that He loved them, and if He loved them He would be apt to talk to them in a way to please and do them good. Children always are quick to

O

find out those friendly to them. And wherever Christ preached, He generally had boys and girls present in the congregations that gathered about Him. I think Christ spoke in a way to interest the young. He could tell them how to overcome their faults, and could help them in their efforts to live kind and dutiful lives. It was a great treat for this boy to hear what Christ had to say, and I presume it led him to resolve to try harder than ever to live as Jesus would have him.

II. Another lesson taught us is *the use Jesus can make of even a boy.*—No one in this multitude, it seems, except this lad, brought anything to eat. Whether this was a lunch his parents put up for him, or what he brought along with him to sell, we do not know; but we are greatly interested in seeing how useful he became. The fact that he had the loaves and fishes is mentioned to Christ by one who seemed almost ashamed afterwards that he said anything about it. Jesus, however, did not consider it of no importance. For He called the boy to Him, and then took what he had, and made his few loaves and fishes answer for the wants of all. It must have made the lad feel happy that Christ thus took notice of him, and made use of what he had brought with him. Nor could any one have been more astonished than the boy himself to see how those loaves and fishes lasted. Christ can use children if they are willing, and sometimes they have been of great service. He can use their gifts, whether they be the pennies which they have earned, or some piece of handiwork they have made. None are too young to serve Jesus, and such have often been employed by Him to accomplish good.

III. And then we also learn that *it is always best to keep in good company.*—This boy would have missed a great deal if he had not gone out that day to see Jesus. If he had given himself up to having some fun with his comrades he would not have been honoured as he was by Christ. There is a time appropriate for everything. And the secret of a happy, useful life is, be careful as to what you get interested in. Boys ought to find that which will benefit them in going to church and Sabbath school. If this boy had told his mates that he was going to hear the wonderful Teacher, whose fame was filling the whole country, they might have ridiculed him and tried to persuade him to go with them; but by bravely following out his purpose to see and hear for himself, he not only was gratified therein, but was noticed and used by Jesus. I think that proved to be the most noteworthy day in his life. What he heard and what happened to him at this time he could never have forgotten, and it probably influenced him as long as he lived. He may have become a follower of Jesus from that day, and a preacher of the Gospel to others when he grew up to be a man.

M. G. D.

LXV. The Bread of Life. JOHN vi. 41-58.

THE passage is a difficult one for all to understand, and it is especially difficult therefore for children to understand. It was found to be very difficult by those who heard it, and it is not surprising therefore that you have a difficulty in comprehending the meaning of the passage. The Jews who heard it, however, did not have the same difficulty as you. They did not, I think, find much difficulty when our Lord said: "I am Bread, you must feed on Me." But when He said: "I am the bread which came down from heaven," they did not understand it. They saw Him a living man before them. They did not know two things about Him which we know.

And what were the two things they did not know about Him? They did not know He came down from heaven, and was born in a different way from other men. And they did not know that in a few months He was going back to heaven. We know these two things. We know that there was something very peculiar in the way He came into the world, and the way in which He went out of the world.

We do not, however, so easily understand Jesus saying: "I am Bread, and you must eat Me;" and the reason is, that the Jews lived in the East, where men talk much more in figures than we do. We speak in plain matter of fact words, and do not try to convey our meaning in picture words. I have spoken, boys and girls, about picture words, and we must try to understand these in our reading about the Bible. You must try to set the key to these picture words. I think you will find the key to this picture about bread in the 57th verse. "He that eateth Me, even he shall live by Me." Just let us think of this.

You know all over the world there are animals preying upon one another. The lion springs upon the small animal, the eagle swoops down upon the small bird, and men live upon sheep and oxen to support their own lives. We do this every day. We take the life of the corn and vegetables; otherwise they would continue to grow and produce other plants. We take the corn and the fruit and destroy them that we may live upon them.

So you see he that eateth anything lives by it. Our Lord, when He says "You must eat Me," does He not mean, "You must live by Me"? "You must get a life from Me which you cannot have without Me"? So when our Lord speaks in this picture language it seems to mean that there is some kind of life about us which we cannot have unless we get it from Jesus. The young children I think can tell me what this life is; the life of goodness, the life of love, the pure life, the holy life which we get from Jesus when we get near to Him and trust Him as our loving Saviour, when we take His words and His example and His cross to our hearts, and ask for His spirit to live in us.

Then we get from Him—what? A holy life. We get to love goodness, and God who is goodness. We get to love purity, and truth, and virtue, and gentleness, and graciousness. We get to possess these things, to be gentle and praying and noble; and all that beautiful and holy life which is the life of Jesus comes into us. And He calls that "eating" Him, dealing with Him, making Him the very support and food of our soul's life, just as you make the food on your tables your bodies' support.

You see it is not so difficult, but it is very precious to know. It is beautiful to think we can get God's life produced in us, in our poor sinful human lives, if we will only take Him in and feed on Him. If we come to feed on Jesus in this way every day we shall come to be like Him. May God grant this for His mercy's sake.

J. O. D.

LXVI. The Bread of Life. JOHN vi. 51. "*I am the living bread which came down from heaven.*"

CHRIST is the Living Bread, the Bread of Life, the Bread of God, the Bread which came down from heaven. Keep these words in mind for they contain the whole Gospel, "I am the Bread of Life." These words from Christ's own lips have been sounding in our world for eighteen hundred years. This has been God's message, Christ's message, the Holy Spirit's message to our world.

I. *The soul is hungry.*—You know what bodily hunger is. But the soul is hungry; it feels a want; it does not know what the want is. We come into the world with an empty heart, a heart without God. We try to get this hunger satisfied, or we try to forget it.

And *what has made us hungry?* Is there any hunger in heaven? None. Up yonder there shall be hunger no more. But there is hunger here. Sin has made us hungry. Until we get quit of sin we shall never cease to be hungry. There are many things connected with us that increase the hunger, but that is the main thing. It is sin that has emptied us of God—that makes us cry, "Who will show us any good?"—that makes us go from once place and person to another, saying, "Give me something to eat, for I am hungry, hungry." There are many who know what this hunger is, but yet they do not know it rightly. They wonder they are not happy. The reason is, God has not filled their hearts. If He had, they would cease to be hungry.

II. *This world has no food in it.*—You may go all round the world, and you will get no food for the soul. Is there food for the soul in heaven? Yes; but we are not in heaven. Men, in various ways, try to get their hunger satisfied. Some say, If I had only enough of money, I think my hunger would cease. Others think if they had their fill of pleasure, their hunger would cease. The theatre, dancing, mirth, will that make a man not hungry? No; not one of these; the man is hungry still, for there is nothing here that can fill the soul. The prodigal tried to get quit of his hunger by eating—*husks.* Will husks feed us? No. The second thing is—*ashes* (Isa. xliv. 20). Here is another, something worse than ashes—*wind* (Hosea

xii. 1). That is a strange thing to feed upon. There is another thing still worse than all that. What do you think it is? We are told about it in Prov. xv. 14: "The mouth of fools feedeth on—*foolishness.*" Now, here are four things the Bible says we try to feed our hunger upon. Remember these four things. These are the things men are trying to feed upon, and it won't do. Their soul is just as empty as ever, for it is a hungry world. Did you not hear, some years ago, about the siege of Paris by the Germans? It was an awful time. The people were starving; for the German armies were all round about the city, and they could not get food. They fed upon all the animals they could get hold of, for the whole city was hungry. What Paris was in that siege, the world is now. It is a hungry world, and there is nothing to feed upon here. You may go from end to end of the world, north, south, east, and west, and you will find nothing to feed the soul.

It is not a wrong thing for you to be merry and to play, there is nothing wrong in that. But will that fill your soul? No; you must have something else than that. You must look for something more, something higher and more lasting than that. When you are playing you should say to yourselves, "Well, this is all very nice, but I must have something more." And when you go home to-night, and think how happy you expect to be through the week, you should say, "Well, but I must have something more than that, for that will not last for ever."

III. *God has sent us food.*—Where has this food come from? From the world? No. From India, China, America, Russia, from the North Pole? No. Where does it come from? Heaven. God has sent us food. He has sent us food because He loved us, pitied us. Did he do this once to the children of Israel? Yes. Where? In the wilderness. What did he send them? Manna. When the Lord Jesus Christ was here, great multitudes came to Him, and He fed them—four, five, six thousand. He said, "I have compassion on the multitude, because they continue with me now three days, and have nothing to eat." What made Christ pity them? They had nothing to eat. He was sorry for them, and accordingly He provided bread for them. He gave them bread to eat just as God had given Israel manna in the desert. And that bread—that manna

—came from God; it was God's gift to a hungry world, God's gift to the hungry sons of men. It was in love God thus fed them in the day of their hunger, with what they could not get with their own hands, or from their fellow-men. But what God did in the desert, and what the Lord Jesus did for the thousands who followed Him, was just a figure of what God does for us. He sends down food from heaven; He sends it down in plenty; He sends the best food—the finest of the wheat; and He sends it free, without money and without price.

My dear children, it is God alone that can feed you, that can make you happy, that can fill the void in your hearts. That which feeds a soul must come down from heaven. That which feeds the body grows upon the earth; that which feeds the soul comes down from heaven. And that which comes down to feed the soul must be full of the love of God, the grace of God.

Can you remember some of the different things that are spoken of food in the Bible? What is the first mention of it? The fruit of the tree of life—that is the first time food is spoken of. Then we have afterwards food spoken of among the children of Israel. There was always bread in the Tabernacle—the shew-bread. It was always there, in the Holy Place; twelve loaves stood there, and these twelve loaves were just the voice of God saying,—I am feeding you; here is food from heaven for you. Then there is something in the Bible about the hidden manna; we do not know what it is now, but we shall know hereafter. In many ways, God speaks of feeding us, and feeding us with what comes from heaven. He gives angels' food—better than angels' food, a feast of fat things, the choice food of heaven. Will you not take what God has provided? In a hungry world you may have plenty for your souls. For God does not stint you; He keeps a rich table, a plentiful table. He invites all, and all things are free.

IV. *Christ is the food God has sent down from heaven.*— "I am the Living Bread which came down from heaven." "God so loved the world that He gave His only begotten Son, that whosoever believeth in Him should not perish, but have everlasting life." That text tells us that the bread God sent down from heaven to us here is His only begotten Son,—the Word made flesh, who was born in Bethlehem, lived at Nazareth, died at Golgotha, and rose again. It is this Christ who is the food of men's souls, so that whosoever eateth of Him shall never die, and shall never hunger, —" My flesh is meat indeed, and My blood is drink indeed." Christ is the food of our souls, the fruit of the tree of life, the manna, the shew-bread, the paschal lamb; He is all these, for in Him we find God. Nothing can fill a soul but God; and when Christ comes in, God comes in; and in filling us with God, He makes us bright, happy, holy; He fills us with that food.

And if you want to know about this bread which came down from heaven, read the four Gospels, which just contain a description of the Bread of Life. These four Gospels contain a fourfold picture or description of the bread of God. Study these Gospels, and, in studying them, you will know what the bread of life is,—the bread of God. You will hear Christ say, "I am the Bread which came down from heaven, that a man may eat thereof, and not die."

You will say, How am I to get it?—Christ is in heaven, and I am upon the earth. God tells us that whoever believes what is written of Christ in these Gospels gets the bread into his soul. It is in receiving what God has written in these Gospels about Christ that we get the bread, and feed upon it. Study, then, these Gospels, that in meditation on them you may have your hunger fed, your soul satisfied—that you may be filled with God.

Remember, we have nothing to pay. The bread is all free. A little child can eat it as well as a grown-up man. All get it in believing—only in believing. Remember, it is for the chief of sinners, the hungriest of the hungry, the emptiest of the empty, the poorest of the poor. "He that believeth hath everlasting life, shall never come into condemnation, but is passed from death unto life." It is said of the forbidden fruit, " In the day thou eatest thereof thou shalt surely die." But of this fruit which is not forbidden, we say, In the day thou eatest thereof thou shalt surely live. Eat, O friends! eat and be refreshed; eat and be satisfied.

Do not think that you have plenty of time before you, and therefore may eat when you like. Days are running fast away; death may be nearer than you think—Christ nearer than you think. The last trump may soon be sounding, and then the bread sent from God is taken away, and we are left without it. Take this bread and live for ever; take Christ and live for ever; take the fulness of the Word made flesh; take Him now, and in Him be satisfied. He contains enough for you!

H. B.

LXVII. The Redeemer's Tears. JOHN xi. 35. "*Jesus wept.*"

YOU know this text to be the shortest in all the Bible. Is it not the sweetest also? Thousands and thousands have blessed God for these two words. Next to the comfort of knowing that Jesus shed His blood, is that of reading that He shed tears.

On the day when Jesus rode in lowly guise into Jerusalem, hailed with Hosannas, we are told that when He came nigh the city, He lifted up His voice and wept over it, saying, "O that thou hadst known, even thou in this thy day, the things that belong to thy peace; but now they are hid from thine eyes." These were tears of grief and compassion indeed—wept for enemies that would not be friends. A great writer, from that scene has drawn a title to a book he published. Did you ever read Howe's treatise, called "The Redeemer's Tears over Lost Souls"? That is the book to which we refer.

On two other occasions we are told of Jesus weeping. A few days later than the incident mentioned, down in a garden at the foot of the same hill of Olivet, He wept by night, in that agony of His, which brought the bloody sweat in great drops from His body to the ground. "He offered up prayers and supplications with strong crying and tears unto Him that was able to save Him from death, and was heard in that He feared."

The other occasion was that of the text. The scene was near the Mount of Olives too; for the village of Bethany stood on the back of the hill. It is this weeping of Jesus we are now to consider.

Notice, however, before proceeding, the difference of character in those three weepings of Christ. In Gethsemane, His own anguish, endured indeed for us, wrung the bitter drops from His eyes. On Olivet, He wept for foes resolved and doomed to perish. Near the grave of Lazarus, He wept in sympathy with loved friends. Those tears of Jesus speaks to us of four things. They are tears,—

 I. Of pain. Jesus suffers.
 II. Of pity. Jesus sympathises.
 III. In pledge. Jesus shows what all may find Him.
 IV. Of example. Jesus sets an example.

 I. *Here are tears of pain.*—Tears are not always painful. Laughter itself at times runs over in tears. Is there not something touching here—that joy should go to the same fountain as sorrow to draw water? But though this be the case, tears are generally the signs of grief. These tears of Jesus were signs of pain within.

A great deal of Christ's sufferings was within. His worst pain was not when they scourged Him, or when the nails went through His hands and flesh, or when He said, "I thirst." The pain of crucifixion was very dreadful, but He had endured worse anguish than the bodily torture. The worst sufferings of men generally are not what can be seen. Perhaps there are walking the streets in health, or sitting in our worshipping assemblies, without a sign of woe, persons whose bosoms are full of a grief worse than bodily pain. God only knows the bitterness and the burden of stricken hearts. Now, never any one suffered so much as Jesus did in His heart, surrounded as He was with sin and its awful fruits in our earth. Think of the constant burden that must have pressed His heart, seeing with His eyes what surrounded Him! To see the bitter wages of sin, to see the sad workings of sin in unbelief and slowness to learn, to see this both in enemies and friends, bowed down His soul in grief.

This sorrow was for us. It was part of the burden Jesus bore for us, that we might be relieved. When He wept, as well as when He bled, He was suffering for us.

 II. *Pity.*—Jesus sympathizes. It is beautiful to see Jesus' tears mingling themselves with those of the sorrowing sisters. He feels that Lazarus was His brother too, and He weeps to think he had been sick to death and now lay in the grave. Jesus must have been fond of Lazarus. You recollect the sisters' message when their brother was ill, "Lord, he whom Thou lovest is sick." Yes, the Jews were right when they said, "Behold how He loved him!" Love shed those tears, love for the dead and for the living. O happy family, equally numerous, or less so, or more so, that can put their own names into that verse about the Saviour's love to the three of Bethany, and read it about themselves!

Some children will be ready to say, How should Jesus shed tears of sympathy with Martha and Mary, when He knew very well that Lazarus was to be raised from the dead? You are quite right in thinking that Jesus knew that he would soon recall Lazarus. There is no real difficulty, for all that, in His weeping meanwhile. Sympathy throws itself into the feelings of others, and sees as with their eyes. It weeps with the present distress, whatever issue be foreseen.

III. *A Pledge.*—These tears speak about the future, and show us what Jesus will always be. Everything done by Christ on earth was done for all time. The meaning of His actions were not confined to the persons and the places of the hour. They stand out as parables to teach the world. When Jesus wept with Martha and Mary, His tears promised that all His suffering followers to the end of time should have His pitying regard. They dropt to the earth for you.

It is true that we must not think now of Jesus shedding tears in heaven. If God wipes away all tears from the eyes of Christ's people, they cannot remain in the eyes of Christ Himself. Tears belonged to the time of His weakness and humiliation. Nevertheless, His heart is as tender and as full of love as ever. You recollect how in the last day, the Judge, who is the Son of man, speaks of the least of His brethren as one with Himself; when they are fed, clothed, visited, He counts all done to Himself. It is because this truth may be read in the tears shed by Jesus at Lazarus' grave that so many thousands have blessed God for the words of the text.

IV. *A pattern.*—The Saviour sets us an example. It is a woful thing to have a hard, unpitying heart. Should any of you be already selfish and stony, woe for you in this suffering world!

If you do not get your heart warmed and softened by

Jesus' grace, it will get like flint and steel. There is so much to pity all around us, that if we will have no fellow-feeling with sufferers, the constant refusal to show kindness will prey on the soul and eat its marrow up. The tears that are kept in will turn to gall and wormwood within us. Pray for a tender, loving heart in your youth. You will have enough to do to keep even such a heart from having its feelings deadened in the years of after life.

The teaching of Christ's tears to us all may be given in Paul's words, "Weep with them that weep." Sympathize with real distress as you find it around you. Then let your sympathy be practical. Let it move your hand as well as stir your heart and fill your eye. Try and take some grains from the great heap of human misery, and add some to the growing pile of human happiness. It is a blessed work; and he who every day dries some tears, is in training for the companionship of angels and of Jesus and of God.

Whether would you have Jesus weep over you, or with you? Over you, as lost, like doomed Jerusalem; or with you, as His loved ones in sorrow, like Martha or Mary? You know what should be your choice!—is it your choice? The place for those over whom Christ grieves is a place of "weeping and wailing and gnashing of teeth." Why should any of you see it?

J. E.

LXVIII. Christ's Drawing Power. JOHN xii. 32.
"And I, if I be lifted up from the earth, will draw all men unto Me."

IF any of us have seen a magnetized tack-hammer, we know that it is a hammer with one end having the property of a loadstone, which takes up the tacks, whilst with the other end they are hammered in. The gospel is something like this hammer. It draws the little tacks, whilst the big nails won't move. Suppose we were to bring near this magnetized end of the hammer a number of fine needles; what would be the effect? It would draw them. They would seem as if they had life. They would spring towards the end of the hammer, and cling to it just as if they had an affection for it; just as a child springs towards its mother, and clings upon her neck. What makes this? Ah, there is some mystery here. We can't explain it. But we can understand the fact for we see it with our eyes. But who are these little needles? They are the little children. And what is it that draws them? It is Jesus. Yes, how sweetly and strongly He draws them. But they must come, or be brought near to Him—for, don't we notice, that if the little needles are not brought near to the hammer, they don't move towards it? But when we lay them close by, then they move and fasten upon it, as if they could not help clinging to it. Oh, beautiful thought! Parents and Sunday-school teachers, think of it. Bring your little ones near. There is a sweet drawing power in Jesus. By teaching and prayer, bring them and lay them near, and see if they are not drawn as by the cords of love into His arms. But we observe that the big ones are not so easily drawn. While the little ones are clustering, as if all alive, around the centre of attraction, the big ones lie as if dead. They don't move at all. Even when the hammer is laid upon them, or strikes a hard blow, they scarcely seem to move. And if children, whilst they are little, and can come to Jesus much more easily, so to speak, keep at a distance—keep too far off from Jesus to feel His drawing power, when they get big they will be like the big nails, and perhaps they will never be drawn to the bosom of Jesus. How dreadful that would be!

There is a beautiful passage in the New Testament, which speaks of Jesus drawing hearts to Him: "And I, if I be lifted up, will draw all men unto Me." Now let us fix that text in our minds, and connect it in our thoughts with the little hammer and the needles. Yes, Jesus was lifted up on the cross by His enemies, in order to render Him ignominious; that is, that all people might scorn one that was crucified. So *they* meant it for evil. But *God* meant it for good, that He might draw all men unto Him. And He did draw even some of His crucifiers unto Him. The Roman centurion, who ordered the soldiers to drive the nails into His flesh, that hard-hearted Roman gazed on the cross, until he felt his heart melted and moved, and he cried out, "Truly this was the Son of God." And the dying thief who was crucified with Jesus, a very wicked man, turned his eyes upon our Lord, and felt his heart drawn towards Him. "Oh," said he, "this Jesus is righteous, but what a sinner *I* am," and he looked at that blood oozing from His thorn-clad brow, and streaming from His pierced hands, and he said, "Surely that blood can wash my sins away." Then he put up a prayer, "Lord, remember me." See how he was drawn. And Jesus did remember him, and took him with Him up to heaven.

Have you been drawn to Jesus? Has His dying love like a secret cord drawn you to this precious Saviour? If so, cling to Him now and for ever, and bring other little ones near Him. Perhaps they will be drawn also. If you have not yet come to Him, oh, come now, while so many are flocking to Him, and clustering around His feet, and nestling, as it were, in His very bosom. "Come to Jesus, come *now*." J. B.

LXIX. The True Way to Heaven. JOHN xiv. 6.
"*No man cometh unto the Father but by Me.*"

ROME is one of the oldest and most famous cities of the world, and is now the capital of Italy. There, eighteen hundred years ago, the Emperor Nero reigned. He was a monster of cruelty, who one day set the city on fire, and put the blame of its burning on the innocent Christians. There too, about the same time, the Apostle Paul was a prisoner, with his right hand chained to a Roman soldier: he preached Christ, and died as a martyr. Its ruined Forum and fallen temples tell of the "story of the Cæsars" long since gone. But if its old heathen religion is dead for ever, another religion, little better, has come into its place, and has its leading seat there. Its priests and monks and nuns swarm like bees about the streets. All kinds of "lying wonders" are invented to deceive the people. Let me tell you of one of them which I lately saw on the morning of "Easter Friday."

Near the splendid church of St. John de Lateran is the famous *Scala Sancta*, or Sacred Stair, supposed to be brought from Jerusalem—the same steps down which our Saviour walked from Pilate's hall of judgment to the hill of Calvary. These steps are twenty-five in number, made of solid marble, and covered with wood to keep them from being worn away by the knees of the climbing pilgrims. Those pilgrims on Easter week come from all parts of the world. They are of different colours and ranks and ages, and I watched them beginning to climb this "holy stair," slowly creeping up, counting their beads, crossing their faces, and muttering their "Ave Marias" and "Paternosters" as they went. Near the top was a full-sized image of the Saviour, made of wood, crowned with thorns, and wearing the marks of His wounds on His temples, and hands, and side, and feet. Around this "image" of Jesus a group of women were gathered. It was sad to see their pitiful looks and hear their groaning prayers, as they beat their breasts and kissed each wound, from the pierced feet to the thorn-crowned head. Poor people! they were quite in earnest, but they were sadly self-deceived. They thought that for every step they climbed, they received indulgence or pardon for the sins of a year! Therefore, when they reached the top they thought that sins of twenty-five years were blotted out; so that, taking their average life at fifty, two visits to the Sacred Stair would carry them to the "gates of heaven."

I thought of a noble man—namely, Martin Luther—who, three centuries ago, found the light of the gospel on that same stair. Dressed as a monk, with his shaven head and bare knees, he was creeping up those marble steps, hoping thereby to calm his troubled conscience and work his way to heaven, when all at once the voice of God was heard crying in his soul, "The just shall live by faith." Obedient to the heavenly voice, he saw his error of trying to earn his title to salvation by his own pains and works; and leaving the city in disgust, he went home to nail his "Theses" to the church door at Wittenberg, and to kindle the fire of the glorious Reformation.

Yes, Luther found the true way to heaven, not by climbing that Sacred Stair on his naked knees, but by simple faith in Jesus, who said, "I am the way, the truth, and the life: no man cometh to the Father, but by Me." If you would ever enter heaven you must do it by the same way.

That way *is an ancient way*. On it the saints of God have walked in every age,—patriarchs like Abraham, prophets like Samuel, judges like Gideon, apostles like Peter, martyrs like Stephen, mothers like Eunice, and children like Timothy, who knew from boyhood the Holy Book, and by it became wise unto salvation.

It is a narrow way; for "strait is the gate, and narrow is the way that leadeth unto life, and few there be that find it."

It is a holy way, "the highway of holiness." Here is God's password to all who enter it,—"Except a man be born again, he cannot see the kingdom of God."

It is a difficult way. All its pilgrims, be they old or young, have some cross to carry. Like Bunyan's pilgrim, they must climb the hill Difficulty, and fight with Apollyon.

It is a safe or well-guarded way, for the angels encamp around it; and as the mountains are round about Jerusalem, so the Lord Almighty is round about its travellers.

Finally, *it is a freely open way,* free as the sun that shines on the evil and the good; free to all men, without money and without price, whatever the colour of their skin or the land of their birth; free to the richest, if they only become poor in spirit; free to the poorest, if they only seek to be rich in faith; free to the wisest, if they only wish to be taught of God! and free to you, dear boys and girls. Only enter it now. You *need* to enter it, for you are not too young to sin, and not too young to die. Death may cut you off very soon, and your bed may soon be the little green grave. Enter it *now,* while your hearts are tender; for the sooner you do so, the earlier and the deeper will be your happiness. Your memory will be filled with fewer regrets when you come to look back on your early years; and your seed of holiness, that grew so fast on the soil of earth, will bear the richer harvest in the paradise above.

> "When we devote our youth to God,
> 'Tis pleasing in His eyes;
> A flower, when offered in the bud,
> Is no vain sacrifice."

A. B.

LXX. The Cross. JOHN xix. 17. "*And He bearing His cross went forth into a place called the place of a skull.*"

THOSE gracious words of our Lord, "Suffer the little children to come unto Me," have been called the "child's gospel." And surely it is "gospel," or "glad tidings," for the young, that Jesus is willing to receive them, takes pleasure in them, opens His arms to them, will have none hinder them. But the "child's gospel" is contained in other texts, too. It is in our text. It is "good news" to the child, that the Saviour, "bearing His cross, went forth to Golgotha," because He did *that* for each child; and thus, and thus only, could there be any hope for eternity. Oh, how interesting should it be to watch every step which He took on that dreadful journey! Jewish boys and girls then alive saw it, and perhaps were sorry—perhaps joined in mocking Him; but they did not *understand* it. They remind us of the birds which went on singing merrily, and the frogs which continued to chirp, when a friend of ours was drowning in a mill-pond. At the last moment his foot felt the bottom and he rescued himself; but he said that what struck him the most strangely and painfully while struggling and crying for help, was the utter carelessness of the various creatures around! So it was with the greater part of those who witnessed the scene before us, as the procession moved along through the streets of Jerusalem more than eighteen hundred years ago.

But, you may tell us, that it is so painful to think closely upon Christ's bitter sufferings. When we love persons we cannot bear to picture them to ourselves in distress; how could we ever look at the portrait of a mother painted on her dying-bed, or of a brother borne wounded and gasping on a litter from the battle-field? No; we have them painted at their happiest times, in comfortable easy chairs by their fire-sides, or leaning on a sunlit balcony. And, of course, it is more agreeable to contemplate the Blessed One in His quiet infant rest in the manger at Bethlehem, or in His dazzling glory on the Mount of Transfiguration, or riding on the favoured ass down the slope of Olivet, with the multitude shouting Hosannas, and strewing His path with branches of palm. But still, are we to turn away from Him now when *for us* He is "bearing His cross" and setting out for "the place of a skull"?—nay, rather, shall we not walk after Him, "beholding and weeping," as the pious women did? Now let us ask,—

I. *Why He bore the cross?*

It was a *heavy* load. Two large pieces of wood, or two rough sticks of timber strong enough to sustain a man's weight, could not have been light, and He was to bear it for a distance, and to bear it up hill. And it was a *terrible* load. It was the instrument of His torture and death. Bad as our culprits may be, we do not make them drag their own gallows. We mercifully keep it out of their sight till the fatal moment has arrived, and the prison bell begins to toll.

If, then, it was so heavy and terrible a burden, why was the Lord compelled to carry it? Certainly He could have found others to carry it for Him,—there were His own disciples, there were men who could have been hired to do it, there was not an angel in heaven but would have flown to relieve Him of it. But it seems that the authorities determined that He should do it Himself, in order to add to His grief and shame, if possible. Crucifixion was the Roman mode of punishment for condemned slaves. It was the lowest and cruelest mode of punishment in the world. And they were accustomed to put the cross on the back of the criminal to signify that he had brought it on himself by his own folly and wickedness; it said to the bystanders, " He has got on his shoulders the accursed tree which he himself planted." It was, therefore, a fresh arrow in His heart, a fresh sting to His soul. It was meant to aggravate His grief and trouble in that dark hour. In America the Indians pack their poor wives with whatever they can strap on—skins, kettles, food, babies—till they groan and stagger, but if they complain they will have extra tent poles added. This is a piteous sight, and you would be indignant at it. But what is it compared to that of the gentle Redeemer, trembling from want of nourishment, sick from want of sleep, torn with the savage scourging, yet bearing His cross!—soon, He knew, it was to be stained with His blood—soon, He knew, He would be hanging in torment upon it; but He has to pull it after Him as if He were Barabbas himself! But we must hasten to ask—

II. *How was it "His" cross?*

St. John says " His " cross. In what sense was it His? There is a proverb which declares that "those who fill their beds with thorns will by-and-by have to lie on them." But of this we are confident, that Jesus was "holy, harmless, undefiled, and separate from sinners." Pilate's verdict, after repeated examinations, and in the face of His accusers, was, "There is no fault in Him." It was not "His" cross then because He deserved it. He was as innocent as the snow-white lambs which for centuries had been slain as types of Him on the Temple altars. But it was "His" cross in that He *was to be nailed to it.* He was really about to be fastened to it. There was to be no escape for Him, as there had been for Isaac, who presently yielded His perilous position on the fagots to the entangled ram.

It was "His" chosen cross, as He had *chosen* to offer Himself upon it. It was no surprise to Him—no mistake; it was His choice, His plan, His determination. The prophecies which foretold it were His thoughts about it ages before. He was expecting it as thoroughly as He was expecting His resurrection; alluding to it He said, "I have a baptism to be baptised with, and how am I *straitened* till it be accomplished."

It was "His" cross, as He *must* be uplifted on it. You are right in supposing that it was not *necessary* for him to consent to it. God used no compulsion. He did not say, "I command you to become obedient to it. I insist on your rescuing that fallen race." But when Jesus had voluntarily undertaken it, He could not withdraw. Then He was bound to the cross as with cords. Then He had to drink the cup, or rebel against His Father's will. Nobody is forced to join the crew of a life-boat; it is left to their taste and courage; they can do it or not as suits them; but if they have joined, then the "must" begins; then they must train, they must report themselves at proper seasons, and when the storm is raging and the vessels are making ashore, and the signal rockets are bursting in the air, then they *must* be at their post, and brave the cold, the waves, the hurricane!

This was how the "must" applies to Jesus. Of His infinite compassion He had engaged to ransom us; and when the price to be paid was due, He had to pay it in agonies, and He had no other desire or intention. That "cross" was even *dear* to Him in this view of it. He would not have had it destroyed, He would not have been delivered from it. The "twelve legions" of celestial guards were waiting His beck, and, it may be, besought

Him to let them interfere; but He said, "For *this cause* came I to this hour. Let the *cross* alone, it is Mine! and let *Me* alone. It is in expiring on it that I shall conquer Satan and win My crown!"

III. *Let us ask whose cross it properly was.*

Strictly speaking it was not Christ's, but ours. He had not proceeded far with it before His strength failed; and the soldiers, perceiving how He was fainting, and impatient to get their wretched task through, laid hands on a certain villager named Simon, who happened to be near them, either gazing curiously, or trying to steal through the crowd into the city on business. They transferred the Lord's cross to him; and resist as he might, and protest as he might, he had to convey it the rest of the journey to Golgotha. And now the cross was on the proper person—a sinful human being. In that Simon represented us. *We* ought to have endured its pangs, for we were the transgressors. We merited it—not Christ; He was blameless—we were guilty. He was worthy of a radiant throne, not of a cross. But we had angered God's justice, and He who would deliver us from the bottomless pit, would have to present Himself a sacrifice in our stead. The cross—anguish of body and spirit (for the cross is the emblem of that)—was our doom, and Jesus here addressed Himself to it.

Do not forget that it was *our* cross. He simply took it upon Himself. He allowed God to deal with Him on it as if *we* were there. He bade Him smite Him, heap stripes on Him, and pour out the scalding vials of vengeance on His head. Thus He was our atonement. God reckoned with Him for us. He *satisfied* the law so that it had no demand left. Our iniquities were an insurmountable wall between ourselves and God's favour; Jesus on the cross broke the wall down to the ground, and opened an effectual door through it. As the converted heathen said to the missionary, "Once I was in a deep valley, with a huge pile of black stones (my crimes) pressing me to the dust. I groaned and writhed, but it was useless. Then you preached Jesus to us, and when His cross touched the pile, it tumbled and dissolved!"

But now what may we learn from this fact, that Jesus thus encountered our cross for us?

Do we not learn His *exceeding kindness* towards us?

What instances of parental affection we have had. A merchant was wrecked on the Atlantic, and floated for days on a raft, with his tiny daughter and a dozen grown-up people. They were short of supplies. The biscuits and the water were regularly apportioned, so much apiece, and then it was such a fragment and spoonful that it scarcely filled the mouth. The merchant nobly denied himself his, to give his "Mary" a double portion. They were picked up, but he remained an invalid to his grave —that self-denial cost him his health. This was a beautiful example of tenderness; but it fades into shadow in the light of Jesus "bearing His cross" and ascending to "the place of a skull!" Let us meditate more earnestly and frequently on this practical proof of His "exceeding kindness" towards us.

Again, we learn from it *that God is willing to be reconciled to us.* He does not now frown upon poor sinners who seek Him, or threaten them with hell! On the contrary, He smiles and invites and promises. If we approach Him with Jesus for our mediator, clinging to His skirt, pleading His cross, God has nothing for us but love. Let us reflect upon this. It was at the foot of the cross that Christian, in the "Pilgrim's Progress," suddenly lost what up to that spot so oppressed him. *There* it is that we are to be rid of what alarms us. Indeed, it is so! Christ on the very cross here mentioned, secured God's salvation for us, and we have but to apply to God for it *through Him.* We learn from it that Jesus is to be *everything* to us! Not merely our cross bearer; but as He was so entirely that, so is He to be as entirely our guide, our pattern, our teacher, our master, our judge. It is mean just to *use* Him for what He did on the cross for you, and then, as it were, refuse Him His claims for your service! He requires that those who visit and embrace His cross for forgiveness, shall visit and embrace it for purification, for advice, for comfort.

Finally, we learn from it *how to bear our trials.* They are crosses—that is, they afflict us; but, ah! are they as awful as Christ's? And yet He had not a murmur. Patiently He bore His, till He sunk under it! Now ours always have many alleviations; and then He will sympathize with us, and succour us, and enable us to bear them cheerfully. An ancient writer says that our crosses are composed of hundreds of fragments, while Christ's was solid. He had to bear His whole as it was! We are laden with ours bit by bit, and we seldom have a second bit added until a former bit has been removed. Thus our cross is nothing to Christ's. But be it solid or in fragments, we will bear it, humbly following Him who went forth bearing His, which was ours, "to the place of a skull."

J. B.

LXXI. Saved by a Cry. ACTS ii. 21. *"Whosoever shall call on the name of the Lord shall be saved."*

ONE summer afternoon a little boy was playing on the bank of the river Clyde, near Glasgow Green. Suddenly falling towards the edge, he rolled into the water. Almost in a moment he sank and disappeared. Then coming up, and stretching out his arms, he cried with all his might, "*Oh, save me!*"

A kind man, near, heard the touching cry; and he at once, and without any apparent hesitation, casting off his coat, plunged into the river, and catching him with his strong arms, bravely brought the boy to the shore.

It was a generous, noble deed, and that afternoon his was the joy of rescuing a little one from an early, untimely grave; and I have no doubt that, as good George Herbert used to say, the thought of what he had done that day would be "sweet music to him at midnight."

That little boy was *saved by a cry;* for had he not cried, his case might not have been discovered until it was too late. Of course, it was not his cry that *actually* saved him, yet it was the means of leading to it. It fetched a saviour near; and doesn't that show how sinners are saved? They are not saved, strictly speaking, by prayer. They are saved by the Lord, in answer to prayer—or, prayer is the cry that brings the Saviour near.

"Whosoever shall call on the name of the Lord shall be saved" (Acts ii. 21).

I. *A cry comes from a sense of danger.*—That little boy wouldn't have cried if he had thought and felt that he was safe. He cried because he was conscious that he was in terrible danger, and that without some deliverance coming to him outside of himself, he would need to perish. So felt Peter when he was sinking in the waters of the Sea of Galilee. He was going down—down, and he saw that unless the Saviour came to his side and laid His hand upon him, he would perish.

And isn't that the very way people feel when they come to see their sins lying on them unforgiven? They feel as if a weight were on them, sinking them down to a lost eternity. For sins bring death. God has said it, and God must keep His word, and so maintain His just and holy character. God could not break His character, even to save a world; and therefore it was that Jesus had to come and take our place and die, the just for the unjust, that through His obedience unto death God might be able justly as well as graciously to receive and bless us.

Now, have you seen your sins? and have you felt their sinking power? and have you cried?

II. *A cry comes from a hope of deliverance.*—For why cry, unless you expect that help will come? That little boy cried in the hope that some helping hand would be stretched out to him. And he was not disappointed. Deliverance came. So with David,—

"This poor man cried, God heard and saved
  Him from all his distresses."

And did not the dying thief on the cross cry to Jesus in the expectation that he would be heard and saved? And was he disappointed? No. And nobody will, who calls on Jesus.

III. *How near Jesus is to all that call on Him.*—What a merciful providence it was that such a kind friend was so near that little boy drowning in the Clyde? Yet the Lord is near us all. He is not far from any one of us.

"He's near to all that on Him call,
  Who call in truth on Him alone."

How near to Moses and the children of Israel at the Red Sea! How near to the three Hebrew children in the furnace; and to Daniel in the lion's den! And how near to the disciples in the storm! The Lord is a *very present* help in trouble.

IV. *How simply we may obtain the help we need.*—We

have but in earnest to cry; we have but to tell Jesus all our case, and He will hear and help us.

> " For thou hast not forsaken them
> That truly seek Thy face."

Oh, how easy, to us, is God's gracious plan of saving us!

Say,—have you seen your sins, and felt their load! And have you cried for salvation, and received Jesus as your Saviour? "For every one that asketh receiveth, and he that seeketh findeth."

A. A.

LXXII. Ananias and Sapphira. Acts v. 2. *"And kept back part of the price."*

This story of Ananias and Sapphira is full of sadness. In going over the story let us remember that it is there in the Bible to bring a message for us.

When a telegraph bell rings, what a difference it makes whether we know that it is the arrival of an important despatch for us, or the mere line signals repeating themselves! If it is for us, how we watch and listen and drink it in! So let us do with this message from God to us.

I. *What happened to Ananias and Sapphira?*

They suddenly dropped down dead. A few minutes before, they were walking, looking about, nodding to friends. A few minutes after, they were corpses, lying stiff, cold, speechless, their spirits in another world.

It is a painful thing to die thus, to be smitten without warning? Ananias and Sapphira were cut off in the midst of their iniquity.

Even when our worst criminals are sentenced to be hung, they have a period of repentance allowed them, and chaplains to exhort them to improve it. But Ananias and Sapphira were tried, found guilty, condemned, executed in the space of a single breath! At Peter's word each fell to the earth, dead. Does it not say to us, "Be ye also ready?" We may have the golden thread snapped short and the pitcher broken at the fountain when we least expect it.

II. *When did it happen to them?*

Were they seized with a mortal disease, such as the plague, which slays men as they sit at their meals? No; none of these arrows were flying around. It was bright and tranquil morn. The doctors would have reported that they had no malady, and the coroner that there were no wounds. The whole affair was miraculous, "it was the finger of God." It was His direct doing, and it was done as a judgment upon them. The awful power of Jehovah accompanied His word. An invisible shaft pierced them through and through; or a view of the heinousness of their transgression rushed upon them and overwhelmed them. Intense feeling can do that; it has transformed dark hair into white in a night, and strong-minded persons into raving lunatics. Then we should pray God to keep us in peace, to avert fright from us, so to cover us with His wings that we may have no fears; and that when terrors befall us we may meet them serenely.

III. *Why did it happen to them?*
This is the lesson for us: It happened to them because they told a deliberate lie. They wanted to imitate the noble conduct of Barnabas, who had sold his land and devoted all to the Lord. Ananias sought to have the credit of doing as handsome a thing, so he sold his acres, kept back part of the price (his wife being privy unto it), then brought a "certain part" and presented it to Peter as proudly and plausibly as if it had been the whole. God revealed their hypocrisy to Peter. God Himself said to them, "Depart, ye cursed, into everlasting fire." Their last utterances were deliberate lies.

Thus God was glorified and the Church was warned.

Does it not show to us how God hates lying? Does He not say it is an abomination to Him. Are not liars said to be shut out of heaven. (Rev. xxi.)

"I scorn to lie," said Washington to his mother, when a mere child. But there are those, alas, who do not reckon it as a meanness! They have a lie in their throat, as an adder has poison in his fangs, for every trouble. What wrath they are treasuring up for themselves! How they are trifling with their characters!

IV. *How did it happen to them?*
Through covetousness. They wished for Barnabas' fame, but they could not surrender all, as Barnabas did. This

covetousness was the vice of the Jews. It is now, in their unconverted state.

Ananias and Sapphira had this disease. They would defy God Himself in order to gratify it. Beware of avarice. Guard against miserly propensities. They creep in, and creep on, and creep out most wonderfully.

Especially in dealing with God let us be careful. If you have consecrated, though it be but a penny, to the missionary or any sacred cause, it is Christ's, not your own. "Thy vows are upon me, O God." You cannot withdraw it. It will burn your pocket and devour your flesh as doth a canker.

Where is he or she who ever "kept back a part of the price," and would not sooner or later have gladly paid it in tears or drops of blood!

We should be deeply humbled when we reflect upon our triflings with God. Which of us but has trodden in the steps of Ananias and Sapphira, even if we have not followed them to the brink! Can you say, "I have not." And yet God has spared us! We bow our heads and adore His long-suffering and grace. And shall we not henceforth avoid the appearance of evil and cherish the tender strings which check us in the path of falsehood? Must we have iron hurdles and prickly hedges to restrain us?

Let us cleave closer to Him who is Truth itself, and let us cleanse ourselves now from all our secret faults in that precious fountain to which He bids the vilest, and in which they are washed whiter than snow.

J. B.

LXXIII. The Ethiopian Eunuch. Acts viii. 30.
"Understandest thou what thou readest?"

I WANT to say a few words to you respecting the conversion of a great man, the conversion of a man of Ethiopia, which was brought about by Philip, one of the church deacons, and who was an evangelist.

I will explain to you these two words. He was an evangelist because he announced the glad tidings, the tidings of peace. He was also one of the newly appointed order of deacons. We have that order now among the clergy of our Church, for we have the three orders of

Bishops, Priest, and Deacons. Philip had been appointed one of the three deacons who was to attend to the wants and instruct the poor. The Apostles on the other hand represent the other order, that of priests; and we find later on in this book, the Acts of the Apostles, that there was one named James the Less, the brother of our Lord, the first baptized at Jerusalem. As Philip the deacon was preaching, the angel of the Lord said, "Arise, and go toward the south, into the way that goeth down from Jerusalem into Gaza, which is desert." Now this road is a long and weary road; notwithstanding this, we find Philip immediately obeyed the command. He arose and went, and on the way he found a man of Ethiopia, a portion of Africa. This Ethiopian was a man of quality and position. He had authority under Candace, who was the Queen of Ethiopia, and who had given him the charge of all her treasures, because she placed great confidence and trust in him. Besides that, he was a Jewish proselyte, that is he had been converted to the Jewish religion, and he had come a long distance to Jerusalem to worship. He was now returning, and was sitting in his chariot, reading the 53rd chapter of Isaiah, which speaks of the sufferings and death of Jesus. He read that Christ was to be led to the slaughter without judgment; and then having read this, Philip joined him, and asked, "Understandest thou what thou readest?"

Now notice the simplicity and ignorance of the Ethiopian. He answered, "How can I, except some man should guide me?" And then he permitted Philip to come up in the chariot. And Philip read these beautiful words, full of the history of Jesus, "He is brought as a lamb to the slaughter, and as a sheep before her shearers is dumb, so he openeth not his mouth." And then the Ethiopian said, "Of whom speaketh the prophet this? Of himself, or of some other man."

Philip instructs him and preaches unto him Jesus the Saviour. Now this seems strange to you, the Ethiopian reading these startling words and then to ask this question; but remember the Jews believed then, and still believe, that the Messiah is yet to come. They did not believe that our Lord Jesus Christ was the promised Messiah. They still hoped for the time when their kingdom should be restored to them. Hence the striking words of the prophet had no effect, and did not bring home the real truth to the Ethiopian.

Now, dear children, while speaking of this 53rd chapter of Isaiah, the thought came to me that whenever we select a few chapters out of that best book, the Bible, this is the best. There is in the Book of Psalms a psalm well known to you, beginning with these words, "The Lord is my Shepherd, I shall not want." Again, there is another chapter in John, "Let not your hearts be troubled." But the 53rd of Isaiah is one which many a mother teaches her children, as well as the 23rd Psalm, and that beautiful chapter of John. That chapter in John I often find has an echo in children's hearts.

To return to our history. After Philip had preached to the Ethiopian, and had told him plainly of whom these words were spoken, they passed on along this dreary road. Presently they came to some water, and the Ethiopian was baptized. You may remember in your catechism two things: "Repentance, whereby we forsake sin; and Faith, whereby we stedfastly believe the promises of God." This Ethiopian was a penitent. He is now a believer. He says, "I believe Jesus Christ is the Son of God," and then he is baptised.

We are told nothing more in holy Scripture respecting this Ethiopian; but we hear from tradition that after his return to Ethiopia he became a missionary and went about preaching the gospel of Christ. The evangelist had preached to him and he preached to others. We hear from tradition, also, that this Ethiopian suffered nobly for the Christian faith. Notice, first, here is a man of great mark. He leaves his own country to attend to his religious duties at Jerusalem. This should teach us a lesson, that we should not stay away from church for a trifle. And does it not also teach us that beside public prayer and public devotions, we should not let anything interfere with our private prayer. You see that nothing prevented this Ethiopian from coming a long distance to worship. No trifling pretence, no excuse, prevented this man coming along that dreary road up to Jerusalem to worship.

Again, let us think of these words, "Understandest thou what thou readest?" Oh, let us endeavour to understand with our hearts and minds what we read. It may be in reading books for our lessons, but above all in reading the best of books, the Holy Bible, let us understand, and endeavour to do so with God's help.

And, lastly, how are we to understand? We can understand by asking those around us, by instruction from our parents. And the best way to do this is to put faith in them; and, dear children, when you grow up, and those who are with you now may be no more, you can look back and there is still a link between you if you now go to an affectionate parent or friend and ask what you do not know. The great thing in reading the Bible is to read it in a prayerful spirit, and whenever we ask for a right understanding of the Holy Scripture let us also ask for the aid of the Holy Spirit, the Spirit whose teaching is so gentle, who seems to whisper within us and prompt us to do right, and check us when we do wrong. Oh, let us invoke and call from God the aid of the Holy Spirit that we may understand the Holy Scriptures. Let us in reading the Bible at all times utter this prayer, "O God, send down the light of Thy Holy Spirit to guide me, that I may understand what I read. Open thou my eyes, that I may see the wondrous things of Thy law."

J. W.

LXXIV. Paul's Sister's Son. Acts xxiii. 16-24.

"*And when Paul's sister's son heard of their lying in wait, he went and entered into the castle, and told Paul. Then Paul called one of the centurions unto him, and said, Bring this young man unto the chief captain; for he hath a certain thing to tell him,*" *etc.*

WE all know something about Paul who wrote the Epistles, and who was first called Saul of Tarsus. There is not a more Christian man to be heard of than this Paul. Probably there was not a man on the earth, just before the time of his conversion, who so hated Christ as Paul did. For Paul was a very self-righteous man; and the idea of getting his debt paid by another and doing nothing himself, he positively hated, and sought to kill those who believed that was the way of salvation.

Do you know what a Christian is? It is one who has

found Christ crucified to be all his salvation and all his desire. Have you found this, that Christ is a heaven to the sinner? That is what a Christian finds out; that is what Paul found out on the day of his conversion; and from that day he lived together with Christ.

This good man had two friends; they were relations, called Junia and Andronicus. There is a memorable thing he says about these two relations of his. He says, "*They were in Christ before me.*" "They got into the city of refuge before me." He says that as if he envied them, and as if he would say, "I wish I had gone in as soon as they."

Did you ever hear a person who said, I have come to Christ too soon? I never heard any one who said that; but I have found people saying, "Oh, if I had come sooner, how much I might have done, and how much I might have enjoyed!" Junia and Andronicus came sooner than Paul, and probably by their prayers helped to bring about his conversion.

There was an old Puritan called Mr. Doolittle. (Though his name was Doolittle he did a great deal—he was a most diligent worker.) He was once preaching to a congregation. A young man came into a seat near the pulpit, and tried to keep near the end of it, so that he might easily get out; but the people closed up, and the young man was fairly jammed in, and could not get away. He sat still when he found he could do no better. Mr. Doolittle was setting forth Christ, and all at once looked up to the gallery to an old man, and said, "Friend, are you sorry that you came to Christ so many years ago?" The old man rose up and said, "No, sir, I rejoice that I have known Him so long; and He is always becoming more precious to me." He turned to another on the left, and said, "Are you sorry that you came so soon to Jesus?" "No, sir, but I am sorry that I did not come sooner." Then he looked down on the young man, and said, "Have you come to Jesus?" The young man did not know what to say. He said again, "Young man, have you come to Christ?" and got for answer, "No, sir." "Are you willing to come?" And the young man looked up again, and said, "Yes." "And when will you come—now?" Having fully gained his attention, he set before him a waiting

Christ; and the young man was brought to Christ that night.

The text is about the nephew of Paul—the son of Paul's sister.

First of all, he was a Christian—a Christian lad.

Second: He was a lad that had much love to his uncle.

Third: Notice how God made use of him on behalf of his uncle.

Fourth: Notice what we owe to this young man because of what he did for his uncle.

Fifth: Observe that he got a reward, and he is going to get more.

I. I believe *he was a Christian lad.*—My reason for thinking this young man to be a Christian is this: it is quite clear he did not belong to the Jewish party any longer. He was very different from those that lay in wait for Paul's life. We have a good notion what people are by their companions. The Apostle John says, " Every one that loveth Him that begat loveth them that are begotten of Him." Every one that loves Christ loves Christ's family—His brothers, His children. This lad was one of these, and so we infer that he was a Christian; he took his uncle's side, and did it at a time that was very trying. It was at a great risk he took his uncle's side; and yet his heart was with him, because his uncle was on Christ's side.

He must have been a young lad. I don't think he was twenty—I scarcely think he was sixteen. When the chief captain saw him, what did he do? Just what he would have done with a young lad not grown up. He "*took him by the hand*"—doesn't that show him quite a boy?—and said, " Well, my lad, what have you come to tell me ? "

II. *He loved his uncle very much.*—It was natural he should. He must have attracted those that were young. He was a man who was very amiable; and this lad would like his own uncle, and like him for his amiable qualities. And then, grace makes a person have more love to relatives than ever; the more love to Christ we have, the more love to our friends. You might think, " Oh, if I love Christ very much, there will not be room for my friends." But it is just the other way; our love to our friends becomes the stronger and more tender. Have you read what a child said to her parents when dying: "I do not know how it is, I always liked you, but since I loved Christ I like you far better." This young man had much love to his uncle, and the special way he showed it was this :—

His uncle was in the castle, the great tower built at the side of the Temple, which they called Fort Antonia; and you got into it from the Temple by a flight of steps. Paul was a prisoner up in that high tower. He was taken there by the captain; and, when lying there, this nephew of his found out about a conspiracy, for the Jews were talking about it in Jerusalem. He was a lad of a good deal of sense. He does not seem to have told anybody what was in his mind, but just said this to himself, "I will risk my life for my uncle." So he goes to the castle, and asks to be allowed to speak to his uncle, and told him.

His uncle hears it very calmly, as he used to do, and then he says, "Well, let us pray about it;" and they prayed about it. Then he says, "Now, I'll tell you what we will do. When you go out, tell the centurion to speak to me."

You may be sure that this young man risked a great deal for Paul. For what would these forty men not do to him when they found out that Paul had escaped through him? What did you ever risk for the love of Christ and His people? Have you risked the favour of anybody? Can you bear being laughed at? Can you bear a joke against you for being a Christian?

III. *How God used him.*—Paul told him to call one of the centurions. The centurion came, and Paul said to him, "Will you take this young friend of mine to the captain, and say that he has got a certain thing to tell him?" Paul was always favoured by those about him. He was a kindly man, everybody liked him. When he was on board ship going to Rome, why, he seemed to have command of the ship; they all felt his influence. The centurion obeyed him, and took the young man to the captain. God has extraordinary ways of delivering His people when in danger, but sometimes very simple ways. John Knox, in that house of his still standing near the Canongate, was just on the point of being killed by a wicked man firing a pistol through the window; but before the pistol was fired, God put it into the heart of John Knox to rise from his seat and go to another part of the room to get a book. The shot came at that moment, and John Knox was saved in that simple way. Perhaps you may have heard how God saved a Puritan prisoner in England when a justice of the peace was determined to send him to prison. A little child began to play with the prisoner. He was a kindly man, and he soon gained the confidence of the child. He was kept some twenty minutes in the hall, till the little girl and he became great friends; and when the justice, who was the little girl's own father, was going to send him to prison, she said, " You shall not send him to prison. If you send him to prison," she said, " I will kill myself—I will drown myself." She was a little girl, but a great favourite; and her father at last said, " Well, I will set him free for your sake." See what God can do!

Even so He used this nephew to get Paul out of this great danger; and it was very simply done. "You have something to tell me?" said the chief captain; "come away and we will speak of it alone." He was pleased with the young man, finding him to be a modest young man. He must also have been a youth who was very *truthful;* for these reasons: His uncle at once believed what he said; and whenever the captain heard the story, he acted upon it.

You see what it is to have a character for honesty, for truthfulness; and it is possible to have a noble character when young.

The captain acted on the young man's information; and orders out his troops—two centurions, two hundred soldiers, two hundred spearmen, and seventy horsemen with them; and Paul in the midst, surrounded by so many guards, is just as safe, you may say, as if a band of angels were around him. God called out the soldiers of the governor on his behalf, and they marched with him to Cæsarea. What an awful disappointment to these forty wicked fellows! The snare is broken, Paul has escaped—and all through this young man.

Young people, God can use you. Perhaps he has some use for you now, if you will just put yourself in His hand.

IV. *What we owe him.*—He saved his uncle's life at this time. If Paul's life had not been saved, we should not have had some of the rich letters in our Bible, such as the Epistles to the Ephesians and to the Philippians. We should have lost some of the sweet texts we so delight in. You would have lost that text—"Children, obey your parents in the Lord, for this is right. This is the first commandment with promise." Paul would have children as well as grown-up people attended to. And if Paul's life had not been saved at this time, we should not have had his letters to Timothy, and we should not have heard of him "knowing the Scriptures from a child;" and we should not have heard of Timothy's mother and grandmother teaching him. We are indebted to that young man for all these precious things, in a certain way; for he was the instrument in God's hands of saving his uncle's life.

V. Last of all, *about his reward.*—When you do service for God, it is not good to think a great deal about the reward. When you do kind things to one another, it should not be because you expect some advantage. Christ said, "When you give a great supper, do not make it for those who can recompense you; but for the poor, the halt, and the maimed, for they cannot recompense you." This is best of all—to do kind things to people that cannot recompense you. "You will be recompensed in the resurrection of the just." This young man had not the least idea of a reward; but he has had already a great reward—he has got his story in the Bible.

But besides, there is a great reward waiting for him; for Christ has said that if you give even a cup of cold water to a disciple, you shall in no wise lose your reward. He describes the giving of it in the 25th chapter of Matthew, where He says that He regards what is done to His people as done to Himself, and will say to them, "Come, ye blessed."

See how God rewards those that do kind things to His people! If you love Christ, you will love His people, and try to do kind things to them. Are you trying? If you are, God will open a way to you. Do you know any sick person? You could perhaps sing a hymn to that person, or speak a kind word, or drop in for five or ten minutes with just a kind look. Are your parents Christ's people? You should be ten times kinder to them than ever before, for Christ's sake. In every way try to get the reward Christ gives.

But are you one of Christ's children? Oh, it will be dreadful if you are not found in Christ! for you know about Him; and that if you come to-night, you will be a saved sinner. And why will you not come?

There was a man out at the gold diggings who had a large piece of land, and it was said there was gold there. He tried to find the gold, but at last gave it up, and the land was sold to others.

Soon a report went abroad that large nuggets had been found, and every day they were finding more. When the man who had parted with the land heard of it, he gnashed his teeth, and went out of his mind with rage at himself for his folly. Even so, Christ says there are people who will "gnash their teeth," when they see Abraham and Isaac and Jacob in the kingdom, and the prophets, and they themselves shut out!

Paul, when warned of the conspiracy against him, at once took the way of escape from it. There is a far more terrible conspiracy against you; for Satan and his hosts are all bent on your ruin. Why not escape at once, for all things are ready?

A. A. B.

LXXV. The Account. Rom. xiv. 12. "*Every one of us shall give account of himself to God.*"

WHAT is the account? "Of ourselves." I need scarcely explain what this means. There is a boy who left his home in the morning to go to school. At dinner-time he does not appear, and in the afternoon at five o'clock, there is still no word of him. And when his mother goes to make inquiry she finds he has not been at school all day. She becomes anxious about him, afraid lest he should have met with some accident, or have been led away by other wicked boys; or, it may be, even have run off to sea to be a sailor; and the neighbours are all astir, and they are fancying the worst, till at length, when it is just about time for going to bed, the runaway appears, wet, and cold, and dirty, and tired, and hungry. The first thing his mother says to him is, "Johnnie, where have you been? what has come over you? what have you been doing? *Give an account of yourself.*" You all know what she means when she says that.

And there is another boy, who has gone to be apprentice to a grocer. His master is as kind to him as any master can be, for he is an orphan, and behaves to him like a father, and so he is grieved to learn that his young apprentice is going far wrong. He is taking his master's money, and putting away his goods, and wasting his time whenever his back is turned, and taking up with bad company, and learning to drink and to smoke, and going to the theatre, where Satan likes young people to go, because there they learn so much that is evil, and get so quickly ready for doing his work on earth and going to be with him in hell. Well, there is nothing for it but he must turn him away in disgrace; and so he takes him into his little room, and sits down right opposite to him, and looking him full in the face he says, "What is this you have been doing? *what account have you to give of yourself?*" You know what he means when he says that.

Well, just so is the day coming when God shall require account from His truant, wayward, disobedient children, His unfaithful, ungrateful servants. Few people think of that, whether children or men and women. They go on in their sin, and enjoy themselves the best way they can, and disobey God, and forget God, and serve the devil, as if they had nothing else to do, as if nothing else were expected of them, as if there were no account to be rendered. Solomon seeing them in his day, just as now, living as if they were mere butterflies, as if they had no precious souls to be saved or lost, and no heaven or hell to look forward to, and no God to answer to, puts in the solemn warning, "But know thou, that for all these things God will bring thee into judgment."

Yes, dear children, hear what God's word says, "It is appointed unto men once to die, but after this *the judgment!*" Have you ever thought of this "judgment," in which we shall have to give account of ourselves? It is an account of *ourselves* we have to give, not of other people, not of our neighbours, not of this or the other boy or girl, but each of himself and herself; and that is the most difficult account of all, the hardest, that which people like worst. It is an easy thing to give an account of others, we are all ready enough to do that, whether young or old —we can tell what this one and the other one has done. But to give account *of one's self!* and to have no way of getting away from it! that is the difficulty.

It is a dreadful thing to think of *living* with such a load of sin to account for; it is a more dreadful thing to think of *dying* with it. How can you be happy in such a case— how can you live happily, committing sin every day—sin still unforgiven? How can you expect to die happily, while this text stands written in the Bible, "Every one of us shall give account of himself to God." Can you lay down this book as you took it up—careless? Can you go to rest this night again, unpardoned? What if you should never awake? Will you not go straightway and offer up the prayer, "Lord, have mercy upon me, and take away my sins, for Jesus' sake"? You know there are some substances that take out marks made by ink: nothing in all the world but one can take out the marks of sin. Who can tell me what it is? THE BLOOD OF CHRIST. "The blood of Jesus Christ, God's son, cleanseth us from all sin." The dying time is coming, will you not get ready for it? will you not be like that young Hindu, just about to die, saying, "Sing, brother, sing"? "What shall I sing?" "Sing of salvation through the blood of Jesus. Sing, thanks be to Him who giveth us the victory through the blood of Jesus;" and then he sinks back and dies.

J. H. W.

LXXVI. Living Epistles. 2 COR. iii. 2, 3. *"Ye are our epistle written in our hearts, known and read of all men: forasmuch as ye are manifestly declared to be the epistle of Christ ministered by us, written not with ink, but with the Spirit of the living God; not in tables of stone, but in fleshy tables of the heart."*

AN epistle is a letter. The true Christians at Corinth served as letters to recommend both Paul the servant and Christ the Lord. The neighbours whether Jews or heathens, learned from the holy life of the converts that the minister who taught them was true, and that the Saviour in whom they believed was Divine. The Apostle starts with the thought that the Corinthian disciples were a certificate in favour of himself as a minister, but he soon glides from that thought into a greater thing; he goes on to speak of the Corinthian disciples as being like written letters, in which all men may read of Christ.

It is of this second and greater thing that we propose to speak. Our subject is: Christians are epistles of Christ. The text tells five things about this kind of letter :—

I. *The Paper*, or the material on which the marks are made. Many different substances have been employed in successive ages of the world to receive and retain written words, but one feature is common to them all: in their natural state they are not fit to be used as writing materials; they require a process of preparation. The reeds, and leaves, and skins which were used as writing materials by the ancients, all needed a process of preparation; and therein they are like the living epistles of Jesus Christ, who must be renewed in the spirit of their minds ere they show forth the Redeemer's likeness in their life. But the preparation of modern materials for writing, although it was not directly before the Apostle's mind, contains in fact more points of likeness to the renewing and sanctifying of believers than any of the ancient arts.

Although the text does not directly refer to paper—a substance invented long after it was written—there is a remarkable likeness between the method of its manufacture and the work of the Spirit on a disciple's heart and life in preparing them to be epistles of Christ. " Filthy rags " are the raw material of the manufacture. These are with great care and labour broken very small, and washed very clean; they are then cast into a new form, and brought out pure and beautiful, ready to get a new meaning impressed on their smooth, bright breast. Paper from rags is, in an obvious and important sense, " a new creature."

Such a process of breaking down and building up again takes places every time that the writing material is prepared for an epistle of Christ. You might as well try to write with pen and ink upon the rubbish from which paper is manufactured, as expect legible evidence for the truth of the gospel in the life and spirit of one who has not gotten "a clean heart"—who has not been born again.

Christ does not find on earth any pure; He makes them. Those that stand around the throne in white clothing were gathered from the mire. They were once darkness, though they are now light in the Lord. Let no one think that he can be taken to heaven because he is good; but let no one think Christ will not receive him because he is evil. Him that cometh, Christ will in no wise cast out. "The blood of Jesus Christ cleanseth us from all sin."

Not on tables of stone, like those on which the Law was graven, but on tables of flesh must the mind and likeness of Christ be written. Give the Lord your heart. He desires that His own name and holiness should be written there. Surrender it to Him, that He may blot out its stains, and mark it for His own.

II. *The Writing*, or the mind and meaning which is fixed on the prepared page. It is not Christianity printed in the creed, but Christ written in the heart. The mind of Christ is so graven in the heart that His likeness shines through in the life.

It is well understood that a person's character may be best learned from his letters. These seem to be windows in his breast through which you may see his nature. How eagerly the public read the letters of a great man, if they are printed after his death! People expect to know better by these than by any other means what the man really was.

As our Redeemer left no monument of Himself in brass or marble, so He left no letters written by His own hand. He did not write his mind on tables of stone or on sheets of parchment. Even Rome, with all her rage for relics, does not pretend to show the Saviour's handwriting. Yet He has not left Himself without a witness. He has left "epistles of Christ." True disciples, whether young or old, when He desires to let the world know Himself, He points to you! The world judges of Christianity chiefly from the life of Christians.

III. *The Writer.* The letter is written by the Spirit of the living God. Some writings and paintings look well enough for a while, but are easily rubbed off by rough usage, or grow faint with age. Only fast colours are truly valuable.

How shall we get a writing or a likeness made durable on the human heart? One thing we know, many beautiful things in book and lip, which people admire for a day, are blotted out soon. Lessons that human hands lay on are not able to stand the world's rough usage.

No writing on a human soul is certainly durable except that which the Spirit of God lays on. It is when the truth from the Bible is pressed into the soul by the Holy Spirit that any one becomes a new creature. Old things pass away, and henceforth the Christian bears about upon his character the likeness of Christ.

IV. *The Pen.* In writing the new name and new nature on the tables of the heart, the Holy Spirit employs some instrument. It is expressly said in the text that Paul and the young evangelist who assisted him had a hand in the work. The terms, "ministered by us," show the place of man in the work of conversion and purifying. It is not a high place that the minister stands in, but it is the right place, and he cannot be dispensed with.

In photography it is the sun that makes the portrait. There is no drawing of the outline by a human hand, and no shading of the figure according to rules of the painter's art. The person stands up in the light, and the light lays his image on the glass. Yet in this work there is room for the ministry of man. Without the ministry of man the work could not in any case be done. A human hand prepares the plate for securing the picture, and adjusts the instrument for throwing the light at the proper moment on the prepared surface. Although in the real work of making the picture the artist has no hand at all—although he has nothing more to do in the end than stand still, as Israel did at the Red Sea, and see the work done by the sun—his place is important and necessary.

A similar place under the ministry of the Spirit is given to the ministry of men. God does not send angels to make the gospel known. We learn it from men of flesh and blood like ourselves. Cornelius and his house will be saved, but Peter must go from Joppa to Cæsarea and open up to them the way of salvation. Nor does he confine Himself to any class of instruments or any age. " Ministering children" are often used to bring the word home in power, where older ministers are not admitted. A child forgiven through the blood of Christ, and loving the Lord that bought him, may be employed, like a little vessel, to convey the water of life to another child whose heart is like the dry ground.

V. *The Readers.* They are a great number, and of various kinds. The words have a very wide range, for it is said that these letters are "known and read of all men." The meaning is, that the writing is not a letter sealed or locked up in a desk, but exposed daily to public view. These epistles walk about upon the streets, and mingle with the crowds in the market-place. Every one who likes may read them : they are open to all. Some who look on the letters are enemies, and some are friends. If an enemy see Christ truly represented in a Christian, he may be turned thereby from darkness to light ; but if he see falsehood and envy and anger and worldliness in one who is called a Christian, he will probably be more hardened in his unbelief. Those who already know and love the truth are glad when they read it clearly written in a neighbour's life—are grieved when they see a false image of the Lord held up to the eyes of men. Christians, old and young, seeing that you are epistles of Christ open to public gaze, read by friend and foe, what manner of persons ought you to be in all holy conversation and godliness?

Take some lessons from this subject :—

(1) Every one's life is an open letter. Some are epistles of Christ, some are epistles of vanity, of covetousness, of selfishness. The spirit that reigns within is more or less visible outwardly in the life.

(2) Some letters are forgeries. Some lives are forgeries too. They give out that they are epistles of Christ, while they are not.

(3) The letter should be clearly written, and so easily read.

We shall not be of much use in a blinded world until the mind of Christ shall have been so substantially embossed upon our whole life that in the various jostlings of the world those who shut their eyes to the doctrine of the gospel shall be compelled to feel, as they press against us, what it is to be a Christian   W. A.

LXXVII. A Gift. 2 Cor. viii. 5. "*They first gave their ownselves to the Lord.*"

It happened thus. One day a man came to the place where these people lived. He was not a handsome man. He was not a rich man. He was not a man of rank or of style. He came there only to preach. He told them that he had dreamt, and in his dream had seen one pointing to that very place, and crying, " Come over and help us." And so he had come, and all the help he could offer was —to preach. But oh, he did preach. A Chinese Christian once said, " We want men of hot hearts to come and speak to us of the love of Christ." The hot heart was in the preaching of that man. Well, then, the people listened. Some sneered, " Oh, he is mad." Others exclaimed, " Oh, he is a fanatic ; we have no time for such new-fangled doctrine." But others thought and felt. They made three grand discoveries. A Roman Catholic once sat down to read the Bible. He was interested, and he said to his wife, " Let us read a part every night." They did so for about a week, when the man stopped. " Wife, if this book is true, we are wrong." Two or three evenings passed. Again the man stopped. " Wife, if this book is true, we are lost." Now deeply anxious, he continued to read. And by-and-by again he stopped ; but his face was lighted up with a new joy. " Wife, if this book is true, we are saved." The Macedonians, hearing the preacher with the hot heart, said to themselves, first, " We are wrong ;" next, " We are lost ; " and then, " But we are saved." And as they looked to the Saviour whom he set before them, they gave themselves to the Lord.

I. *You are to give your ownselves.*—Does that mean that I am to say my prayers, and read the Bible, and go to church, and do what is kind and good ? Certainly ; but you may do all this with your ownself not given. There is something more. When you give your own to another, this is an action with knowledge, with heart, and once for all. Keep this in mind, and you will see what it is to give yourselves to Jesus.

It is the present of *a thoughtful mind.* You remember the line in the hymn, " I'll pause before I further run, and give myself to God." Let every girl or boy pause, think, decide. Your parents gave you to God when they presented you at baptism. The name of the Father, Son, and Holy Ghost has been named upon you. You are under solemn covenant to be the Lord's. But *you* are not giving *your ownself*, unless calmly, earnestly, you give your Amen, knowing that you do so, and what your doing so means. Have you thus consented to take Jesus Christ to be your Master, and to be guided in all things by Him?

It is the present of *a loving heart*. That is no right gift which does not come from the heart. What is sought is your heart. There is a desk not far from me which has a secret drawer. The only thing needed is to find the spring. When you touch it, the drawer flies open. So it is with us. The secret drawer in our ownselves is the heart, and the spring of the heart is love. Whoever can touch that has the way to the drawer. Get any one's love, and you get that one's self. A poor Indian, listening to the story of Christ's love, was moved. The spring was touched. "Massa," he cried, "I give Jesus my gun." Then he thought of something more. " Massa, my dog." Something more still. "And here my buffalo skin." "Oh, but Jesus does not want these," said the missionary. "Then I will give myself." Love is never content until it says to the loved, "Here am I." The present of a trinket, of even the costliest article, will not suffice. Personal devotion, personal service—"Here am I"—that must be. Who of you has that for Christ?—your ownself given to the Lord.

Then follows the present *of this self once for all*. Is it not a shabby thing, when you intend to give a present, to be thinking how much you will need to give, and how much you may keep for yourself? Is it not a shabby thing also, when you have once given, to be asking or seeking back again? There is nothing of that if the gift comes from love. Now, let me remind you of a Bible-picture of true self-giving ; let me remind you of what was done by the priest in the old time to one who was to be cleansed. The priest took some of the blood of the trespass offering and put it on the tip of the right ear, and on the thumb of the right hand, and on the great toe of the right foot. What was that to teach? The *right* hand or foot, you know, is the strongest: all his strength was to be given. The ear is the organ of knowledge: all his power of receiving is to be given. Hand and foot are the ways of serving: all his capacity of serving, of working, of being of use is to be given. You have seen a crystal glass with a light in the middle. The light shines through every part of the glass. Well, when love to Christ is in the middle of the heart, its light shines through eye, ear, hands, lips, body, soul, spirit, saying to all, "Whatsoever He saith to you, do it." "Yea, let Him take all," is the cry.

"Take myself, and I will be,
Ever, only, all for Thee."

II. *The reason why you should give yourselves.*—When any one gives a present there is some reason for it. What is the reason for this gift? There are many reasons, but we shall only mention three:

(1) To give your ownselves to the Lord is right. God has a right to what He has made. Jesus the Redeemer has a right to His purchase. The Holy Spirit has a right to make your hearts His dwelling-place.

(2) It is for your good and happiness. You give yourself, and in so doing you have God himself. This is your happiness; it satisfies all your longings; it gives you an object to live for, which ennobles all your energy. "How sweet it is," said one who had given himself to the Lord in the gloom of the prison, "to hear the bird in the bosom sing!" So every boy and girl may have this singing bird, this fount of music and joy in the soul, if they first give themselves to the Lord.

(3) It is for the world's good and happiness. So it was with these Macedonians. No sooner had they made themselves over to Christ than they felt joined by a new love and desire to those for whom He died. They were poor, but in their poverty their liberality abounded. Christ needs such Christians now. This world would be a wholesomer and happier world if there were more of the love and unselfishness and free-souled giving which flows from the first gift—" their ownselves to the Lord."

J. M. L.

LXXVIII. God's Unspeakable Gift. 2 Cor. ix. 15.
"*Thanks be unto God for His unspeakable gift.*"

WHO does not like a "gift"? It may not be worth much, it may be far inferior to what we have every day of our lives, but there is something so pleasant about it—as in a garden, a single bright-winged butterfly attracts and entrances us more than the flowers do, however varied and beautiful they may be. Is it not because the flowers are our own, we are familiar with them; but the butterfly is a surprise, and we feel flattered by his free-will visit to us.

Who does not remember the toy presents of our childhood—the dolls, the Noah's ark, the hobby-horse; and then the more solid present of our boy or girlhood—the charming books, and the live animals entrusted to our care? and even when we are grown up we are not above them. No Christmas turkey eats so sweetly as that which arrives with a card and compliments; and no cloak and hood so become "baby" as those which a kind friend smuggled into the house in a band-box. The custom of making presents is as old as the Bible. We read of them in Genesis. Jacob, for instance, was remarkable for them. We read of his gift of a coat of many colours to Joseph; his gift of sheep and cattle to his brother Esau; his gift of "a little honey, spices, and almonds" to the ruler of Egypt. Araunah's kingly gift to his monarch is another Scripture example; so is the wise men's gift to the infant Jesus, and Mary's precious ointment poured on His head.

Now New Year is the season for gifts. The shop windows crammed full of them tell us that,—our own recollections tell us the same, and so do our feelings. Who, at such a time, does not wish to send presents to those we love? Let us then think awhile of God's "unspeakable gift" to us.

I. *Notice the Giver of the gift.*

St. Paul says that this is God: "Thanks be unto *God* for *His* unspeakable gift." Directly you have a gift you enquire, *who sent it?*—for a deal depends upon that—whether it comes from a friend or an enemy, from a poor person or a rich person. You would not expect much from those who are struggling for a living—it is almost painful to have them bring you of their poverty; but if the queen gives anything, it is taken for granted that it will be splendid—a gold watch, or a diamond pin, or a pearl bracelet. If she condescended to enter a cottage, people would be sure to look on the chair for a five-pound note or a pile of sovereigns. We should say, " She is so liberal, so noble, and so wealthy, she drops presents as an engine does sparks, wherever she goes."

Now God has " every good and perfect gift " in His hand; they are but the crumbs which fall from His table. He has been *giving from the foundation of the world*, and yet He is not in the least impoverished. How can a Creator be! A Being who by a word can turn water into wine, and multiply a baker's loaf into bread for thousands of hungry mouths! And He is as willing to give as He is able. It is His delight to load us with benefits. No mother is happier in kissing her darlings, decking them with her own furs on a cold morning, and seeing them leap for joy around her, than is our heavenly Father in dropping blessings on us, and crowning us with His tender mercies. And yet He is so infinite, and we so feeble; He is so holy, and we are so sinful. The Psalmist turned from considering the moon and the stars, to cry, " Lord, what is man, that Thou art mindful of him!" How well may we turn from considering God's unspeakable gift, and join in that cry!

But so it is. God *is* mindful of us—the glorious God; and the unspeakable gift is actually *His* present to us.

II. ·*Notice the gift itself.*

It is Jesus, the meek and lowly Jesus of the Gospels; and everything else such as forgiveness, grace, eternal life in Him.

A white carrier dove alighted upon a prisoner's floor; the prisoner said, " It is merely a pigeon;" and he threw it a crust, and then went on with his work. By-and-by he tried to drive it away. At length he was struck with its tameness, and catching it up, he found tied beneath its wing a letter, promising him aid in escaping, and enclosing a latch-key and a sum of money. The dove had been thrown in from the street on this errand.

Now, similarly, Jesus is nought to us until we receive Him into our bosoms as our own;—then, with and in Him, we have whatever is needful to deliver us from Satan, and insure us God's immediate and everlasting favour! God intends that He shall fetch us back to more than Adam lost in Eden; that He shall be our "righteousness" and our "strength." Jesus is yours and mine, if we open our hearts to Him. " Unto us a *child is given*," said the prophet Isaiah. The angel re-echoed that when he said to the shepherds, "*Unto you is born* this day in the city of David a Saviour, which is Christ the Lord." The Apostle is sending it on here to us, when he says, "Thanks be unto God for His unspeakable *gift*" to us,—Jesus.

It was the gift of a *Redeemer*, without whose death we must have perished.

It was the gift of a *Teacher*, without whose instruction we must have wandered on in ignorance,

It was the gift of a *Brother*, without whose sympathy we must have fainted at the prospect of duty and trial.

But this anticipates our third point.

III. *Notice the greatness of the gift.*

He could have given us myriads of things which would have excited our astonishment, but they could not have helped us. What could a planet or a comet have done for us, though they were to be called after us, and obey our orders? But He chose for us what was superior to the whole universe; just what we required, but what we could not have dared to hope for—He gave us His dearest, His best, His co-equal!

It was indeed an "unspeakable" gift, for it was *so amazing!* It was next to Jehovah, and it was Jehovah. It was the Owner of the flock giving Himself to rescue the flock from the snow-drift or the precipice. It was the Almighty giving Himself for His creatures. The cherubim and seraphim must have hidden their faces in dismay as they saw Him carrying His cross to Calvary! they had been wont to worship Him, to fly like lightning at His command.

It was "unspeakable," because he is so *surpassingly lovely.* He was lovely in His character, in His speech, in His actions, in His devotion to God and us. What guilt was there in Him? was He not without blemish; the express image of God? What love shot out of Him and hovered around Him! how His garments smelt of myrrh, aloes, and cassia, out of the ivory palaces!

It was "unspeakable," because it was *for such vile objects.* We were so mean and undeserving. How you would admire a princess who walked miles in a burning desert to relieve a company of lepers, or who sold herself into slavery to be of use to a plantation of miserable negroes! But Jesus did more than this for us, who were worms in comparison with Himself.

It is "unspeakable," because it does *such vast things for us.* Without it we were certainly doomed to hell; without it, it would have been impossible for God to pardon us.

It rids us of our burdens; it sheds peace abroad in our consciences; it unfolds to us the smile of God; it is our key to the grave; it is our title to mansions in the skies. When ages upon ages of joy unspeakable have gone by, we shall owe every moment of it to God's "unspeakable gift." Then,—

IV. *Notice the gratitude which becomes us.*

A bedridden Esquimaux said to a missionary, "When you begin to read to me about Jesus, sir, I am as hard as a block of ice; when you finish and go away, I am melted into water." "The story of Jesus," said an African, "is my hymn, my prayer, my Bible. I weep over it when I can't sing about it; and I sing over it when I can't weep about it. This is true, that I thank God for it from the soul of my foot to the top of my head."

And what are we about? Where is our harp? Can we not thank God for it with *our lips?* Ought we not to try to praise Him for it when we wake and ere we sleep, as well as in our churches and chapels? Closet melodies should be as frequent as closet petitions. Have Watts, and Wesley, and Cowper written their exquisite verses for private use in vain? Do they never rise to God from our lips?

Can we not thank him with our *spirits?* When there is no music outwardly, there may be music within. Pious affection may be kindled by recollection, and glow and burn as a fire; and God can make its secret blaze "under the fig-tree."

Lastly, can we not thank him by *our conduct;* by walking before Him so blamelessly and wisely that we may testify to others how faithful His promises are, how easy His yoke, how real and powerful His presence with those who have accepted His unspeakable gift. Endeavour to "adorn" your Christian profession; and then, assuredly, you will be thanking Him for it.

But *have* you accepted this unspeakable gift yet? Suppose I met a royal messenger returning from your door with an ornament which an empress might be proud to wear, and saying: " This is a gift from Her Majesty to that young lady who bears Her Majesty's name, but I cannot obtain admission; I have knocked till I am tired; this is the fifth or sixth attempt at intervals. She evidently listens; but she is too careless or engaged to attend. Once she glanced at it from behind the curtains; and once she unfastened the lock, and was just slipping the bolt, but her pet dog barked, or her parrot whistled, and she sauntered back to them; so I fear I must report it to Her Majesty, and she will change her purpose regarding it." What should I say to that messenger for you? How could I excuse you and plead for you? But beware, lest you are doing that very thing to God's messengers who are commissioned to urge upon you His unspeakable gift.

Is that to be trifled with? Is that to be declined till it suit your convenience? Oh, by the awful consequences of missing it, I beseech you to claim and clasp it as your own this moment!

J. B.

LXXIX. Sowing. GAL. vi. 7. *"Whatsoever a man soweth, that shall he also reap."*

JUST as the early months of the year are the sowing-time of the gardener and farmer, on which the flowers and the vegetables of the summer and the crops of the harvest will depend, so the early years of your life are *your* sowing-time, which will go far to determine what the harvest of your later years and of your eternity shall be (Gal. vi. 7).

I can fancy some mischievous boy scattering vegetable seeds—peas, or beans, or lettuce seeds—over the flower-beds in spring; or flower seeds—Indian cress, or wallflower,

R

or candytuft, or marigolds—over the vegetable-beds. The gardener would call out to him, "Stop, boy; do you know what you are doing? You are *sowing*. It is not as if you were scattering clay, or stones, or bits of wood. These seeds will *grow;* they will spring up again; and what a sight the garden will be!"

Now *your life* is just like that. It may seem mere amusement to some. You may scarcely think what you are doing. But it is as really sowing as in the case I have supposed.

I. The sowers—who are they? We are *all* sowers, every one of us. In the other sowing, it is the farmer or the gardener; but in the sense in which we are now looking at it, everybody is a sower. Every one who *lives, sows.* You are a sower. You are sowing. Your life is a planting of seeds, good or bad, which must all, sooner or later, bear fruit after their kind. I wish I could get you to believe and remember, "I am *a sower!* my life is *a sowing!*"

II. The seed—what is it? Of course, if we are sowers, there must be *seed* which we sow. There can be no real sowing without seed. I have seen infant scholars going through the different trades, imitating the workmen in each. I have heard them singing, "This is the way we sow the corn," suiting the action to the word. But it was not real sowing, for there was no *seed.* It was mere imitation. It was *playing* at sowing. But ours is *a real sowing,* for there is *real seed.* And if you ask, "What is the seed?" I answer, *Everything that we do.* My actions are all *seeds,* which I am planting in the field of my *life,* in the garden of my *life.* My work, my play, my lessons at home and at school, during the week or on the Lord's day, my reading, my amusements—each is *a seed* which I am sowing, for this life and for the life to come. And when it comes to an end, your life will be like a field, every part of which is sown with seed.

Have you ever thought of this? Nothing you do is *done with.* You may have forgotten it. But it is no more done with than the seed that is buried in the ground, and will spring up by-and-by. "*Whatsoever* a man *soweth,*" is just the same as saying, "*whatsoever* a man *does.*"

III. The character or kind of the sowing—what is it? All the sowing must be *one of two kinds.* There is endless variety of seed. If you were to take a seedsman's catalogue, you would find an almost endless list of seeds and roots. And so there is no limit to the number and variety of actions which we do. But they may all be divided into two classes. The one is "sowing *to the flesh;* " the other is "sowing *to the Spirit.*" Instead of calling them *good* or *bad*—instead of calling us *good* or *bad sowers*, God's Word divides us thus : " he that soweth *to his flesh,*" and " he that soweth *to the Spirit.*"

"Sowing to the flesh" is just doing what is pleasing to *ourselves*, following our own likings, gratifying our own inclinations, walking in the way of our own heart. " Sowing to the Spirit " is doing, or seeking to do, what is pleasing to *God*, having regard to His will, His law, His glory. Let us take anything we have done during the past year, anything we are about to do now, and ask ourselves, Is *this* sowing "to the flesh" or "to the Spirit?"

That question may be asked concerning everything we do, and *may be answered.* As we are always sowing one way or another, so it is always either *to the flesh* or *to the Spirit. Which is it?* Everything you ever did was the one or the other. You will find the works of the flesh and the fruits of the Spirit mentioned in Gal. v. 19-23. Where there is still the old heart, where there is no true love to God, where Jesus is still kept out of the heart, all we do is a "sowing to the flesh." When the heart has been surrendered to Him, the "sowing to the Spirit" begins. What is *your* sowing to be?

J. H. W.

LXXX. Children of Light. Eph. v. 8. *"Walk as children of light."*

THE word "walk" here is not used in the ordinary sense of taking a walk. The word used to mean in old English a man's manner or habit of life. And so St. Paul says to all the children of Christ, " Let your life be worthy of the One whose name you bear. Walk as children of light."

Now what is meant by "children of light"? It means children who have the same nature as the children of God. Children of darkness are those who are dark and bad in their hearts ; children of the light are those who have the very nature of light.

Now there are three things in the making of light, three things which ought to be what we call the characteristics of the children of light. The light dispels darkness, and always brings joy and hope and opportunity of work, and always shines for the sake of others. Now there are, children, three things in which you are to show yourselves as children of light. All living things love light. You know how the birds rejoice and sing when the light appears ; and some love the light so that you will see them waiting on the side of the mountain where the sun rises and in the evening they will gather on the side of the mountain where the sun sets, and men have seen these birds pass from one bough to another in the tree as the sun sinks down, so as to retain the light of the sun as long as possible. And so all living things love light ; but the light we are to love and walk in as children of it, is not the sun that can set, but the Sun of Righteousness that can never go down on any distant horizon. The light you are to walk in is, remember, children, pureness, unselfishness, truth, love, the light that comes from the very heart of God Himself.

This light dispels darkness. You cannot have darkness and light together. You know that in the world. You know that, when you open the shutter of the dark room, and the light streams in, the darkness must go. It is just so with the light we have from God. My dear friends, these two things cannot be together,—selfishness and unselfishness, right and wrong, truth and falsehood, purity and impurity ; these things cannot be together. Where the light of the one comes, then the darkness of the other must disappear. You must give up all darkness when once the light of God's love and mercy streams into your life and dispels darkness.

Have you ever watched in the sick room and heard the sick lips say, " Is it nearly light ? How long will it be before morning ? " If so, you would know the value of the light. It brings with it joy to those who can work, and opportunity for labour. When the sun begins to rise, man goeth forth to his work, and the city streets, which had been so silent, get alive, and the country becomes alive with the song of living birds. And so it will be when this very light of God shines into your heart. It will bring you the joy of knowing that you are walking in the light of God's countenance. And then remember the uses of the light. First, the light must dispel the darkness; the light must bring joy and activity; and the third point is, that the light never shines for its own sake. Do you think that the candle burns for its own sake? It is alight to give light, not to keep light. And the sun. Do you think the sun shines for its own sake? Was not the sun given to give light on the earth? And so it will be with this light. When this gets into your heart you will reflect light, like the stars and the moon reflect the light from the sun. We shall reflect in our lives, for the sake of others, the light of God's righteousness; and when you have this light in your hearts then let it shine from your hearts in deeds of tenderness and mercy and love, to make glad and joyous the lives of others. And so St. Paul said to his children, and we say, "Walk as children of light."

We are told of a figure of a king with a harp in his hand. He loved the harp so dearly, for every morning when the sun shone upon it its strings gave forth wondrous music. Your hearts are like that, and as the Sun of Righteousness shines upon them they ought to make music for God's sake. The day shall come when all the hearts of men will be as harps. The knowledge of the love of God shall cover the earth even as the waters cover the sea, and there shall spring from every human heart a song of gratitude for Christ's sacrifice, and endless joy and abundant praise.

O children, you are not children of darkness but children of the light. You have been purchased with an awful price, the blood of Christ. Let the light drive away darkness from your souls. Let it bring joy and work with it in your lives, and let the light shine upon others so that men may see it in your works, and so that they may glorify your Father who is in Heaven. Amen. T. T. S.

LXXXI. Obedient Children. EPH. vi. 1. *"Children, obey your parents in the Lord, for this is right."*

I WAS ministering one day at a sick-bed. The sick person was an old man, weary and worn out with the toil of a long life. I read to him the story of Enoch walking with God, and Cowper's hymn, "Oh, for a closer walk with God!" When I had finished, the old man said in tones of Christian penitence, "Minister, I wish my life had been like that hymn." I thought the old man's words were a beautiful description of obedience. An obedient child may be called a child whose whole life is like a hymn of praise to the glory of God.

I. *Obedient children are the children who obey the voice of the Lord.*—To obey means to hear, to listen, to attend to. But there must be something to hear, something to listen to, something to attend to. What is that something? It is the voice of the Lord through which He makes known to us His will. I knew a mother who was giving her boy an advice as he was leaving her home in the country to begin life in a great city. She gave him words of warning, words of instruction, words of loving cheer; but she summed up her parting words with this wise counsel—"And remember, John, always to serve the Lord, and you will best serve yourself, and your master, and your father, and me." This is the great rule of the life of Christ's obedient children. They speak the truth, for that is the will of God. They are honest, for that is the will of God. They are kind to one another, for that is the will of God. They honour their father and mother, for that is the will of God. They are diligent in any work they are called to do, for that is the will of God. What is not the will of God they dare not do. When they are doing the will of God they are doing all that man can require of them.

II. *Obedient children are the children who obey the Lord because they love Him.*—A gentleman once met a little girl carrying a big baby boy on her back on a hot summer day along a dusty country road. Her face was glowing with heat, and streamlets of perspiration were running down it, and her hair was flowing in the summer wind. The gentleman was struck with the romping fresh child, but thought she was overburdened. He stopped her and asked if the baby was not too heavy. She looked up through a mist of golden hair and a wave of smiles and said: "Oh, he is not the least heavy, he is ma brither." Love was the spring that made her burden light, her duty well done; and love is the secret of the obedience of all Christ's children. The obedience that is born of fear is hard, heartless duty, not good for ourselves and not glorifying to God. The obedience that springs from love is free, happy service, the service of children, not the service of slaves. God wants all that we do for Him to proceed out of the love of the heart that He has made clean and glad by His grace. What we do for Him depends greatly on how we do it. He thinks more of a mite that unselfish love gives than of a million that is given from selfish fear.

III. *Obedient children are the children who obey the Lord in all things.*—Children are sometimes tempted to think of God only on Sundays or at times when engaged in religious services—that He is to be obeyed in worship. But He is to be obeyed in work, and in all the work that His children are called to undertake. There is a story told of a very small congregation in America. It consisted of only twelve persons, but they all agreed to do something in the service of God. They had a meeting to arrange plans and appoint "to every one his work." They began at the oldest and came down the list of members to the youngest. Some agreed to teach the young, some to visit the poor, some to conduct "little prayer meetings," some to circulate tracts. This was all good, useful work. The youngest member was a servant girl. She was asked what she would undertake. She was very shy and felt herself very helpless, but she modestly answered, "I will try and serve God in the trifles of my common life." It is said that the old minister, on hearing this, replied, "Brethren, the youngest member will beat us all." That "youngest member" certainly teaches us all a lesson. To serve God in the "trifles of our common life" is the duty and the privilege of God's obedient children. We are called upon to be living epistles of the Lord Jesus Christ, and on every side of our life there must be written in Christian deeds the gospel we have believed.

IV. *Obedient children are the children who find in obedience its own reward.*—It is not wise always to be asking, "What wages am I to get for serving God?" I remember sitting beside an aged minister who had lived a long useful life. He spoke of the many things that God had done for him, of his own deep peace and the joy of a happy trust; and he spoke of heaven. He was going there with clear bright hope. But he said a thing about heaven that made my young heart wonder. " I do not think of heaven as a place where God will reward me for what I have done for Him, but as a place where I will praise Him for what He has done for me." Surely this is the right view of looking at the rewards of obedience. Everything we do for God should be regarded as an oblation of praise for what He has done for us. At the end of the page we come back to the truth with which it opened—an obedient child is a child whose whole life is like a beautiful hymn of praise to the glory of God ; and the reward of obedience is in being made by grace and truth like a Christian song. We are called upon to keep the commandments of the Lord,—His grace in Jesus is given for this great end, and the Scriptures tell us that " in keeping of them there is great reward."

G. W.

LXXXII. The Children's Book. EPH. vi. 17. *"The word of God."*

EVERY New Year's Day is like a milestone on our journey towards eternity. On one side of the milestone we can read the number of the miles we have already passed. But can we read on the other side how many miles are still before us? No, we do not know whether many years or only a few days will bring us to the end of our earthly pilgrimage. But if we love God, we may read this inscription on the other side : " Surely goodness and mercy shall follow me all the days of my life, and I will dwell in the house of the Lord for ever."

On looking over the past, resting at a new milestone, I have beside me one good and faithful companion, who has been with me since my early childhood. He has been a wise counsellor, an unerring guide, a patient and wonderful teacher of things earthly and heavenly, a loving comforter,—in short, everything that you could desire in a friend. His voice was sometimes very solemn and grave, but so earnest and affectionate that I could not forget his words ; and, because they were truth and love, I had to return to him and acknowledge my sin and folly, and ask him to continue to guide me, though it was by rebuke. This friend understood all my thoughts, and, what is more wonderful, he understands that hidden and mysterious thing the heart, out of which the thoughts come. He led me to the fountain of life, of peace, and of love; he showed me how God forgives sin and renews the sinner's heart; he spoke to me of God's wonderful works and acts in the past, and of His great purposes in the future. And in all this he always spoke of Jesus Christ, the Son of God, the Saviour and Shepherd, who died for the flock, and lives now to bless them.

Now, when I was a child, he spoke to me as a child. He told me beautiful, wonderful, and touching stories, which I can never forget. I fancy even now that I hear his voice as I heard it then, when he told me of the creation of heaven and earth; of man, made in the image of God; of the garden of Eden; of righteous Abel, the first shepherd and martyr; of Noah, how he feared and trusted God, and built the ark. I think I still see the rainbow as I saw it in my mind when he first told me that God set it in the clouds, to assure us of his mercy; and that I still see the stars, as he told me God showed them to Abraham, and promised him to be the father of many nations. And so many other stories—of Joseph, of Moses, of David, of Daniel; and in all these stories the first and chief and last was always God.

And as I grew older, this friend appeared to me to grow greater, wiser, more wonderful; and I am still a little child before him, and he teaches, corrects, and guides me.

Now you know that this friend is the Bible. I like to look at the books which I read as a child. But the Bible is the only book that grows with us; and, when we come to die, we still feel as little children and disciples and learners. The Bible is indeed, as the word itself tells us, *the* Book. There is none like it. It is given to us of God, to lead us to God. It is written by the inspiration of the Holy Ghost, the good, loving, and infinite Spirit. It reveals to us Jesus Christ, the Son of God, the Saviour of sinners, the heir of all things. It tells us how to glorify God, and to enjoy Him for ever. It tells us the wonderful history of creation and of the fall. It tells us the wonderful history of God's ancient people. It tells us the most wonderful history of all times,—the life, death, resurrection and ascension of Jesus Christ. It tells us what will be the end of all things, when Jesus will return, and God will make new heavens and a new earth, wherein dwelleth righteousness. This book is given to us of God, because He loves us, and it is to make us wise unto salvation, by faith, which is in Christ Jesus.

I. God intends and wishes children to read His word. God never forgets the little ones. When He brought the Jews out of Egypt, He especially remembered the little ones. When He instituted the festivals, He remembered the children, and foresaw that they would ask questions as to the meaning of the ceremonies, and commanded the parents to instruct them. When He gave the five books of Moses, He commanded the fathers to read them to and with the children, and to speak to them about His great and merciful works. God wishes children to know, love and serve Him. Think of Samuel, and how God spoke to him. Think of Josiah. "Josiah was eight years old when he began to reign, and he did that which was right in the sight of the Lord." Fancy a little boy, only eight years old, being raised to the throne. He was one of the greatest reformers that ever lived, and from his tender childhood he loved God. Think of Timothy, who knew the Scriptures from a child; and when his great teacher and friend, the Apostle Paul, was about to leave him, he wrote to him not to be afraid of false teachers and perilous times, but to cleave to the word of God, which he had known from the days of his childhood.

II. God has therefore caused the Bible to be written in a simple and attractive way. There are no stories so beautiful, so wonderful, so interesting, as the Bible stories. There is no book in which we find such grand and touching poetry, such terse and deep sayings. Here is something for every one—the soldier, who likes to read of battles; the sailor, who likes to read of storms and shipwrecks; the lover of nature, who likes descriptions of scenery and of the glories of creation; the philosopher, who likes to study the anatomy of the human heart; the sorrowful, the weak, the sick, the aged, the dying, all find here food for their minds, and comfort for their souls.

God repeats in the Bible what is important, that we may

understand it clearly, that we may not forget it. He very often repeats and sums up what He has said before. So the ten commandments are summed up into two; and many short and simple verses contain a great many pages of the Bible condensed. John iii. 16 Luther calls "the Bible in miniature." Then the types and parables are like pictures and models—striking, attractive, compact, easily remembered, and yet very deep.

III. The Bible is a deep book, and we never can exhaust it. But if we know *Jesus as our Saviour*, we know the sum and substance of the Bible. I was one day in Carlsruhe, the capital of Baden. The duke has a palace there, and all the streets in the city lead to this palace. The city is built like a fan: wherever you are, if you go on a little you come to the palace. It is thus in the Bible: all prophets and apostles testify of Jesus, that He is the only Saviour and Lord.

IV. Lastly, the Bible is the children's book. *Only* children can understand and profit by it. Except we become like little children, we cannot enter into the kingdom of God. When we are humble, when we feel that we are very ignorant, that our hearts are very sinful, that we are very unworthy, that we are very weak, then God the Holy Ghost teaches us out of His own book, and makes us very happy in Jesus.

A. S.

LXXXIII. Lights. PHIL. ii. 15, 16. *"Shine as lights in the world; holding forth the word of life."*

MANY of you will remember what is written in "Pilgrim's Progress" about the shining ones; how, when Christian and Hopeful drew near to the great deep river of Death, they met two men, whose raiment shone like gold, and whose faces shone as the light; and how the same two shining ones waited for the pilgrims when they came out of the river, to lead them into the city. You may have thought when reading this that it was only a picture of angels, and had nothing to do with you. It has a great deal to do with every one, whether old or young, who confesses that Jesus Christ is Lord. Does not the text say that you are all to be shining ones? Well, let us try to gather some portion of the truth which St. Paul would teach us, by answering three questions, beginning with three short words which you can all keep in your minds—*Where? What? How?*

I. *Where* are the lights to shine? "In the world," is the reply. Our blessed Saviour, when He was about to leave the world, would not pray that His beloved disciples might be taken away with Him out of it; all He asked was that they might be kept from everything which would dim the brightness of His glory in them. He sent them into the world that they might shine. Now, think—What kind of place is it into which you send or in which you set a light? Is it not a place either dark or dangerous? This world, in which it is Christ's will that we should live and move, is full of darkness and full of danger; therefore you and I are to shine.

The world is a *dark* place. Very lately you got all sorts of presents, and cards, and kind greetings, the expression in which was, "A merry Christmas!" Why do you associate Christmas with great joy? Is it not because, in the words of Isaiah, "the people that walked in darkness have seen a great light"? My dear young readers, the best mirth that you can put into this weary world of ours is of the same kind—a shining in darkness. Yes, darkness! When you pass through the streets in the day-time, you see here and there iron posts supporting lamps. *Then* you don't feel the good of these lamps. But by-and-by, as night approaches, you are grateful to the lamplighter; you understand the use of the lamps he has lighted. That is the very use we are to be in this world. It lies in darkness because it lies in wickedness. You may have seen what is called a missionary map, with a great many black spaces in it—these black spaces marking out the countries and islands which the light of the gospel has not yet reached. How thick the darkness sometimes is! When Narayan Sheshadri was in this country, I heard him say—"I was brought up to believe that I myself was a god on earth; that all men, women, and children ought to worship me." This, because he belonged to a particular caste! And you know what frightful superstitions and horrid cruelties prevail in Africa and China—in a great, far too great, part of the world—among the hundreds of millions of heathens. Is that all the darkness? Alas! there are spaces as black as those on the map in Christian countries,—ay, close to your own happy homes. Wherever Christ is not known, loved, obeyed, there is the shadow of death. And every one whom I address should be like the lights which God created to divide the day from the night; shining as a light whose very presence marks out separation from sin—" a light in the world."

If I add, the world is full of *danger*, as well as darkness, you will see an additional need for the light. Some of you may have sailed in the lovely Firth of Clyde, or out of the harbour of Leith, going north or south. Don't you recollect noticing, here and there along the coast-line, revolving lights? These lights are all marked in the captain's chart. He knows, as he looks at one—" There is a bad reef there; I must keep clear of it." And so, as to every one, it is a warning or a guide. I cannot resist telling a story about a lighthouse keeper: it is so often told that you may have heard it, but I must risk the repetition. One day the light would not revolve. What did the keeper do? He ran to the right position, and with his hand kept revolving the light until he was utterly wearied; then he called another man : and thus, all night long, the light was kept in motion. Afterwards a friend spoke to him about his anxiety. "Why, sir," he answered, "there might be a hundred seamen looking out from the storm to catch a gleam of this light. If it don't move, it may be mistaken for another; and in their uncertainty they may lose the channel and be wrecked." My young friends, there are dangers very many; rocks and quicksands, some so sunken that they are not discovered until the soul's peace and health are destroyed on them. And each of you should feel as that lighthouse keeper felt—" There may be some looking out from the darkness, and if they don't see a true light in me, or if by what I say and do they are turned away from God and lose the right channel, they may be wrecked, and the fault will be mine." Be sure of it, each boy or girl is, to some other boy or girl, a light. You have two hands : use the one to keep back from the danger, from what is bad and ugly; use the other to point and help to what is good and right. Some years ago a young man went up from Aberdeen to London. He was taken into the employment of an eminent publisher. One afternoon Mr. Irving came into the shop. He noticed the youth; and on being told that he came from Scotland, went kindly to him, and said: "Young man, you have come to a very wicked place,"—that was the hand holding back; "but," he added solemnly, "the grace of God is in it,"—that was the hand bidding onward. The young fellow never forgot the words; amidst the dangers of the great capital, the memory of that saying was as a light to him. God help you and me to be such lights in this world, so full of darkness and so full of danger.

II. But it is time to think, not merely of where the light is to shine, but also of *what* the light is. And I will tell you something about the phrase "lights," as it is used by the Apostle, which at once explains this. The phrase means *luminaries*; it is the same phrase as in Genesis i. 14, "Let there be *lights* in the firmament of heaven:" so that you see the Christian is to be like one of those stars that "come twinkling one by one from out the azure sky." A hymn, with which no doubt you are familiar, thus gives the thought :—

> "Make me thy child—a child of God,
> Washed in my Saviour's precious blood :
> And my whole heart, from sin set free,
> *A little vessel full of thee.*
>
> "A star of early dawn, and bright,
> Shining within thy sacred light ;
> A beam of grace to all around ;
> A little spot of hallowed ground."

There are two things which I would like you to remember about these luminaries.

They are *reflecting lights*. I referred you to the first chapter of Genesis, which speaks of the creation of all things. Well, if you read that chapter, you will find that on the first day God created light, and on the fourth day He made lights. People used to cry, "How strange! How could there be light without light bodies?" Science has confirmed the word of the Bible. And the account in Genesis is true of another creation,—"If any man be in Christ, he is a new creature." Christ is the Light. Whose is in Christ is a light only because he received the Light. Until Christ comes into and dwells in the heart, the heart is dark. When you go out at night and look up to the moon and stars, you exclaim, How glorious! Yes; but the glory is not in the moon—it is a dark body, with no light except what it gets from the sun. Jesus Christ is to us what the sun is to the moon. It is He who is and who gives light, and all our shining can be only the sending beyond us of the beam which has come from Himself. It is when our heart really opens to Jesus; when "the old, old story of Jesus and His love" ceases to be a mere story and becomes a living truth in us; when we are turned right toward the Saviour, feeling ourselves poor lost sinners, but knowing and seeing in Him a perfect Saviour and a perfect salvation, and we give ourselves as we are to Him as He is, it is *then* that the light is received, and all things become new in their interest, and claim, and blessing, as, having received, we walk *thenceforth* reflecting the light of the Lord. Blessed *then*—may it be fulfilled in you!

Now, this further as to the *thenceforth*. The lights are a *growing, increasing kind of light*. They shine "more and more unto the perfect day." Long centuries ago there was a glorious temple in Jerusalem, and in that temple there was a fire, as to which the charge given to the priests was, "You are to keep it always burning; it is never to go out." Now, the light which Christ gives is to be always burning and shining, Sunday and Monday, at home and from home, in health and in sickness, at play and in church, all times and all ways giving forth something of Jesus' spirit, and becoming more and more brilliant the longer it shines. Therefore, if we would be lights in the world, we must be getting always new and fresh supplies of light from Jesus. And we shall get if we obey Him with our whole heart, and trust Him fully, and pray to Him, and read His Holy Word. He will give us then His Holy Spirit to dwell in us,—to be, as it were, a new anointing, a new light of life every morning, making us better and truer and wiser the longer we live.

III. One point remains,—*How* the light is to shine. We often speak of persons shining. Such and such a boy, we say, shone at school; or such and such a one shines in society. That is not the way of the shining to which we are called. That kind of shining is often false and ruinous. One evening I saw the harbour light kindled at St. Andrews. "What a mercy that light is!" I thought. "Ah!" said the gentleman with whom I was walking, "sometimes it betrays. The seaman mistakes it for the light at the mouth of the Tay, makes for it, and finds out, at a terrible cost, his mistake." All shining which springs from mere ambition, or love of gaiety, or love of the world, or selfishness, betrays. And there are many such betrayers, many such antichrists in the world. May you be delivered from them!

In the first clause of the sixteenth verse, you find the manner of the Christian shining. "*Holding* forth the *word of life.*" We are so to let this candle shine out, so to hold forth what we are taught in the blessed word of God, in our lives, in our talk and walk, in our conduct towards those whom we may meet, in what we are and do, that they may see a light of heaven in us, and glorify our Father which is in heaven.

This is how you are to shine. And, remember, you *are* to shine. What is God's mind about the stars? He lights them for us and for His world. What do you do? And we have light in Christ not that we may live nursing a solitary goodness, but that we may let light go out from us. Would that we were all taught of God to hold forth the Word of Life to the perishing around us.

J. M. L.

LXXXIV. Giants. 1 Tim. vi. 12. "*Fight the good fight of faith.*"

"I wish that I had a 'sword of sharpness' and 'shoes of swiftness,' and could go about killing off big ugly giants like that Jack in my book. I like my giant-killer book better than the stories of good boys that get ill and die. I would like to live and do something. The giants were horrid, putting men and women in their dungeons, and devouring up children. Blunderbore and Cormoran were the worst. It is a good thing that they were stupid and greedy, and ate too much, and went to sleep often. Jack was splendid; so clever and never afraid, and everybody said,

> 'This is the valiant Cornishman,
> That slew the giant Cormoran.'

But that was long ago, and there are no giants nowadays."

Are there not, my boy? Indeed there are; all, I suspect, that ever there were. There are a great many horrid, cruel giants that do sore mischief to men, women, and children, and you will not require to travel to Wales or to Cornwall to find them. *They are everywhere about.* You may find and fight them, if you choose. In fact I may tell you that you will be obliged to fight them. You cannot get out of it. If you do not conquer them, they will be sure to conquer you. One way or other it is certain to be. Either *you* must get the upper hand or *they* will. There are some that are especially cruel to children.

I. One is called BADTEMPER. When he gets hold of any boy *he puts him under enchantment.* He alters his face so that he would not know himself in the glass; knits his brows, makes his eyes glare, changes his voice into a bear's gruff growl or a wolf's howl, makes him feel like to strike every one and break everything round about, turns all the wholesome blood in his body into vinegar and gall, puts toad's venom on his lips, and tortures him until he feels himself the most miserable little wretch existing.

That is a very bad giant indeed, and a very hard one to get the better of. He comes to life again and again, when you think he is finished. But you must by all means be sure to conquer him if you hope to have any happiness in this world.

II. Another is a wicked, two-faced giant, called FALSEHOOD. The boy who, unfortunately, falls into his power, *loses immediately the proper use of his tongue.* Two little words in particular he grows unable to say. They are quite short words, one has only two letters and the other three; one is "yes," and the other "no." But the poor fellow is no longer able to say these at the proper time, and in the right place. He says "yes" when it should be "no," and "no" when it should be "yes." His tongue stammers and hesitates, and tells things all wrong, and upside down, and not as they really are. His description is blurred and twisted, like a bad photograph. No one can trust his story. His cheeks grow red and hot and uncomfortable, and he is in such a flutter of fear that *he is afraid*

S

even of his own father and mother. I am very sorry for the boy who gets into the clutches of this giant. It is a kind of madness, and he may not get out of it all his life.

III. Then there is DISOBEDIENCE. But by this time I daresay you have found me out, and know what I mean. *The giants you have to fight with are all kinds of sins and evils.* So, without making a giant of it, disobedience is another of the things you must strive against. Remember that *everybody has to obey*, and is happiest when obeying. Your father has to obey; the Queen even. Perhaps you imagine that when you are older you will then do as you like. Not at all, nobody can do that. The soldier obeys his officer, the sailor his captain. In all the offices and shops somebody gives the orders, and the rest obey. On the railway everybody, all the guards and porters, look to the time-table and obey it. If all of them did as they pleased, sent the trains and stopped them anywhere and at any time, such collisions and accidents would be! Therefore, do not be stiffnecked and rebellious. Obey your parents, and when older *obey your conscience and your God;* otherwise there will be confusion and terrible accidents.

IV. Then there is SELFISHNESS. Strive against it, think of others, be kind and helpful. It does not matter how young and little you are. You can always do something in that way. A mouse, you know, once did a good turn to a lion. You can watch baby, or run an errand upstairs to spare old, tired limbs. Opposite the house where I once lived stood the cottage of a poor widow, with a few flowers outside, that were all her delight. The woman took ill, and lay long in bed. Many people showed her kindness. From my window I could see the doctor go in at the door, and kind ladies who brought comforts both for body and mind. But there was one who showed her a very real, unobtrusive piece of kindness. It was a little neighbour girl. She did not call to inquire, nor go in at the door, nor make herself seen in any way. But she came bringing her watering-pot and watered the poor woman's flowers, that would certainly have died in the hot summer sun. This she continued to do every day, till their owner was better again. The very first day the widow was able, she came tottering out to see her pets, and there they were, all alive and well. I wonder if she ever knew who kept them alive! I do not know.

But I saw the little girl do this, and remembered it, And I know God saw it and remembered it, and has written it in His great Book. Every kind thing you do is certainly written there.

I could tell you of some more—giants shall we call them again? But these are the worst that you will probably meet, and if you get the better of these, you are not likely to have much trouble with any others. Old people encounter a few others. For instance, I saw a man the other day knocked about and abused by Giant INTEMPERANCE in a way to make you shudder. He tossed him from one side of the way to the other, bemired him, tore him, disfigured him, and at last threw him before the wheels of a car and ended him. I know a giant called MAMMON who keeps a great many poor slaves, chained neck and heel, grubbing all their life long in his dirty mines, till, with the constant glitter of gold and silver, the unhappy creatures lose the power of their eyesight for anything else in this world. But there is no need to say anything of such in the meantime, and when you have slain those I have mentioned, you will have grown so skilful in the business that you will polish them off quite easily when you come to meet them.

I hope that all your life you will be a brave fighter against *every kind of wrong and evil*, both for your own sake and for everybody's, and will help to make the world, and this part of it we live in, a safer and better and happier place for us all. There is a great deal to do. Oh, the groans and miseries of men, women and children! Some houses are only *giants' dungeons*, where the inmates lie in darkness and squalor and horrid cruelty. Help to get everybody out, if you can, into the sunshine. Some are doing the best they can. I hope you will do better than **any**, and perhaps some day people may say of you,

> "This is the valiant British man,
> That strives for goodness all he can."

T. P. J.

LXXXV. The Word of God. 2 Tim. iii. 16. "*All Scripture is given by inspiration of God, and is profitable for doctrine, for reproof, for correction, for instruction in righteousness.*"

Our subject is the Word of God, and we shall consider some of its titles.

I. God's Word is "a hammer."

See that block of whinstone, and now see that little instrument lying on it—a hammer. Yonder skilful workman can with it break that block into pieces, which can then be applied to any purpose that he may think them fit for.

When our first parents were created their hearts were soft, and therefore easily impressed by Divine things, and their affections were pure and warm, but when sin entered and took possession, the heart became as hard as the hardest stone and the affections became like ice. And so they naturally continue to be. When, however, the Word of God is duly applied to the hardest heart, it breaks it into shivers, after which it is formed anew like Christ. This is "not by might, nor by power, but by My Spirit saith the Lord."

II. "The Sword of the Spirit."

Each one, young and old, who has come to the Lord's side has been enlisted to be a soldier of the cross. A soldier must have on his armour when placed before the enemy; so, to be of use, we must have on our armour constantly, for the enemies—the devil, sinful thoughts and desires—are always in our way. We have five pieces of armour—the helmet, the coat of mail, girdle or belt, sandals, and, over all, "the shield of faith." These are all for defence. We have only one for attack—the Sword of the Spirit, the Word of God.

See Jesus, thrice tempted in the wilderness by Satan, and each time smiting him with His sword, and thereby completely vanquishing and silencing the great enemy of souls. The three strokes of the sword were taken by Jesus from that wonderful book Deuteronomy.

The Bible is a "*two-edged sword.*" The edges are the Law and the Gospel. The Law wounds but cannot heal.

The Gospel, be it in the Old Testament or the New, wounds, and, when applied by the grace of God, can heal.

III. The Word of God "a *Lamp*."

How we are cheered by light when it causes the darkness to pass away and shows us all around. But a lamp, though made of the finest gold, filled with the purest oil, and having the best of wicks, would be of no use to us in our hand in a dark place unless a flame were applied to it. The Bible is the darkest and most mysterious book in the world if it is not lighted for us by the Holy Spirit, but when thus illuminated it is infinitely the brightest book, and shows us clearly the way through this dark world of sin and sorrow to our Father's habitation in glory, where there shall be no darkness, but where the Lord shall be our everlasting light.

IV. The Bible "*a Looking-glass or Mirror.*"

When first we look into the Word of God we see our own character, and read that we are poor and miserable, and wretched and blind, and naked of holiness, and stand in need of all things. We also see, as if in the background of the past, men and women whose lives are recorded therein. We admire much in them, but they are not perfect. There is One, however, completely holy and loving, and altogether loveable. This is the Son of God, who casts a lustre over all.

We see His marvellous goodness to us in the marks of the nails and spear in His hands, His feet, and His side, and we are filled with gratitude and love to Him, and desire earnestly to be like Him; and so we commune with Him in His Word, this mirror, and grow liker and liker unto Him, even though only seeing Him as through a glass, dimly, until we become perfected in Him, and then see Him in glory as He is.

The hammer and sword, to be effectual, must be applied by the infinitely wise and Almighty Spirit, and He alone can light up the lamp and the mirror.

Jesus, the Friend of little children, tells us our heavenly Father "will give the Holy Spirit to them (whosoever they are) that ask Him."

There are millions on millions of little children, whose souls are as valuable as ours, groping their way through this dark world towards eternity, who have never seen even the outside of a Bible. What a cheerless desert this world would be to us without the "Word." Let us earnestly seek that it may be soon brought within the reach of the whole human family, so that each may have it in his power to say, like you and me,

> "Holy Bible, book Divine!
> Precious treasure! thou art mine."

R. F. F.

LXXXVI. Faithful Children. TITUS i. 6. "*Faithful children.*"

THE island of Crete, now called Candia, once had a hundred churches. They all began through the ministry of Paul and Titus. No doubt Paul, in his memorable voyage to Rome, looked toward "The Fair Havens" and "Lasea" (Acts xxvii. 8), with prayer that the people there might be saved; and in after years a great harvest was reaped in that island.

May we not trace the spread of the truth in that island, in some large measure, to the "*faithful children*" of the believers? Believing households were seed-corn all over Crete. And if so in Crete, an island famed for lying and gluttony, why may that not be in our own island too? Let us think a little on these "children."

1. *There were families where the children were "faithful."*

Whole families of saved children! How blessed! and how cheering! And that, too, in such an island as Crete. And this word "*faithful*" means two things. 1. *Full of faith.* The young souls were led by the Holy Spirit to receive Christ, and become believers. Yes, they became followers of "faithful Abraham." They accepted the "faithful saying," that "Christ Jesus came into the world to save sinners." For young people need the same Saviour as old sinners do; they must look to the same Brazen Serpent to be healed; they must slake their thirst at the same Fountain of living water. 2. *Truthful*, or full of fidelity. That is, they were children who spoke the truth, and were true in their actions; not deceitful, like other Cretian children. They were like the "little maid" who was servant to Naaman's wife—so truthful that her mistress could trust every word she spoke. Dear young people, whoever knows Christ, who is "the Truth," will certainly seek to be like Him.

II. *We might have expected to find such families.*

We ought to expect to find as many young souls saved as old ones; and it is the duty and privilege of young people to seek and find Christ in their very childhood. Do you not remember the children in the Temple crying, "Hosanna"? and how Jesus spoke on that occasion to those who wondered at it and thought it folly? Jesus said, "Have ye never read, Out of the mouths of babes and sucklings thou hast perfected praise?" (Matt. xxi. 16). Dear young people, think upon these words of Jesus, how they tell us that we should expect early conversions; and think, at the same time, of the families in the island of Crete, where there were so many instances of this early conversion. There is a Saviour for you to-day; will you come to-day?

And your parents surely should rejoice in this fact about the children of Crete. Your teachers, too, even when they know that the scholars of their classes are living in streets or houses where all around them is drunkenness, and dishonesty, and evil. The children of Crete were "lilies among thorns;" for there were gluttony and lying on every side of them. And so, also, let us pray for and expect the conversion of the *young in heathen lands;* for they are not situated in circumstances worse than the children of Crete. God's gospel, the good news about the life, death, and resurrection of His Son, is the Spirit's mighty instrument in changing old and young.

Children of believing parents, are you "faithful"? You of all others are surely privileged, having your parents' prayers, your parents' example, your parents' counsels, and the Divine offer made to you in baptism, "I will be your God"—your parents' God, to be a God to their seed after them (Gen. xvii. 7). What if the children of heathen parents rise up against you in the judgment!

A. A. B.

LXXXVI. Out of the Depths. TITUS iii. 3-7. "*For we ourselves also were sometimes foolish, disobedient, deceived, serving divers lusts and pleasures, living in malice and envy, hateful, and hating one another, etc.*"

WE have seen a great continental river after it had flowed for many miles within a comparatively narrow bed, bursting suddenly into the dimensions of an inland sea. At the lower end of that expanse it again became a stream confined within its banks; and at another stage became another sea. The St. Lawrence, in North America, is the grandest example of this in the world.

The Scriptures, especially in these Epistles of Paul, resemble such a river. In some parts its bed is narrow, and you can easily see from bank to bank; but in such a portion as our text the current breaks at once through and spreads into an ocean where we can neither feel a bottom nor see a shore. Here, in a few lines, lie all the loss of man, and all the salvation of God. This portion of Scripture, although a connected whole, is made up of three distinct parts.

The first (verse 3) reveals our low estate.

The second (verse 4-6) explains how the fallen are raised.

The third (verse 7) points to the high place on which the saved stand.

It is a Pilgrim's Progress from the city of Destruction to the city of the living God.

I. The low condition in which the fallen lie. "For we ourselves also were sometimes foolish, disobedient, deceived, serving divers lusts and pleasures, living in malice and envy, hateful, and hating one another." What a sea of wickedness! It cannot rest. "Who are these and whence came they?" Listen to one who has been rescued and he will tell what the imprisonment was. He who in this verse describes the condition of the sinful, is now among the saved. It is only after he has been delivered that he can or will bear true witness regarding the bondage in which he was held. This missionary, Paul, after his own deliverance, was ever ready to tell of his unconverted state.

The characteristic marks of the lost estate constitute a connected series.

(1) "Foolish," that is, thoughtless or heedless.

An infant or an idiot may be on the bank of some yawning gulf, and yet be entirely unconscious of danger. He laughs, but you shudder. You know his danger; he does not know it himself. This represents one feature of an unrenewed, unpardoned sinner's case. Although sin lies on him, and wrath before him, he eats, drinks, and is merry.

(2) "Disobedience," implying that the warning voice has come and has been neglected. This is His commandment, "That we should believe on the name of His Son Jesus Christ, and love one another." This commandment every prodigal disobeys every day and all the day long, until he arise and go to his Father.

(3) "Deceived."

This speaks of those who have lost their way and are wandering.

It is the distinguishing character of the evil heart of unbelief that it departs from the living God. Deceived by the corrupt bent of his own heart, the person who does not come near to God in the Mediator, is always going further off by a law of his being.

(4) "Serving divers lusts and pleasures."

He is a slave too, although he does not think so. Lust or pleasure needs only to say "Go, and he goeth," "Come, and he cometh." None walk at liberty except those whom the Son of God has made free, and guides by His Spirit.

(5) "Living in malice and envy, hateful, and hating one another."

It is a dreadful picture; and the last lines are the darkest. Slaves far from home and serving the stranger, might have their distress greatly mitigated by a gentle heart within each bosom, and mutual love in common sorrow; but these slaves of sin are neither contented in their own minds, nor at peace with each other. Such is the low condition of the unrenewed and unforgiven.

II. How God raises up His own from the depths.

God is our helper. Ah, how guilty, suspicious human hearts misinterpret the mind of God! Marks of His fatherly tenderness are scattered everywhere in heaven and earth. That was a true estimate of our heavenly Father's character, which was formed and expressed by a godly woman in ancient times—"If the Lord had been pleased to kill us, He would not have showed us all these things" (Judges xiii. 23). Bravely spoken, Hebrew matron; thy happy hopeful word rebukes our dark suspiciousness. We must look unto Jesus if we would measure the depth of God's philanthropy. His love to men was embodied in the "unspeakable gift."

The act of saving us from our state of sin is an act of pure mercy. It is in no measure of the nature of a bargain; it is wholly a gift. This may seem to some a narrow point; but it is a turning point, and to take the wrong side of this narrow point is to miss God's salvation.

III. The high place on which the redeemed stand. "That being justified by His grace, we should be made heirs according to the hope of eternal life."

Not possessors yet, but heirs. What is implied in "eternal life" we cannot fully understand. Eye hath not seen nor ear heard it all.

It is a great mistake to suppose that godless young people enjoy this world well, and that godly young people renounce the happiness of this world to make sure of the next. In the nature of the case, they can best enjoy whatever good is going in the present life, who expect a better when this is done. I love my home on earth: but if I have no other home in prospect the dread of one day losing my all keeps me in terror.

If I am the heir of an eternal life, I enjoy all the good which the present life contains, and when its sorrows come, my weary spirit is soothed by the certainty that they will soon be over.

In these verses, then, we are led near the mouth of a horrible pit; the veil is drawn aside and we look down on that seething sea of wickedness. But as you gaze and grieve, a light from heaven, above the brightness of the sun, attracts your notice. It is the philanthropy—the man-love of God our Saviour. Silently but resistlessly the Light of the World draws some, draws many out of the deep and lifts them upwards to Himself. Purified in the process, they soar away like clouds, and cluster round heaven's gate, waiting for the time when an abundant entrance will be administered to them into the joy of their Lord.

What of those who are still in the pit? To them the invitation comes: Come out of her My people. "Now is the day of salvation."

This portion of Scripture is a religious tract, and it is one of the narrative series. A sinner saved tells the story of his own redemption, that the saved may glorify the Lord that bought them, and that the unsaved also may arise and, on the footprints of that returned prodigal, return to his Father and their Father, to his God and their God.

W. A.

LXXXVIII. Roots of Bitterness. HEB. xii. 15. *"Looking diligently, lest any man fail of the grace of God: lest any root of bitterness springing up trouble you, and thereby many be defiled."*

HERE is a whole parable in a single verse. The apostles had learned from their Lord to employ pictures in order to make their lessons more striking and memorable. Their pictures were taken sometimes from the history of human life, sometimes from the habits of animals, and sometimes from the growth of flowers and trees. The lesson which this verse teaches is found growing in the ground. Under the likeness of a root, this text teaches us something about the nature, the source, the effects, and the cure of sin.

I. The nature of sin.

(1) It is a root. In many points sin is like a root. The root is always below ground; it is never seen. So often is it with sin. There are times when no evil word can be heard from the lips, and no wicked act can be seen in the life, and yet the person may be very sinful all the while. As the stalks grow up at one season of the year, and disappear at another, while the root which bears them remains alive at all seasons under the ground, so the sinful words and deeds may break out into great strength at one time, and at another time cease, while the root of sinfulness grows still strong in the heart, and is ready to bear its fruit

whenever an opportunity is offered. Again, the root is always growing as long as it is left living. It is in its nature not to stand still, but to be always increasing. Such also is sin in the heart; the longer it remains the stronger it grows. If the sinful desires that grow in your heart this year be not crushed and killed, it will be more difficult and more painful to kill them next year.

In yet another point you may observe a likeness between sin and a root; while it is easy to destroy the flower and fruit, and even the branches of any hurtful plant, it may be next to impossible to tear the root completely from the ground. A farmer is often sorely disappointed after he has cut over the weeds, and even tried to pull out the roots, to see the old enemy growing up as strong and thick as ever on the spot.

Ah, parents have often found, after wicked actions have been checked by chastening, that the evil disposition has been left lurking in secret, and has burst into wickedness again whenever it found an opening!

(2) *The root is bitter.* Everything depends on the nature and kind of the root that grows in the soil. Good and evil trees may grow beside each other in the same field. The fruit follows the root; no matter how rich the ground, how abundant the rain, how bright the sunshine, if the root be a "root of bitterness," bitter also will be the fruit.

Thus sin growing in the heart turns all the powers of our nature into evil. The understanding mind and the glowing affections, the nimble feet and the cunning hand—all are turned into poison by the corrupt desire that nestles deep in the soul like a root underground.

Saul of Tarsus possessed learning and eloquence and energy, and a fiery, unfainting heart; but the bitter root was in the man, and it turned all into fruits of wickedness. All his varied powers were employed in hunting and murdering the innocent disciples of Jesus. But when the bitter root was turned out of him on the way to Damascus, by the flash of Christ's redeeming love, and the plant of a renewed nature left living in its stead, all his powers were forthwith exerted in serving God and saving men.

II. *The source of sin.*

We do not at present speak of the first tempter and the first temptation. Our business is with ourselves and with the awful truth—that the roots of bitterness are not planted by other people, but spring up within ourselves. In the text we do not read, " Lest any root of bitterness be brought in," but, " Lest any root of bitterness *springing up* trouble you." When we see a stream rushing downward to the sea, we sometimes ask, "Where is its source?" Thus, when a sinful life is flowing like a stream, and any one asks whence it comes, Jesus leads up to the sinner's own heart, and bids us see it " springing up " there. " Out of the heart proceed evil thoughts, murders," etc. (Matt. xv. 19).

Every child should first watch his own heart, where sin springs up of itself; and next be careful of the company he keeps, lest he learn from others wicked words and ways in addition to his own.

III. The effects of sin.

We do not now trace out all the poisonous fruits which the bitter roots of sin bear in time and eternity; we speak only of the two named in the text, "trouble and defilement."

(1) Sin troubles you. It troubles the world, a nation, a Church, a family, a single person. Observe, although the bitter root springing up often disturbs the peace of a country and rends asunder a Church, the root never springs from the ground between two persons or two companies; it always springs in the persons themselves. The troubler is within us; and if he were not allowed to dwell within us, he never could contrive to disturb the peace between us and our neighbours.

The root of bitterness that grows strongest in one child is selfishness; in another, anger; in another, falsehood; in another, disobedience to parents. They are alike in that all have sharp prickles, and these pierce the flesh of all who come within their reach.

The stings of conscience in time and the wrath of God in eternity are the fully ripened fruits which these roots of bitterness bear. " Sin when it is finished bringeth forth death."

(2) Sin defiles others. If a careless farmer permit thistles to grow and ripen and run to seed on his own field, he injures thereby the field of his neighbour. Many grown men, and not a few children, take the name of God in vain

and utter profane language. These sounds from foul lips fly through the air, like thistle seeds on the wind, and falling on the ears of the young deeply defile their hearts. Beware! Let no word or act proceed from you that would corrupt another. Each of us is our brother's keeper; and if by our sins we defile his soul, God will require his blood at our hands.

IV. The cure of sin.

It appears from our text that two things go to the cure of sin—our diligence and God's grace. "Looking diligently, lest any man fail of the grace of God." This does not mean that we owe our salvation partly to ourselves and partly to God. No; Christ is all our salvation; He alone has finished the work, and it is His free gift to poor sinners. But it is also true, that God expects us to watch and pray, and strive for the salvation; our diligent look cannot work our salvation; but we are told to look diligently lest we should miss this precious salvation, which has been completed by Christ, and is offered free to all.

The grace of God means His undeserved goodness to sinners, His free gift. If Christ dwell in your hearts by faith, sin will not be allowed to dwell along with Him; but on the other hand, if He is kept out, all sorts of evil thoughts and habits will live and thrive within.

W. A.

LXXXIX. Resisting the Devil. JAMES iv. 7. *"Resist the devil and he will flee from you."*

ONE day standing by the brink of a stream, we watched a little water-rat at play. How frolicsome it was!—now nibbling the grass, now rolling itself over and over like a ball. Who would have guessed that there was a blood-thirsty eye following it everywhere? But so it was. All of a sudden, out leapt a weasel from its ambush. The next moment it had its teeth in its throat. We were too late to save it. Though the weasel skulked off from us, the poor little water-rat had just strength enough to crawl to its hole and then it heaved a sigh and died.

And who that sees a child running about so happy, so free, so light of heart, would imagine that there was a murderous being hovering near it, laying snares for it, bent on its destruction? Yet so it is. "Your adversary the devil goeth about as a roaring lion, seeking whom he may devour." Never does he appear so hateful as when he endeavours, as he always does, to ruin those whom the very brutes refuse to harm. A wolf found a child in a forest, and nursed it, and fought for it; but Satan plots how he may destroy the loveliest and tenderest.

Do you not feel him at work?

1. Whispering evil thoughts, as he did to Eve in Paradise, and to our Lord in the wilderness. There they are before you know it, and without your leave.

2. Stirring up naughty desires and passions in you. The heart is naturally sinful, and Satan can somehow make it show its love of sin, as bubbles rise to the surface of a bowl, as snakes creep out of the rocks.

3. Alluring you by outward pleasures or wicked examples. He says, "Here's a sweet thing; you may have it, you must have it. Never mind if it is a little bit bad."

Thus he tempts you. Each of you is a city besieged by him. This being so, what a word of comfort is this from God: "Resist the devil and he will flee from you."

I. The charge to resist him—not to attack him—that might be to expose yourselves unnecessarily to danger. Do not be careless about him—that is madness; but resist him. Do not be afraid of him or yield an inch to him, but resist him.

But how? (1) By stopping your ears and shutting your eyes. Ear-gate and Eye-gate are the chief entrances to the town of Mansoul. The fall came of Eve's listening and looking, and half our falls come of the same.

Lately we saw a robin on a pathway, fascinated by the calls and charms of a robin in a cage. Close by was a man holding the string. Now that robin's peril lay in its looking and listening. If it would but turn and fly away out of sight and sound it would be delivered; but it listened and looked and then it hopped into the cage and was captured. Don't dally or parley with Satan; but resist him by shutting your eyes and ears to temptation.

(2) By silencing your heart. If a temptation gets in at Ear-gate or Eye-gate, it rouses our hearts, and they begin to crave and clamour like a pack of hounds when the huntsman holds the fox in the air above their heads

"They will devour him," you say. No; he fetches out his whip and shouts to them, "Down, dogs—be quiet," and they are as still as stones. So we must silence our hearts when they cry out for what is wrong. We must say "get thee behind me, Satan."

(3) By lifting our shield. "The shield of faith, wherewith ye shall be able to quench all the fiery darts of the wicked one." Faith is a covering thing. It comforts and encourages. A drummer-boy used to wander about fearlessly in front of Sebastopol picking up bullets and cannon balls. When asked how he dared to do such a thing, he replied, "Yonder, hidden in that trench, are fifty rifles, ready to shoot the first Russian who attempts to touch me." It was his faith which filled him with fearlessness. And if we remember, "Thou God seest me," we shall not fear. Satan will perceive that we "abide under the shadow of the Almighty." If our faith fail not, he will be foiled.

(4) By drawing our sword. "The sword of the spirit, which is the word of God." Satan cannot stand before cuts and thrusts from this weapon. Jesus plied it when they fought together. We may not understand *how* it is, but *so* it is, that a verse of the Bible is to Satan what a brandishing of a sword in our faces is to us.

(5) By falling on our knees. You think that is a queer way to fight. If a soldier went on his knees in battle there would not be much chance for him. But it is different in this warfare. Prayer fetches Omnipotence to our succour. Just lift up your heart in prayer when "oppressed of the devil," and you will receive heavenly aid, help from the sanctuary. There was a little girl who got the name in her family of the "silent sister." When she was worried, or when she saw any one in distress, she had a way of sitting perfectly still, as if lost in thought for a minute or so; then a smile would steal over her face and she was as cheerful as anybody. She had formed the habit of "looking to Jesus," casting her care upon Him, begging Him to undertake for her. She resisted Satan by prayer. These are some of the recipes for resisting the devil. They are of God's own providing, and He expects that children, no less than grown-up people, will avail themselves of them. Children have to eat and drink for themselves, or they will die; and run away from danger, or they will be hurt; and chil-

dren must resist the devil for themselves, or he will lead them captive at his will. A sailor lad was floating about in the Polar seas. He was in a small boat with nothing but an ice-hammer to defend himself with. The bears came swimming towards him, roaring and gnashing their teeth, but as fast as they set their paws on the gunwale, he struck them with his hammer; and so defied them till his companions rejoined him. Now if he had said, "I am only a lad, I cannot be expected to beat off these bears by myself," what would become of him? But he did what he could, and God did all the rest for him.

II. The promise that he shall flee. " He shall flee from you."

A tiger would not flee if a child resisted him—a robber would not—but Satan is stronger than either, the most powerful of creatures, and yet, if resisted, he shall flee from you! Jesus has overcome Satan. He has bruised his head. If we confront him in Christ's name and strength, he will quail before us. In Christ's presence Satan is an utter coward. He may and he will repeat his assaults, but every time it will be with fainter hope of success, while our former victories will bear us to a firmer resistance. A child who repels the "God of this world" is a hero indeed! Jesus says of him, "Well done."

Are you resisting the devil? If not, be sure he is mastering you. He only wants you to be submissive, and he will bind you with silken cords.

"You can snap them when you please!" Mark this— they will grow tougher and harder and stouter every month you wear them, till at last they will get to be iron manacles in which, bound hand and foot, you will be his helpless captive.

You have no time to lose. It is not even now too late to resist him, if you do it relying on the grace of Jesus. Oh, if he did but know it, the most wretched prisoner in his innermost dungeon might escape if he would! Nothing is too hard for the Lord.

J. B.

T

XC. Precious Blood. 1 Pet. i. 19. "*The precious blood of Christ.*"

During the days of Holy Week we commemorate our Lord's agony, and on Good Friday our Lord's death. And so I should like to say something to you about this very solemn week, when our thoughts should be about the precious blood of Christ with which we have been redeemed.

I. About the blood of Christ. Of course you know what blood means in itself; and we hear of a great deal of bloodshed throughout the Old Testament and the New. When the Israelites were to go out of slavery in Egypt they were to kill a lamb, and the blood of that lamb on the door was a sign for the angel to pass by. You remember the sacrifices that used to be offered to God, and you remember in the New Testament how our Lord's blood was shed on the cross, and St. Peter says: "We have been redeemed with the precious blood of Christ." Like a red thread in a skein so this crimson blood runs through the history of the Old and New Testament. You are not to think that the blood of an animal or the blood of Christ as man is anything in itself—the reason of its value is, the blood is the life. It was our Lord's life that He gave for us. In the Old Testament they were told not to taste the blood of the animal, because the blood was the life. You are not to think only of the blood, but the pouring out of that blood meant the giving up of His life. If you poured out your blood through a wound it would mean your life. He gave His life for us to save us. If you were perishing in the waves, and a man jumped into the sea to save you, and died in so doing, he would give his life and not merely give an example. Christ left an example, but by the shedding of His blood for us are we saved.

II. Now Peter says the blood of our Lord Jesus is precious—"The precious blood of Christ." Boys and girls, if you were to live till you were eighty years of age I could not teach you more than this, that you are saved from sin, and made pure and holy for ever. I could not teach you more than there is in those few words—"The precious blood of Christ." You will learn more and more, as you grow up, how precious beyond all price, beyond all you can think of in any way, how precious that blood is. Oh! if you learn that lesson you will have learned much; if you have not learnt that lesson you will have learned nothing. If you are to know everything about astronomy —of the history of the great kings and men who ever lived, and thought, and died—all about everything that is around you, the earth, and the trees, and the skies, everything that man can speak about—even if you learn all that and do not know that the blood of Jesus Christ is precious, you have learned nothing—nothing that can help you in the hour of death and the solemn day of judgment. So, boys and girls, try to learn how precious the blood of Jesus Christ is.

What makes it precious? There are some things whose value is in themselves. A beautiful landscape as you see it—you cannot purchase it. The simple beauty of the evening with the stars dying out one by one; when you gaze on it you are lost in awe. And so with the glories of the sea. All these things have values in themselves and you cannot buy them. Again, some things have great value because they are rare, because there is not much of them. You know, boys and girls, that gold would not be of more value than lead if it was as abundant as lead. So it is with the value of diamonds. Thus you see some things are of great value and precious because they are rare. And some things are of great value at different times. You know that a sovereign is of more value sometimes than at other times. One hundred pounds were, years back, of much greater value than they are now. You see things are precious and valuable in themselves because of their rarity and because of what they can buy.

Now think of the precious blood of Christ—the life of Christ. How beautiful, how precious. Think of the beauty of that tender life He lived on earth and the beauty of the eternal life He has lived from the beginning. Think of the purity and love of Christ's life. Think of how rare it is. Not one other life in the universe is like the life of the Son of God. And, boys and girls, think of what was *bought* by it, of the immortal souls of millions and millions of men, of how ten thousand times more precious must be the precious blood of Christ—precious because of the beauty and holiness of its life—precious because it is the only life of its kind in the universe—precious because it has purchased the immortal souls of men.

You know who used these words—St. Peter. He knew how precious it was. You remember how he denied Christ, and said, "I know not the man," when he was afraid that being a friend of Jesus might get him into trouble. But he was forgiven by Jesus, and he counted the blood of Christ precious because it had saved him.

Now, what does Christ want you to do for all this? What does He want in return for giving His precious life for you? Think of what Jesus went through. Soldiers spat upon Him, and beat Him, and reviled Him, blindfolded His eyes, and then striking Him, said: "Can you tell who did that?" What have you given Christ in return for this? What He wants is that you give Him your trust and love and the joy of His salvation. I can tell you, boys and girls, when your father or mother give you something, whatever it may be, their true joy is in seeing you take it thankfully; and that is Christ's real joy, as we are told in the Bible. The Bible says, "He shall see of the travail of His soul and be satisfied." Do not you, boys and girls, like to satisfy Christ? It is the greatest joy of His life when He sees us, who have denied Him and revolted against Him, accept His salvation; and it is the greatest sign of His love that we are thus enabled to give Him joy and satisfaction.

I read not long ago about a ship that was coming to this country, from another distant land, and there was a lady missionary on board who had been living and working among the heathen. One girl, a pale and delicate girl, she had converted, was with her. A great storm arose and the captain told the passengers the ship could not hold out. They got out a boat and in this was the lady and the little heathen girl. There they were in this boat days with only a few biscuits to eat. They were maddened with hunger and thirst, and there seemed no hope for them; and this lady, nearly worn to death by the cold and wet and hunger, could not sit upright. She found herself leaning on the frail girl beside her. She tried not to press too heavily on the girl, and as she fell into a kind of swoon she heard the poor girl whisper to her, "Oh, if you love me lean on me." The lady swooned away and did not awake till she found herself on board a vessel which had rescued them; but there seemed to be a voice from heaven saying in tender accents, "If you love Me, lean on Me."

This is the voice of Christ. We shall be rocked on the wild sea of life and sin. No help for any one of us with the waves of sin dashing over us in the frail bark of life. Oh, children, above the storm, hear the words of your Saviour: "If you love Me, lean on Me." That is what He wants to say. And I can tell you that of all the millions and millions through the ages who have heard that tender voice, and have leant upon Him, not one has He ever failed —not one.   T. T. S.

XCI. The Adversary. 1 Pet. v. 8. *"Your adversary the devil, as a roaring lion, walketh about, seeking whom he may devour."*

In Dr. Moffat's "Missionary Labours and Scenes in Africa," there is a story about a lion lying in wait for a man. The man had gone to a pool of water, and then had lain down on a sloping rock to watch for any stray antelope that might come to drink; but while so doing he fell fast asleep. The heat of the sun reflected from the rock awoke him; but, when he would have risen from his position, he saw a large lion within little more than a yard of his feet, with its eyes glaring in his face! After a few moments he made a motion toward his gun, which he had laid down whilst he slept; but the lion no sooner saw him move than it gave a tremendous roar. Again, after an interval, he made the attempt, when again the lion started up as if enraged at his daring to seek a weapon of defence. The sun's rays soon made the rock like a heated plate of iron. At length the day closed. The night passed on, and yet every hour the lion was on the watch. The sun rose, the rock was soon as hot as yesterday, only by this time his feet had become past feeling, roasted by the intensity of the heat. About noon, the lion rose up and walked leisurely to the pool of water, eyeing the man all the while, so that when he once more stretched his hand toward his gun, the lion, enraged, made as if he would spring upon him. This day passed over, and another night also. But in the forenoon of the following day the lion again walked down to the water, and while there was arrested by a noise from another quarter, which caused him suddenly to plunge into the bushes and disappear. It was only now that the unhappy man was able to make his escape, worn out and barely half alive.

It is thus that Satan watches souls; and if he sees one anxious to escape, oh, how he springs forward in his rage! His frightful roar has terrified many a soul that had nearly put its hand on the shield of faith. "If you become Christ's," he says, "you must make up your mind to lose everything." In India, how he eyes every movement of those who have been made to feel the heat of wrath, and would fain escape. What uproar he excites! how incessant are his assaults day and night! Until the Lord interpose, arresting this mighty foe, the awakened soul is kept miserable, by fightings without and fears within; but the Lord does come in the hour of need, by His Spirit, and it may be by His messengers too. Let us often pray, "Arise and disappoint the foe, and cast him down, O Lord" (Ps. xvii. 13).

A godly woman was one Sabbath afternoon returning home from church. Her way was up the slope of a steep hill, passing the ruins of a shepherd's cottage. It was a fine summer day, and she was slowly moving on, meditating on the word and ways of God, when her attention was directed to a hawk flying swiftly round and round the old hut. She wondered why the hawk should be thus circling the hut, but soon she noticed that he was in close pursuit of a little bird, which sought to escape by making for the broken window of the ruin. The little bird, however, in its alarm and confusion could not make out the window, but flew past it again and again. But now, as the good woman who observed the scene drew near, the hawk's eye rested on her; his pursuit was not so keen as before—and while he abated his chase, the little bird got presence of mind to dart in at the broken window, and escape. The good woman found it fluttering and breathless, though in a few minutes it was able to fly off, unhurt, to its nest. She said she thought of a poor soul awakened, anxious to enter into rest, and always looking *towards* Christ in whom the sinner is saved; but always prevented coming into the cleft of the Rock by Satan hotly pursuing, raising up opposition, suggesting difficulties, and presenting wrong views of the Saviour. But at length, in a time of love, Jesus draws near; perhaps by sending some one like Philip (Acts viii. 29). Satan flees, and the soul finds the entrance.

Is this your case? Has it ever been your case? I am sure if you have ever felt thus, you will pity others. You will have an intense desire to send to others such messengers of peace as Philip, who was sent to the Ethiopian eunuch; you will pray that such may be sent to souls at home, and to souls in heathen lands, and to any among the Jews who may be moaning, " Thou huntest me as a fierce lion " (Job x. 16); or as Jeremiah, " Mine enemies chased me sore, like a bird" (Lam. iii. 52); but who might soon sing, if you sent them the knowledge of the Saviour, " Our soul is escaped as a bird" (Ps. cxxiv. 7); ay, as the bird that, dipped in the blood of its fellow, was let loose in the open field—emblematic of a soul bathed in the blood of Him who was our fellow, and whose death is our life (Lev. xiv. 7).

A. A. B.

XCII. The Shining Word. 2 Pet. i. 19.

"*We have also a more sure word of prophecy; whereunto ye do well that ye take heed, as unto a light that shineth in a dark place, until the day dawn, and the day star arise in your hearts.*"

Now I must ask you to pay particular attention to these three words, *Night, Lamp, Day*, as our talk will be about them.

I. *Night.* The light shines in a dark place. The world is in night. Three things make it dark: 1. Ignorance; 2. Sin; 3. Sorrow.

Are there parts of the world where people are ignorant of God? Yes. What do they make instead? Idols. They worship gods made by themselves. You could take one, and carry it about with you; yet the heathen bow down to these bits of wood and stone. Do you remember what Isaiah, in his 44th chapter, says about the silliness of worshipping a god made by man? He describes a man going away into the forest, and hewing down a tree with his hatchet, and then making an idol out of it; then taking the chips, and putting them into the fire, and roasting his dinner at it. Yet he goes and worships a bit of the tree, part of which he burnt in the fire. You remember the story of a woman in India, with her young husband, who had ordered an idol from the carpenter for their new house. Well, the carpenter was rather a long time in getting it ready; and whilst they were wondering and wearying for it, a missionary came and read a part of that chapter, and the young wife said to herself, "That is a very curious bit of reading to be in that book; it must be a very wise book. Our carpenter is just doing the very thing that book says. I think we might do without his idol." And so, by and by, they had their eyes open, and they came to worship the true God.

But we may be in darkness here, although we may know what the Bible is saying to us about God; and that brings me to the second thing—Sin. Although I say God made me, and He is almighty, holy, good, and a great many things of that sort, yet if I sin, it is dark down in my heart. Sorrow, too, makes hearts dark. Suppose some time at night an angel should come down to London, and say to you: "Come, and I will show you what houses have dark hearts in them. What houses there are where the people do not know God—where they are all distressed with their sins—where they have death, and sorrow, and affliction." Do you think there would be a great many houses that would be bright? Not a great many; for make the houses dark where there is ignorance—make the houses dark where there is sin and where there is much sorrow, and there would be comparatively few left. It is the night season with us all—it is the night time.

II. *Lamp.* But, secondly, what do we have to give us a little light at night, that helps to cheer and drive away the darkness? We have the stars, but they are not always visible; and sometimes we have the moon, but not all round the month. Now, suppose we had neither the stars nor moon to shine for us, what would we have to help us a little? We might have a lamp. Well, that is what the text says we have in dark places. What is the lamp that burns down here in the dark night to guide our steps? The Bible. Prove that from Psalm cxix. 105—"Thy Word is a lamp unto my feet and a light unto my path." Well, then, that is the lamp. Prove from the same psalm that young people should take very good heed to this lamp—unto its shining—9th verse—"Wherewithal shall a young man cleanse his way, by taking heed thereto according to Thy Word." Did you ever try to go out in a dark night with a lantern? You require to take care how it shines; you might have a lantern and confuse yourself with it. You must hold it so that the light will fall in front of you. You see a coachman driving a carriage on a dark night—does he sit in the light? No; the lamps are so placed that they throw their light on the road before him, so that he can see if he is going all right while he sits away back in the dark. Then suppose a man had a lamp in a dark house. He says: "I have got a lamp," there it is; but he never lights the lamp; do you think it would help him much? No. Then he puts a wick into the lamp, but doesn't put any oil; will that help him? No, it would not. Then he puts a little oil; wouldn't that give him a light? It would be a very poor light; but when he puts in more oil the light will get brighter, and he says, "See what a nice lamp I have got." Well, suppose this man, having got the nice bright lamp, was to go and put a bushel over it, and cover it up, would it give much light then? No. Who is it that speaks about that? Jesus Christ. "No man having lighted a candle putteth it under a bushel, but sets it on a stand to give light to all that are in the house." So that is the way in which we must take heed. We must keep the lamp well trimmed. What is the lamp that shines all through time? It is the Bible; and to take heed to it is to read it, and to think of what it says to us, and to act according to it, "taking heed to our way according to Thy Word"—that is doing what the Bible tells us. If a person does what the Bible tells him, will he fall into the ditch in the darkness? No; but if you don't mind your Bible lamp, you will be going on one day, thinking you are doing very nicely and safely, and you will fall into the ditch because you didn't take heed.

III. *Day*. Is this Bible-lamp to burn all through the night of Time? It is. God will not take it away all through the night of Time. But will it burn after the day comes? It will not be needed then. I don't know what God will do with His Bible then—I don't suppose it will live in *this* form

—made of paper, and printed with ink, and bound with leather; but the light that is in the Bible will be in heaven, for what is the light that is in the Bible? It is the Holy Spirit, or, you may say, it is Jesus Christ revealed there by the Spirit. Now prove that Jesus Christ is the light of heaven from Rev. xxi. 23 : "And the city had no need of the sun, neither of the moon, to shine in it: for the glory of God did lighten it, and the Lamb is the light thereof." Well, that is the day—the coming of Christ. Who is the daystar in that verse? Jesus Christ. What is the daystar? The sun must be the daystar. Hence we have in our hymn—

> " Christ, whose glory fills the skies,
> Christ, the true, the only Light,
> Sun of Righteousness, arise,
> Triumph o'er the shades of night;
> Dayspring from on high, be near;
> Daystar, in our hearts appear"!

Christ Jesus, who is to come and shine over the world in the Resurrection. Suppose now, when wicked men are raised up, and Jesus Christ is in the heavens, coming with great glory all round about Him, will it be clear day to them do you think? No, it will not: they will be terribly afraid of the glory. Suppose a man were to go to heaven, and go in without the daystar of Christ in his heart, would it be a bright and happy place to him? No, it would not; because he has no eye to see its light. He has not the love of Jesus Christ in his heart, and so it is all dark with him. Suppose I had an image of wood in the centre of the hall, and I was to say to it: "Do you see much just now?" and there was no answer. I say: "Oh no, it is dark to that image, bring me a light, and throw it upon the eyes of the image, would it see then?" No, it would not. You see, then, you must not only have a light, but you must have the heart to receive the light, and so it says: "The day star shall arise in your heart." Well, that will be in heaven, when Christ comes to those that will have Him, and He will shine in their hearts, and when He shines in their hearts all will be glory, and they will not need any sun nor moon.

J. E.

XCIII. Drinking of the same Well. 1 John i. 7.
"The blood of Jesus Christ His Son cleanseth us from all sin."

OF all the thousands of bullets that have been discharged during a battle, or during the course of a siege, perhaps not one could be pointed to as having brought more than one foe to the ground. Long ago an arrow was sent from the bow of a skilful archer into the right eye of Philip, king of Macedon; but that same arrow never did a like service again. Very different, however, is the case in spiritual warfare, and with weapons drawn from the armoury of God. The same text of Scripture that has wounded one, has often wounded many besides. Like an arrow feathered that it may fly the better, the truth of God is expressed in memorable words; and perhaps each such memorable text has, in every age, done work for God in the case of hundreds of souls.

We wish you to feel that the same word of God that has been blessed to you may be blessed to others, that so you may eagerly seek to make known the truth at home and abroad. We wish also to impress upon you, that if you are still a stranger to the truth in its power—still a heathen, with salvation within your reach—you, even you, may find it where it has been found by other souls.

We could mention some six or eight cases that occur to us at this moment, in which that one verse, 1 John i. 7, has been blessed to bring in amazing light and joy to sin-burdened souls. Thirsty soul, stay at this well—"The blood of Jesus Christ His Son cleanseth us from all sin." It is the water in that well, not anything in you, that is to remove your burning thirst. It is the truth in that text— the truth that God's own Son poured out His life to remove from us the sentence, "Thou shalt die"—it is that which He has done, and not anything in our own character or life, that is God's reason for putting away sin from any of us sinners. And He is never weary in applying Christ's blood, never unwilling. Never does He upbraid us for the past; never does He delay when we come.

We could mention at this moment not a few cases, from the Ethiopian eunuch downward, where the reading of Isaiah liii. has been water of life to the thirsty. They were led truly to drink in the truth that God provided the

Lamb for the sacrifice; and that it is the living and dying of this Lamb of God, and not any suffering, self-denial, sorrow, obedience of ours, that is taken by the Father as atonement. Drink of this well, and having drunk yourself, tell it to Jew and Gentile, tell it to great and small, tell it to the whole creation.

The poet Cowper, when first led to see the black cloud of his sins, was guided by the Holy Spirit into peace and joy by one day reading the words of Romans iii. 24, 25, "Being justified freely by His grace, through the redemption that is in Christ Jesus, whom God hath set forth to be a propitiation through faith in His blood." He saw, as he sat musing on the words, how God waits not for merit in us, but advances to us from motives of love that spring up in His own bosom; and how he meets what the law demands, by the offering of His own Son—an offering which is held forth for the acceptance of every sinner that has a heart to understand.

It was of this same well, only at another side of it, that Colonel Gardiner drank, when, after his awakening, he had for weeks gone on in gloom, imagining that God's justice must insist on the damnation of such an enormous sinner as he saw himself to be. About the end of October, 1719, he read the words: "Whom God hath set forth to be a propitiation through faith in His blood, to declare His righteousness for the remission of sins, . . . that He might be just, and the justifier of him that believeth in Jesus" (Rom. iii. 25, 26). Here he saw the riches of redeeming grace and love in such a manner as even swallowed up (as he expressed it) his whole heart in love; so that, for seven years after he had thus drunk of this well, he enjoyed a heaven upon earth, from the time of his waking in the morning till evening closed his eyes.

The same Holy Spirit, the Guide into the truth, liveth still. May He lead thee to these wells of salvation, and bring thee up from them in the spirit of Isaiah xii. 4, 5: "And in that day shall ye say, Praise the Lord! . . . Sing unto the Lord; for He hath done excellent things: this be known in all the earth."

A. A. B.

XCIV. The Love of God. 1 John iv. 8. *"He that loveth not, knoweth not God; for God is love."*

THE first half of the Christian year was given to us to show what God has done for us, and the second for us to learn to serve God. We cannot have the second half without the first. There must come first God's love to us and then our love to God. There must come first all that our Lord Jesus Christ did for us, before we can do anything for Him. That is what our Church means by putting first all the great love and sacrifice of Christ for us, that afterwards we may be able—how could we do otherwise?—to give ourselves as a sacrifice acceptable and well-pleasing unto God. That is part of the Gospel I have read to-day. It is all about love; because we must start by first knowing that Christ loves us, and then loving Christ in return. It is all love. We are told that love is the root of all true obedience before God. And then we are told in the Gospel the story of the rich man and Lazarus, to show how awful a thing it is to neglect our duty towards God. We are told two things: that all work must spring from love, and then we are told of the awful danger of neglecting to do our duty towards God and our neighbour.

Love must be the root of all true work. Suppose you are doing anything for your father or mother: if you do it through love it is a joy to your father or mother. I tell you, boys and girls, your parents would rather have it done badly if it was done through love, than to have the most perfect conduct if it does not spring from love. In this life all true work for those who love us must be done in love to them. So it is and in a much higher sense in our love to Jesus Christ. Our love for Christ must spring from thinking of His great love for us in dying for us.

There may be a certain amount of kindness to animals, and to our fellow-creatures. Boys and girls are naturally fond of dogs, and cats, and pets, and they think it is a religious thing to be kind to animals. And you who have good homes see poor children in rags, and you think what a terrible thing it is, and you help them. This may be done, and without love to Jesus Christ. Here is one little child who is doing her duty every day, because she prays to God morning and evening for strength to do it. And there is another little child who is doing the same thing, and yet not with the same motive. It is just the difference between two flowers. You have got a rose, and it has no root, and there is a rose growing upon the tree, and the latter has roots, and the sap and the life come up into it, and there are the little buds that surround it. That is just the difference between two kinds of work; the things we do because we are united to Jesus Christ, these are the flowers that will continue to blossom for ever, and will be full of fragrance when we are gathered into the garden of the Lord. The others are only cut flowers after all, and the day will come when they will utterly die. All true earnest work for God must be done for love to Jesus Christ.

This love is like a stream that rises in some far distant place and flows down the valley, and on its banks flowers blossom and wild plants are growing into beauty because they are watered by the stream. So all things will be beautiful and joyous that are watered by the stream of love that flows from the heart of God Himself.

Then as to the awful danger of neglecting this. It is not "not doing any particular harm" will save you. The rich man was not a murderer, the rich man was not a thief, the rich man was not a drunkard. We are only t ld what he did *not* do. He did not do his duty to his poor neighbour, and to God. You know the awful ending. In torment he lifted up his eyes and saw Lazarus afar off. And take care, boys and girls, take care of those sins we call "sins of omission." The sins of self-satisfaction, of pride, of feeling "I am everything, other people are nothing." We are all members of one family, the family of which the Lord Jesus Christ is the elder brother; and the day will come, boys and girls, when you who are rich and prosperous in this life will be just as the beggar in the streets, and—though God forbid—if you will do nothing for the sake of Jesus Christ, who gave Himself upon the cross to save you from your sins, you may be infinitely beneath the poorest little one who has felt in his rags the love of God and Jesus Christ our Lord.

Remember, you are not one little atom by yourself; we are all members of the family of the kingdom of God.

A friend wrote me, a short time ago, of an incident that

happened in Germany. The Emperor, a great hero, a grand man, a great soldier, and a great king, is eighty-six years of age, yet still leads his soldiers to battle, and governs his people. And this great emperor while passing through a village a short time ago entered the village school. The boys and girls did not know who the kind old gentleman was. And he asked what lessons they were doing, and he was told Natural Science. That is, you know, about the various kingdoms to which everything belongs. There is the animal kingdom, and the mineral kingdom, and the vegetable kingdom. And he asked the question, pointing to the stones outside the door, "What kingdom do those belong to?" And they said, "The mineral kingdom." Then he pointed to the tree they could see through the window, and asked to what kingdom that belonged. And they answered, rightly, to the vegetable kingdom. And then he said—to give them an example of the animal kingdom—"to what kingdom do I belong?" Most of them said, "to the animal kingdom," for man is an animal. But one tiny child replied, "to the kingdom of God."

And the old man bowed his imperial head, and laid his hand on the little child, and said: "Thank you, my little child, for that." It touched him to remember that he, master of a hundred legions, the emperor of thousands of people, should be reminded by that little humble child that after all he was a member of the kingdom of God. So every one of us is.

T. T. S.

XCV. Idolatry. 1 JOHN v. 21. "*Little children keep yourselves from idols.*"

AN idol is a heathen god. In the second commandment it is called a "graven image." The figure of Dagon, which fell upon its face to the earth before the ark of the Lord; the golden calf, which Aaron cast for the Israelites; the statues of Jupiter and Diana, which the Greeks worshipped; and those of Vishnu, Buddha, and Juggernaut, which are to be found in India and China now—all these belong to the abominable family of idols. Men bow down to them and serve them.

These idols are :—
1st. The works of human handicraft.
2nd. They are foolish.
3rd. They are helpless.
4th. They are hideous.
5th. They are hurtful.

And so the poor heathen sink deeper and deeper in degradation, darkness, cruelty and sin. Pity them and seek to send them the Bible, and pray for the time when they shall fling their idols to the moles and to the bats, and worship the alone true God.

But now you may say, " What have we English boys and girls to do with idols? There are none around us." Thank God that it is so. Thank God that ages ago the last idol vanished out of Britain. Thank God that your parents never taught you to bend your knees to them. And yet here in the text you are told to keep yourselves from idols. The Apostle wrote these words to Christians, not to heathens. By "little children" he means the young and inexperienced; those who are setting out on the heavenly way, or who are naturally weak and simple. But still what are the "idols" which they are to keep themselves from? If an idol is a thing which draws the heathen away from the living God, may not anything which does this be named an idol?

It is possible for " little children " to make such " idols " of certain things, as that they shall quite estrange them from God, who deserves their best thoughts and affections and services; who claims the bloom and dew of their days.

I. Idol self.

This love of self is born in us, and, if not early checked, will be our master. It tempts you to falsehood, to unkindness, to greediness, to pride, for it feeds upon these. You must gratify it at whatever cost, and then it often demands more than you can obtain for it. Self is a dreadful idol. Beware of it.

II. Idol dress.

We like bright colours and nice attire; but there is danger on the other side—danger of thinking more of the " outward adorning " than of those hidden ornaments of neatness and quietness, which are so priceless in God's esteem. You may forget the pearl, in anxiety about its setting. Fashion is a perilous boat for you to venture in, and before you are aware it may wreck you amongst sharks.

III. Idol food.

It cannot be denied that "little children" may be so fond of nice things, so fond of the dainty things of the table, that they are their idols. They dream of them, and clamour after them, and are angry when they cannot have them. The wholesome things are despised because they are plain. They are ever on the watch for the opening of cupboards, the uncovering of jars, the approach of eating shops. We hope you can say "That is not my idol."

IV. Idol pleasure.

Do not little children encourage the passion for exciting amusements till they are miserable without them, though so many innocent recreations remain to them? They must have the fruit of the forbidden tree. It is as if a bee should be sighing in the middle of a clover and cowslip meadow, because he missed a dandelion here and there! We have known children whose Sundays were a "weariness" to them, and their studies a positive punishment. That should not be so. Their pleasures were their idols. Now you are exhorted to keep yourselves from them.

(1) You can implore from above daily assistance against them. If they are too heavy for you to move, beg God to aid you, and in His almighty strength you can lift the sturdiest and cast it out of the bosom, if not at once, yet by degrees.

(2) Be vigilant against them. Search yourself to discover if they are within you. Faithfully say to yourself, "Am I the temple of this or that idol?"

If you are heedless they will creep in.

(3) Be self-denying. This is a capital cure for these idols. It may be hard to flesh and blood to do it; but it is a bit which we must thrust into our own mouths for our own advantage! Without it, we shall be as those who ride wilful horses, which won't stop or turn, and which pitch them over directly they touch them with whip or spur. If you can "deny yourself" you have the secret of victory over these idols.

(4) Yield your heart to God. You have not two hearts; therefore if God has your heart, these idols cannot have it.

Endeavour to occupy it for God, to present it to God

continually, to view it as consecrated to God. Implore the Saviour to dwell in it by His Holy Spirit, and with Him reigning there all "idols" will be banished—you shall be kept from them, though you are but a "little child."

J. B.

XCVI. Heaven. Rev. vii. 1-17.

OUR subject is Heaven. When a person is going to visit a far-off country, he is generally very much interested in that country, and consults maps and guide-books, so that he may know something about it. We all hope to spend an eternity in heaven, so it is well to know something about it. The glories of heaven are many. We will consider four of these glories :—

I. *In heaven there is work without weariness.*—God made man for work, and we never can be truly happy without it. It is a great mistake to suppose that they are happiest who never need to work unless they choose, and who never choose to work. Employments and enjoyments go together. If you work with a will, you will have great pleasure in work. There are no idlers in heaven. In Eden there were no idlers. "Therefore are they before the throne of God, and serve Him day and night in His temple" (ver. 15). They have abundance of work. They work not at their own will. It is said that they *serve* God. There is a great difference between work and service. The will of God is law to them. They do what God commands, and they do it with their whole heart. There will be plenty of work serving God, and no one will be weary. They are like servants standing before the throne of their sovereign, ready to do all that he commands. They are to be ready to do the work of God; and a large part of that work is worship, and the special part of worship is praise. The church is like a little heaven, for in heaven, they love worship.

A woman went to her minister for a certificate. She was going to America, and had to leave some of her family behind her, but she said that she regretted most of all that she had to leave the church. She had something of the spirit of heaven. A young man got a fine situation in the country with a large salary, yet he said that he did not want to leave the church were he had first worshipped God from the heart. All work on earth makes us weak and weary. Honest work, heartily done, gives pleasure, but weariness soon spoils that pleasure. In heaven they have no weariness. They serve as angels. Life is kept in the body by means of some muscles in the heart, through which the blood flows to all parts of the body. Men would die if they stopped for a single minute. These muscles go on working day and night, yet they have no weariness. Our bodies in heaven will be like these muscles, so that we shall work day and night without weariness.

II. *In heaven there is joy without sorrow.*—You may have joy in this world. If you have health and common sense, and, above all, the grace of God, life will be to you a source of joy. The gospel is a joyous message, and the Christian life is a joyous life. It is not the religion of Jesus, but the want of it, that makes people sad. If you have not some drops of sorrow in every cup of joy, you will be the first child of Adam in such a condition. The sorrow is sent to remind us that our souls must rise above earth, and seek joys without sorrow. Health is a joy, but sickness comes. Food is a great blessing, but with many the wolf comes to the door. A happy home is a blessing, but all homes have their own dark shadows. Youth is a great blessing, but old age comes. It is not so in heaven. All these joys are there without sorrow. "They shall hunger no more, neither thirst any more, neither shall the sun light on them, nor any heat" (ver. 16). In the East, sunstroke often brings sickness and death. Some people call this world a "vale of tears." This world is like a valley with a river flowing through it filled with tears. Look at the last part of the 17th verse: "And God shall wipe away all tears from their eyes." There shall be no tears there. Those who have had many sorrows on earth, so that they go into heaven almost with wet cheeks, will be comforted by God, for He will wipe away their tears with His own hand, and turn their sorrow into joy.

A gentleman was praised for his missionary work. He rose up and said that he only wished to get from man what he hoped to get from God: "Well done, good and faithful servant, enter thou into the joy of thy Lord." This is a joy which children may have. It is not a joy of the body, nor of the mind, but a joy of the heart and soul, coming from love. People must become as children before they can enter heaven, so these joys are for children.

III. *In heaven there is safety without danger.*—Jesus is called the Saviour because He saves us, or makes us safe. The chief blessing which Jesus brings is salvation. Salvation is a Latin word meaning safety. There is always danger on earth. There are many passages in the Bible warning even the best about their danger. Those who wrote the Bible seem to have had a loving fear. The path of life is full of snares, and even the best may fall. During last year 631 partridges have been picked up on the South-Western railway, killed by flying against the telegraph wires. Who would think of danger to little birds from the telegraph wires! All of us are in danger. There is hope of every sinner so long as he is out of hell, and there is fear of every saint so long as he is out of heaven.

You have heard about the Welsh colliers, who were ten days in a mine, buried without food and without water. Men at the peril of their lives bravely rescued them. Crowds of people went to the colliery during these ten days. When the news came that the colliers had been reached, and when the first collier was brought up, there was a death-like pause, and then the crowd shouted with joy, because the men saw their comrades saved. But their joy was soon checked when they were told that these poor men were so weak that they were still in great danger. They were safe *with* danger. The mighty multitude in heaven is safe *without* danger; they have everlasting safety without any danger. "And (they) cried with a loud voice, saying, Salvation to our God which sitteth upon the throne, and unto the Lamb" (ver. 10). There they sing songs in praise of salvation. They sing of salvation in its fullest sense. They all join in taking up the hymn, and saying, in the 12th verse, "Amen."

IV. *In heaven they have rest without end.*—The Book of Revelation is a book which tells us a great deal about heaven. When the Apostle was writing to the poor Christians, he comforted them by saying, "There remaineth a rest for the children of God." He was addressing those whose lives were a sore battle. Read the 17th verse. What a beautiful picture of rest! You have all heard of a book called Richard Baxter's "Saints' Everlasting Rest."

Baxter was in ill-health, so he did not often get a good night's rest, but he knew of a better kind of rest. This does not contradict the statement about work. Almost all the enjoyments you have are just work. Holiday rest is just loved work. A poet says, "The want of occupation is not rest."

What a beautiful home heaven is!—work without weariness, joy without sorrow, safety without danger, rest without end! What boy or girl would not wish to dwell there? Homes on earth will be taken from us. A little girl cried when she was told that her father's house was to be taken down. She was told that her father had got a new house, but she asked if it might not be pulled down too. They answered her that it might. Then she said they would go and live in a boat on the sea. She saw that that would not do, and then she said, "We must all die and flit to heaven. Every home on earth will be pulled down."

This chapter begins by describing an earthquake. Humboldt travelled far to know what an earthquake was. When he was in South America, an earthquake visited the place where he was staying. In a moment he said that all his feelings of safety were gone. Houses were falling, trees moving, the very mountains were reeling; and when he went to the harbour, the sea had fled, and the ships were on the dry ground. Every refuge failed him; but when he looked up, the heavens were calm and unmoved. That is just John's picture of the end of the world. Those who live to see the end of the world must look up like the German philosopher. If they have faith in Christ, they will look up to heaven. Some will be shut out of heaven. You must be heavenly here if you would go there. Think about heaven. Many hate the thought of leaving this earth, so God has told us about heaven that we may love to go there.

A lady whose father died said she had never been able to consent to her father going away, until one day she was reading in the Bible about heaven, and she exclaimed, "Oh, what a blessed place!" She could not wish her father back when she thought of the joys of heaven. John Bunyan tells about Christian and Hopeful going through the river. The king's messengers came for them, and it seemed as if all the hosts of heaven came to meet them. Then they opened the gate, and he got a glimpse of the city, "which when I saw, I wished myself among them." Open the eyes of your soul, and the thought of heaven will not make you feel strange.

"And one of the elders answered, saying unto me, What are these which are arrayed in white robes? and whence came they?" (ver. 13). The elder was astonished to see so many men of a sinful race there. A gentleman once heard Mr. Arnot preaching in the open air. He said that he used a beautiful illustration. It was a fine summer evening. There was a thunder-cloud right above them. He looked up to the cloud, and said, "What are these which are arrayed in white robes?" The sides of a thunder-cloud are often lined with silver. He explained that the water which formed that cloud was drawn from the most filthy pools, as well as from the beautiful rivers, by the heat of the sun. So the Sun of Righteousness shines on all, and they are drawn up and made heavenly in heart. "They have washed their robes, and made them white in the blood of the Lamb." J. W.

XCVII. Whosoever will. REV. xxii. 17. "*Whosoever will, let him take of the water of life freely.*"

HAVE you anything to pay?—nothing. There is a story of a gentleman that got into a railway carriage. Another gentleman came in after him, and his friend on the platform said, "Are you insured?" He answered, "Yes." The gentleman who was first in the carriage—a Christian man—said to his fellow-passenger, after he was seated, "How long are you insured for?" "For a year," he replied. "Only for a year!" said the other; "I am insured for ever." "But that must be very expensive!" "Oh, no! I am insured for ever, and it cost me nothing, and will cost you nothing. My insurance cost God His own Son, but it cost me nothing."

It cost much to dig the well of salvation; but it is dug—dug deep—and it will cost you nothing to drink. Remember that this is the last invitation in the Bible. You have a great many invitations in the Bible, but this is the last. God has never spoken from heaven since this last chapter of the Bible was written. It is the last message He has sent, and a very loving message it is.

God wants you to be holy and happy, and for this purpose He gives you the water of life. And when He said these words, did He mean you? Yes, He meant you—everybody. It is long since these words were spoken—more than eighteen hundred years—but He means those that live in this present age just as much as those living in the time when the words were spoken. "Whosoever will, let him take the water of life freely."

There is a well for the world—think of that—so deep that it can never be dried up. And it is an old well; people have been drinking of that well for six thousand years, and it is not dry yet. It is a clear well,—beautiful water, and cold, so as to refresh the weary, flowing up, and flowing ever. Its waters are for you. From beginning to end this Bible tells us of the well of living water,—free love in Christ Jesus, free pardon and everlasting life to the sons of men.

"Water of life." What does that mean? It means water that gives life. The water of life is something that man cannot give. It is that which God has given,—that which God has sent us in His Son, the Lord Jesus Christ; so that he who has Christ has the living water, the water that gives life to the soul.

This water of life is that which God has provided for making you holy and happy. This well is full of the love of God, the peace of God; he who has it has the love of God, the peace of God. God has sent His message of love in Christ Jesus, His message of peace in Christ Jesus: "God so loved the world, that He gave His only begotten Son, that whosoever believeth on Him should not perish but have everlasting life."

You all want to be happy. This is the thirst which is in your soul. When you are playing, that shows that you want to be happy. When you are going about from day to day with your companions, or when you are in the house, you want to be happy. But you don't know how. You go to every other well but the one that will make you happy. Now God says, You want to be happy, and I will tell you how to have your soul filled with happiness: here is the well of the water of life for you. If a man drink of this, he will live for ever; for when a man gets this great peace and love of God into his heart, he is holy and happy for ever.

The next thing to notice is that word "freely." How much have we to pay!—Nothing at all. In our country water is cheap. But in the East it is dearer. If you were in Alexandria or Cairo, you would see a man with a great skin over his shoulder, crying, "Water for a para!"—about a farthing. But when we go for this water, we get it for nothing. "Ho, every one that thirsteth, come ye to the waters, and he that hath no money." Freely, freely, freely; he that hath no money—nothing to pay! That is God's message about this living water. Do you pay anything for sunshine?—No, nothing. How much do the crows pay for their dinner every day? How much do the lilies pay for their whiteness?—Nothing. So all we get from God is free. And He says, "Open thy mouth wide, and I will fill it." Thus He feeds the ravens, paints the lilies and says, "Open thy mouth wide, and I will pour the water of life into it freely."

"Jesus the water of life will give
Freely, freely, freely."

Notice the word "take," in the next place, Just take it. God doesn't say, Now, come and wait for it, and after you have waited a week, a month, or a year, then you are at liberty to take it. No; He says, Take it just there. God doesn't keep us waiting for pardon, If we haven't it now, it is because we don't take it. He does not keep us waiting for life. If we haven't it now, it is because we don't take it. When Christ was here, He fed the multitudes, sometimes five thousand, sometimes seven thousand. How did He get the bread? He made it. Did He make them pay anything?—No. What had they to do?—Just to take it, that was all. Did He do so on the spot?—Yes. He gave, they took. Now the whole thing in regard to the water of life, pardon, peace, salvation, is just this,—God gives, we take; that is all.

And this message is sent to everybody. "Whosoever will, let him take of the water of life freely." H. B.

INDEX OF SUBJECTS.

Abide with us, 178.
Abraham's Trial, 5.
Account, The, 227.
Adversary, The, 277.
Ananias and Sapphira, 216.
Ark of God, The, 37.

Bad Company, 75.
Bad Habits, 107.
Bethesda, The Pool of, 191.
Bread, The Living, 197.
Bread of Life, The, 195.

Centurion, The, 116.
Children's Book, The, 248.
Children, Faithful, 262.
Children of Light, 243.
Children, Obedient, 245.
Christ in the Storm, 136.
Christ, The Blood of, 131.
Christ's Drawing Power, 204.
Cross, The, 208.

Demoniac of Gadara, The, 139.
Devil, Resisting the, 270.

Ethiopian Eunuch, The, 218.
Evil Spirits, 137.
Excuses, 167.

Fear of the Lord, The, 53.
Fig-tree, The Barren, 165.

Gates, 97.
Giants, 256.
Gideon, 25.
Gift, A, 234.
Gift, God's Unspeakable, 237.
Go Forward, 17.
God, the Creator, 1.

God, The Love of, 284.
Good Example of Four Wise Creatures, The, 80.
Grapes, A Bunch of, 104.

" He took them up in His Arms," 149.
Heaven, 290.
    „   The True Way to, 206.
Herodias's Daughter, 143.
Hospital Sunday, 117.
House of Wisdom, The, 70.

Idolatry, 287.
Isaac, 8.

Jairus' Daughter, 141.
Joseph and his Brethren, 13.
Joy over one Penitent, 169.
Joyful Sound, The, 61.

Knocking, 159.
Knowledge and Wisdom, 68.

Loaf and the Hungry Multitude, The, 193.
Lamb Slain, The, 94.
Lamb of God, Behold the, 180.
Leaf, The Fading, 102.
Left to Himself, 77.
Lent, 133.
Lemuel, The Words of King, 83.
Lights, 251.
Living Epistles, 229.
Lost Sinner and the Seeking Saviour, The, 175.

Maid, The Little, 48.
Ministering Child, A, 28.
Message, An Easter, 151.

Nathanael, 186.
Net, The Spread, 62.

One Thing, 156.
Out of the Depths, 264.

Parting Alike, 43.
Paul's Sister's Son, 221.
Precious Blood, 273.
Pride, 109.

Refreshment Sunday, 146.
Rock of Ages, 87.
Roots of Bitterness, 267.

Samuel, 32.
Saved by a Cry, 214.
Sea, On the, 123.
"Send and fetch him," 39.
Solomon's Prayer, 45.

Sowing, 241.
Storms of Life, The, 113.
Strength, The Secret of True, 89.
Summer and its Lessons, 58.

Tears, The Redeemer's, 201.
Time, The Waste of, 129.
Treasure Trove, The, 65.

Well, Drinking of the Same, 282.
Witnessing Children, 124.
What is it to be to Me? 23.
What shall we do? 153.
Where to carry our sins, 51
White Garments, 85.
Whosoever Will, 294.
Why Children should Come to Jesus, 171.
Word of God, The, 260.
Word, The Shining, 279.

INDEX OF TEXTS.

GENESIS.	PAGE
i. 31	1
xxii. 2	5
,, 10	8
xlv. 2	13

EXODUS.	
xiv. 15	17

JOSHUA.	
iii. 4	23

JUDGES.	
vii. 5-7	25

1 SAMUEL.	
ii. 18	28
iii. 7	32
iv. 10, 11	37
xvi. 11	39
xxx. 24	43

1 KINGS.	
iii. 7	45

2 KINGS.	
v. 1-27	48

PSALMS.	
xxxii. 7	51
xxxiv. 11	53
lxxiv. 17	58
lxxxix. 15	61

PROVERBS.	
i. 17	62
ii. 1-15	65
ix. 1-5	70
x. 14	68
xiii. 20	75
xxix. 15	77
xxx. 24	80
xxxi. 1	83

ECCLESIASTES.	PAGE
ix. 8	85

ISAIAH.	
xxvi. 4	87
xxx. 7	89
liii. 7	94
lxii. 10	97
lxiv. 6	102
lxv. 8	104

JEREMIAH.	
xiii. 23	107
,, 15	109

NAHUM.	
i. 3	113

MATTHEW.	
viii. 5-14	116
ix. 12, 13	117
xiv. 22-36	123
xxi. 15	124
xxvi. 8	129
xxvii. 25	131

MARK.	
i. 13	133
iv. 35-41	136
v. 1-20	137
,, 15	139
,, 38-42	141
vi. 25	143
viii. 1-8	146
x. 16	149
xvi. 7	151

LUKE.	
iii. 10-15	153
x. 42	156
xi. 9	159
xiii. 6-10	165

	PAGE
xiv. 18	167
xv. 10	169
xviii. 16	171
xix. 10	175
xxiv. 29	178

JOHN.	
i. 29	180
,, 48	186
v. 1-16	191
vi. 9	193
,, 41-58	195
,, 51	191
xi. 35	207
xii. 32	204
xiv. 6	206
xix. 17	208

ACTS OF APOSTLES.	
ii. 21	214
v. 2	216
viii. 30	218
xxiii. 16-24	221

ROMANS.	
xiv. 12	227

2 CORINTHIANS.	
iii. 2, 3	229
viii. 5	234
ix. 15	237

GALATIANS.	
vi. 7	241

EPHESIANS.	
v. 8	243
vi. 1	245
,, 17	248

PHILIPPIANS.	
ii. 15, 16	251

1 Timothy.	page	Hebrews.	page	2 Peter.	page
vi. 12	256	xii. 15	267	i. 19	279
2 Timothy.		**James.**		**1 John.**	
iii. 16	260	iv. 7	270	i. 7	282
				iv. 8	284
				v. 21	287
Titus.		**1 Peter.**		**Revelation.**	
i. 6	262	i. 19	273	vii. 1–17	290
iii. 3–7	264	v. 8	277	xxi. 17	294

STANDARD RELIGIOUS BOOKS.

The Clerical Library.

THIS SERIES of volumes is specially intended for the CLERGY, STUDENTS AND SUNDAY SCHOOL TEACHERS OF ALL DENOMINATIONS, and is meant to furnish them with stimulus and suggestion in the various departments of their work. Amongst the pulpit thinkers from whom these sermon outlines have been drawn are leading men of almost *every* denomination in Great Britain and America, the subjects treated of being of course practical rather than controversial. The best thoughts of the best religious writers of the day are here furnished in a condensed form and at a moderate price.

Five volumes in crown 8vo are now ready (*each volume complete in itself*). Price, $1.50.

NOW READY—FOURTH EDITION.
300 OUTLINES OF SERMONS ON THE NEW TESTAMENT.

By 72 Eminent ENGLISH and AMERICAN CLERGYMEN, including

Archbishop TAIT.	Canon LIDDON.	Rev. Dr. H. CROSBY.
Bishop ALEXANDER.	Canon WESTCOTT.	Rev. Dr. Pres. MCCOSH.
Bishop BROWNE.	Rev. Prin. CAIRNS.	Rev. Dr. M. R. VINCENT.
Bishop LIGHTFOOT.	Rev. Dr. M. PUNSHON	Rev. Dr. JNO. PEDDIE.
Bishop MAGEE.	Rev. Dr. W. M. TAYLOR.	Rev. Dr. C. T. DEEMS.
Bishop RYLE.	Rev. PHILLIPS BROOKS.	Rev. C. H. SPURGEON.
Dean CHURCH.	Rev. Dr. R. S. STORRS.	Rev. Dean STANLEY.
Dean VAUGHAN.	Rev. Dr. W. G. T. SHEDD.	Rev. Dr. A. RALEIGH.
Canon FARRAR.	Rev. Dr. T. L. CUYLER.	*And many others.*
Canon KNOX-LITTLE.	Rev. Dr. J. T. DURYEA.	

OUTLINES OF SERMONS ON THE OLD TESTAMENT.

AUTHORS OF SERMONS.

G. S. BARRETT, B.A.	J. OSWALD DYKES, D.D.	Canon LIDDON.
Dean E. BICKERSTETH.	E. HERBER EVANS.	J. A. MACFAYDEN, D.D.
Bishop E. H. BROWNE.	Canon F. W. FARRAR.	ALEX. MACLAREN, D.D.
J. BALD. BROWN, B.A.	DONALD FRASER, D.D.	Bishop W. C. MAGEE.
T. P. BOULTBEE, LL.D.	J. G. GREENOUGH, B.A.	THEODORE MONOD.
J. P. CHOWN.	W. F. HOOK, D.D.	ARTHUR MURSELL.
Dean R. W. CHURCH.	Bishop W. BASIL JONES.	JOSEPH PARKER, D.D.
E. R. COUDER, D.D.	JOHN KERR, D.D.	Dean E. H. PLUMPTRE.
T. L. CUYLER, D.D.	Canon EDWARD KING.	JOHN PULSFORD. [D.D.
A. B. DAVIDSON, D.D.	Bp. J. B. LIGHTFOOT.	W. MORLEY PUNSHON,
ROBERT RAINY, D.D.	WM. M. TAYLOR, D.D.	M. R. VINCENT, D.D.
ALEX'R RALEIGH, D.D.	S. A. TIPPLE, B.A.	W. J. WOODS, B.A.
C. P. REICHEL, D.D.	H. J. VANDYKE, D.D.	C. WADSWORTH, D.D.
CHAS. STANFORD, D.D.	Dean C. J. VAUGHAN.	G. H. WILKINSON.
Dean A. P. STANLEY.	JAMES VAUGHAN, B.A.	Bp. C. WORDSWORTH.
W. M. STRATHAM, B.A.		

Sent on receipt of price, charges prepaid.

A. C. ARMSTRONG & SON, 714 Broadway, New York.

THE CLERICAL LIBRARY—(Continued).

OUTLINES OF SERMONS TO CHILDREN.

With numerous Anecdotes. Crown 8vo. Cloth, $1.50. (Being the 3d vol. of the CLERICAL LIBRARY.)

"*These sermons are by men of acknowledged eminence in possessing the happy faculty of preaching interestingly to the young. As an evidence of this, as well as of the character of the teaching, it is only necessary to mention such names as those of* WILLIAM ARNOT, THE BONARS, PRINCIPAL CAIRNS, JOHN EDMOND, D.D., Drs. OSWALD DYKES *and* J. MARSHALL LANG, *besides many others.*"—*Canada Presbyterian.*

"This book contains a very high grade of thinking, with enough illustrations and anecdotes to stock the average preacher for many years of children's sermons."—*Episcopal Register.*

"They are full of suggestions which will be found exceedingly helpful; the habit of using apt and simple illustrations, and of repeating good anecdotes, begets a faculty and power which are of value. This volume is a treasure which a hundred pastors will find exceedingly convenient to draw upon."—*N. Y. Evangelist.*

PULPIT PRAYERS BY EMINENT PREACHERS.

Crown 8vo. Cloth, $1.50. (Being the 4th vol. of the CLERICAL LIBRARY.)

The British Quarterly says: "*These prayers are fresh and strong; the ordinary ruts of conventional forms are left and the fresh thoughts of living hearts are uttered. The excitement of devotional thought and sympathy must be great in the offering of such prayers, especially when, as here, spiritual intensity and devoutness are as marked as freshness and strength. Such prayers have their characteristic advantages.*"

London Literary World: "Used aright, this volume is likely to be of great service to ministers. It will show them how to put variety, freshness and literary beauty, as well as spirituality of tone, into their extemporaneous prayers."

Anecdotes Illustrative of New Testament Texts.

With **600** Anecdotes. Crown 8vo, **400** pages. Cloth, $1.50. (Being the 5th vol. of the CLERICAL LIBRARY.)

London Christian Leader says: "*This is one of the most valuable books of anecdote that we have ever seen. There is hardly one anecdote that is not of first-rate quality. They have been selected by one who has breadth and vigor of mind as well as keen spiritual insight, and some of the most effective illustrations of Scripture texts have a rich vein of humor of exquisite quality.*"

The London Church Bells: "The anecdotes are given in the order of the texts which they illustrate. There is an ample index. The book is one which those who have to prepare sermons and addresses will do well to have at their elbow."

N. Y. Christian at Work: "AS AN APT ILLUSTRATION OFTEN PROVES THE NAIL WHICH FASTENS THE TRUTH IN THE MIND, THIS VOLUME WILL PROVE AN ADMIRABLE AND VALUABLE AID, NOT ONLY TO CLERGYMEN, BUT TO SUNDAY-SCHOOL TEACHERS AND CHRISTIAN WORKERS GENERALLY."

N. Y. Observer: "A book replete with incident and suggestion applicable to every occasion."

Sent on receipt of price, charges prepaid.

A. C. ARMSTRONG & SON, 714 Broadway, New York.

STANDARD RELIGIOUS WORKS.

TALKS WITH YOUNG MEN.

By J. THAIN DAVIDSON. 12mo, in handsome cloth binding, illuminated cover. Price, $1.25.

"These talks are direct, practical and pungent, such as young men like to hear. They are crowded with points of counsel and direction; they will be invaluable to any young man, and all so plainly and forcibly told, and so fully illustrated, that one can but pursue the reading of them to the end. The graphic descriptions of human nature, and sharp laying open of motive in worldly and selfish living, show an unusually keen sense of observation and understanding of the human heart. It should have a wide circulation."—*N. Y. Evangelist.*

Rev. Mr. SPURGEON says: "The author gives young men fine advice—full of grace and thought—enlivened by story and proverb, fresh with sympathy, and on fire with zeal. These short talks are just what they should be, and all that they further need is to be largely distributed among the crowds of our advancing manhood. **TO BEGIN TO READ IS TO BE BOUND TO CONTINUE; THE TALKS ARE SO SENSIBLE THAT NO ONE WISHES TO SILENCE THE TALKER—BY LAYING ASIDE THE BOOK."**

N. Y. Christian Advocate and Journal says: "This volume will find readers wherever it is known. The talks are fervent and **DIRECT APPEALS TO THE HEART. THE STYLE IS ANIMATED AND PICTURESQUE, AND THE BOOK WILL BE READ BY ALL WHO BUY IT."**

The Parabolic Teaching of Christ.

A Systematic and Critical Study of the Parables of our Lord. By Rev. Prof. A. B. BRUCE, D.D. 1 vol., 8vo, cloth, 527 pp. Price, $2.50.

"A work which will at once take its place as a classic on the Parables of our Saviour. No minister should think of doing without it."—*American Presbyterian Review.*

American Literary Churchman says: "We recommend this book with the most confident earnestness. It is a book to be bought and kept; it has both depth and breadth and minute accuracy; it has a living sympathy with the teaching of the Parables and with the spirit of the Master."

ENGLISH NOTICES.

"Prof. Bruce brings to his task the learning and the liberal and finely sympathetic spirit which are the best gifts of an expositor of Scripture. His treatment of his subject is vigorous and original, and he avoids the capital mistake of overlaying his exegesis with a mass of other men's views."—*Spectator.*

"The studies of the Parables are thorough, scholarly, suggestive and practical. Fullness of discussion, reverence of treatment, and sobriety of judgment, mainly characterize this work."—*Christian World.*

"Each Parable is most thoughtfully worked out, and much new light is thus thrown on the difficulties which surround many of these beautiful and suggestive examples of Divine teaching."—*Clergymen's Magazine.*

"This volume has only to be known to be welcomed, not by students alone, but by all earnest students of Christ's oracles. On no subject has Dr. Bruce spoken more wisely than on the question why Jesus spoke in parables. The one end the author sets before himself is, to find out what our Lord really meant. And this he does with a clearness and fullness worthy of all praise. **Familiar as we are with some of the best and most popular works on the Parables, we do not know any to which we could look for so much aid in our search after the very meaning which Christ would have us find in His words."**—*Nonconformist.*

Sent on receipt of price, charges prepaid.

A. C. ARMSTRONG & SON, 714 Broadway, New York.

STANDARD RELIGIOUS WORKS.

New and Enlarged [**4**th] Edition, in Cheaper Form,
OF

CHARLES L. BRACE'S GESTA CHRISTI.

A HISTORY OF HUMANE PROGRESS UNDER CHRISTIANITY. With New Preface and Supplementary Chapter. 540 pp., cloth.

Price reduced from $2.50 to $1.50.

"It is especially adapted to assist the clergyman and religious teacher in his struggles with honest, thoughtful infidelity."

"*It presents a storehouse of facts* bearing on the influences of Christianity upon such important topics as the paternal power, the position of woman under custom and law, personal purity, and marriage, slavery, cruel and licentious sports, and all matters of humanity and compassion, etc. THE THOUGHTFUL READER WILL HERE GATHER INFORMATION WHICH COULD ONLY BE OBTAINED FROM LIBRARIES OR MANY VOLUMES."

Rev. Dr. R. S. STORRS *says:* "IT IS A BOOK THAT DESERVES THE VERY WIDEST CIRCULATION FOR ITS CAREFULNESS AND CANDOR, ITS AMPLE LEARNING, *its just, discriminating analysis of historical movements as initiated or governed by moral forces, and for the fine spirit which pervades it.*"

"The skill and industry with which Mr. Brace has gleaned and sorted the vast accumulation of material here gathered together, the better to show forth the power and influence, direct and indirect, of Christ's teachings, is not only praise-worthy, but even in a certain sense wonderful. He has a complete mastery of his subject, and many chapters in the book are of exceeding value and interest."—*London Morning Post.*

A NEW and REVISED EDITION, with NEW MAPS and ILLUSTRATIONS,
OF

STANLEY'S SINAI AND PALESTINE.

In Connection with their History. By Dean A. P. STANLEY. With 7 Elaborate and Beautifully Colored Maps, and other Illustrations.

Large Crown 8vo Vol., Cloth, 640 pp. Price reduced from $4 to $2.50.

The late Dean Stanley published a new and revised edition of his "SINAI AND PALESTINE." In it he made considerable editions and corrections, giving the work the final impress of his scholarship, taste and ability. This edition has been carefully conformed to the last English edition—including the new maps and illustrations, and is herewith commended anew AS THE MOST READABLE AS WELL AS THE MOST ACCURATE WORK ON THE SUBJECT IN THE ENGLISH LANGUAGE.

Rev. Dr. H. M. Field, Editor of "*N. Y. Evangelist,*" *says of Stanley's* "*Sinai and Palestine*"*:* "We had occasion for its constant use in crossing the desert, and in journeying through the Holy Land, and can bear witness at once to its accuracy and to the charm of its descriptions. *Of all the helps we had it was by far the most captivating.*"

Sent on receipt of price, charges prepaid.

A. C. ARMSTRONG & SON, 714 Broadway, New York.

www.ingramcontent.com/pod-product-compliance
Lightning Source LLC
Chambersburg PA
CBHW022104230426

43672CB00008B/1271